Papal Primacy
From Its Origins to the Present

Klaus Schatz, S.J.

Translated from German by
John A. Otto and
Linda M. Maloney

A Michael Glazier Book
THE LITURGICAL PRESS
Collegeville, Minnesota

A Michael Glazier Book published by The Liturgical Press.

Cover design by Greg Becker.

This book was originally published in German as *Der Päpstliche Primat: Seine Geschichte von den Ursprungen bis zur Gegenwart* © Echter Verlag 1990.

Library of Congress Cataloging-in-Publication Data

Schatz, Klaus.
   [Päpstliche Primat. English]
   Papal primacy : from its origins to the present / Klaus Schatz ;
translated from German by John A. Otto and Linda M. Maloney.
       p.   cm.
   "A Michael Glazier book."
   Includes bibliographical references and index.
   ISBN 0-8146-5522-X
   1. Popes—Primacy. I. Title.
BX1805.S3413   1996
262'.13—dc20
                                          96-8001
                                            CIP

"When once you have turned back, strengthen your brothers."

—*Luke 22:32*

CONTENTS

ABBREVIATIONS

ACO E. Schwartz et al, eds., *Acta Conciliorum Oecumenicorum* (1914ff.)

AHC *Annuarium Historiae Conciliorum*

AHP *Archivum Historiae Pontificiae*

CCL Corpus Christianorum, Series Latina (Turnhout, 1954ff.)

CSEL Corpus Scriptorum Ecclesiasticorum Latinorum ("Wiener Kirchenväter," Vienna, 1866ff.)

DG *Decretum Magistri Gratiani*, in E. Friedberg, ed., *Corpus Iuris Canonici, P. I.* (Leipzig, 1872)

DS H. Denzinger, ed., *Enchiridion Symbolorum definitionum et declarationum de rebus fidei et morum*, newly edited by H. Schönmetzer (Freiburg, 1965)

Mansi G. D. Mansi et al, eds., *Sacrorum Conciliorum nova et amplissima collectio*, vols. 1–53 (1759–1927)

MGH *Monumenta Germaniae Historica* (1826ff.)

PG J. P. Migne, ed., *Patrologiae cursus completus. Series Graeca*, vols. 1–161 (Paris, 1857–1912)

PL J. P. Migne, ed., *Patrologiae cursus completus. Series Latina*, vols. 1–221 (Paris, 1844–1864)

SC Sources Chrétiennes (Paris, 1941ff.)

ThPh *Theologie und Philosophie*

INTRODUCTION

Histories of the popes or of the papacy—written from a Catholic or non-Catholic perspective, profusely illustrated, biographical studies or institutional histories, solid and scholarly or popular and provocative—it is a highly competitive field, simply because of the explosiveness of the topic. This is connected with the fact that both the current manifestation and the history of the papacy as institution have emerged as challenges for Catholics and non-Catholics: they provoke very different responses, but scarcely anyone can remain indifferent to them. Whether the papacy is seen as a liberating force that can break the bonds of Church establishment or other constrictions, as oppressive and hostile to faith, as the "rock of the Church" or "a stone of stumbling," it remains a reality present at the heart of almost every ecclesiastical problem and constantly provoking controversy. An essential factor in the controversial discussions is knowledge of the history of the papacy, without which the papacy itself cannot be understood.

The purpose of this book, on the one hand, is to respond to the current interest to which I have alluded above; still, it is not meant to add one more book to the pile of papal histories. Instead, it offers to those who are interested in history and theology the essentials of a history of papal primacy. In fact, despite the great number of histories of the popes or the papacy to date, there has been no book devoted specifically to the history of papal primacy. The only work of this type is the two volumes of Erich Caspar's history of the papacy (1930–1933) treating the topic of papal primacy up to the middle of the eighth century, but there has not yet been any comparable work by Catholic church historians.

What do I mean when I speak of a "history of papal primacy" in contrast to a history of the papacy? Vatican Council I (1869–1870) defined the specific meaning of the primacy of the bishop of Rome over the whole Church (the pope as primate in Church governance and in preserving true doctrine) as an essential institution of the Church that can never be relinquished. This primacy is thus a structural element in Catholic understanding of the Church, something not to be surrendered in ecumenical dialogue and without which there can be no single, complete Church community. According to the Catholic belief given magisterial sanction in that council, it has its foundation in the will of Christ and in Peter, who figures in the New Testament. But it was by no means complete and perfected from the beginning; instead, it has had a very lively history, not always proceeding along straight lines. At the present time—differently from the era of Vatican I—acknowledgment of this fact does not present any problems within Catholicism.

How, in what stages, and as a result of what historical factors did papal primacy come to be what it is? We will thus be investigating the historical origins of the primatial structures and papal rights that were later to be regarded as essential and as matters of doctrine not to be surrendered. We are not concerned with those aspects of the institutional history of the papacy that touch its internal self-concept only superficially, such as the development of the Roman curia, papal finances, the papal states, or its sociological embeddedness in Roman society. But obviously we cannot be content to present merely a history of ideas; we must also ask whether, to what extent, and under what conditions the papal claims have corresponded to their historical and ecclesiastical realization.

Thus this book is primarily historical, but it does not avoid the question of how this historically developed primacy can be a matter of dogma never to be abandoned, that is, "instituted by Jesus Christ." A demonstration of the reasons for the primacy in terms of fundamental theology lies outside the scope of this book, but the author does not wish to avoid asking how the reality of history can be harmonized with Catholic faith resting on binding Church dogma, and thus on Vatican I. This Catholic point of view, which is a matter of course in light of its further development at Vatican II and the newer theological investigations legitimated by that council, is here presumed. In this light we will ask how history can be interpreted theologically and in harmony with faith.

The book is intended for persons interested in theology and history and possessing some degree of knowledge of those subjects. The notes are confined to citations of sources and additional readings in support of some summary remarks that may be new even to specialists or matters of controversy requiring further documentation. A selection of the most important additional bibliography is offered at the end of each chapter.

Part One:
The Development of the Primacy
in the First Five Centuries

I. Stating the Problem: Preliminary Questions and Answers

There appears at the present time to be increasing consensus among Catholic and non-Catholic exegetes regarding the Petrine office in the New Testament. Scholars agree that

- Not only the three classical Petrine texts (Matt 16:13-19; Luke 22:31-34; John 21:15-17) but also many others, including especially the presentation of Peter as first witness to the resurrection (1 Cor 15:5) testify to Peter's position as leader of the Twelve and of the primitive community in Jerusalem, a role conferred on him by Jesus and exercised by virtue of that commission.

- The fact that the very writings that contain the strongest witness in favor of Peter were composed after his death testifies to the primitive Church's abiding interest in the person and function of Peter. Apparently he was not merely a figure of historical significance. He remained for the Church an especially important and reliable guarantor of the Jesus tradition.

- The further question whether there was any notion of an enduring office beyond Peter's lifetime, if posed in purely historical terms, should probably be answered in the negative. That is, if we ask whether the historical Jesus, in commissioning Peter, expected him to have successors, or whether the author of the Gospel of Matthew, writing after Peter's death, was aware that Peter and his commission survived in the leaders of the Roman community who succeeded him, the answer in both cases is probably "no."

But for a responsible hermeneutic this does not provide a negative response to the underlying question, which encompasses more than the perspective of Jesus himself and that of the New Testament. Even if they were not "aware" of such an office, that does not mean that the figure and the commission of the Peter of the New Testament did not encompass the possibility, if it is projected into a Church enduring for centuries and concerned in some way to "secure" its ties to its apostolic origins and to Jesus himself.

If we ask in addition whether the primitive Church was aware, after Peter's death, that his authority had passed to the next bishop of Rome, or in other words that the head of the community at Rome was now the successor of Peter, the Church's rock and hence the subject of the promise in Matthew 16:18-19, the question, put in those terms, must certainly be given a negative answer. That Peter worked in Rome and suffered martyrdom along with Paul, probably in the local persecution of Christians by Nero about 64–67 is something that can be asserted with a degree of probability bordering on certainty. The activity and the death of these two apostles at Rome was first attested in the "Letter of Clement" from the community at Rome to that at Corinth around the year 95.[1] It is also presumed in the letter from Ignatius of Antioch to the Romans around 110, probably reflecting the conviction of eastern Christian communities also that Peter had been at Rome. Added to these are references from this period in two apocryphal writings (the Ascension of Isaiah and the Apocalypse of Peter) as well as the location at "Babylon" in 1 Peter 5:13, which is probably to be interpreted as a reference to Rome.

In the second century, at any rate, there is an unimpeached tradition in both East and West, and there are no reasons deserving serious consideration for doubting the historicity of this information. That Peter was martyred by crucifixion is apparently presumed as something known to the readers of the final chapter of the Fourth Gospel (John 21:18-19) and can therefore be regarded as highly probable. It is not equally certain that the excavations under St. Peter's Basilica have found the genuine location of Peter's tomb, especially since there is another Roman tradition of venerating Peter at St. Sebastian on the Appian Way.[2] What these excavations do reveal with certainty is that Christians in the second century were already convinced that Vatican Hill had something to do with Peter's grave, for the Tropaion discovered during these excavations stems from that time; it, and the Pauline parallel on the road to Ostia, are described by the presbyter Gaius around the year 200 as "the trophies of those who founded this church."[3]

Nevertheless, concrete claims of a primacy over the whole Church cannot be inferred from this conviction. If one had asked a Christian in the year 100, 200, or even 300 whether the bishop of Rome was the head of all Christians, or whether there was a supreme bishop over all the other bishops and having the last word in questions affecting the whole Church, he or she would certainly have said no.

But are these the right questions? Is a negative answer not inevitable if we approach the first centuries using the yardstick of our modern, fully developed doctrine of primacy, or especially the standards of Vatican I? Is such an inquiry really historical? If we ask the questions in such a way as to evoke a negative answer, are we not precluding any serious theological investigation? In fact, we everywhere encounter this kind of alienation by means of a later concept of primacy and all the historical associations, especially negative ones, connected with it. This is usually the case to a greater degree for those who reject any notion of primacy in these texts than for those who think they can discern one. In such cases it is usually said that a juridical superiority of one church over another, or certainly anything like papal primacy of jurisdiction was completely foreign to Ignatius, or Irenaeus, or even Augustine; they knew nothing of any bishop being placed over another, and so on. If one then cites evidence that establishes a certain higher status accorded to the Roman community but not subject to description in familiar legal categories, they are immediately measured against the concept of primacy in later times, or even that of Vatican I. The conclusion that follows is that such a primacy can by no means be derived from those documents. In the present state of research, this kind of conclusion, of course, is not a scholarly achievement; it is simply a truism.

What is lacking is not critical historical knowledge, but historical hermeneutics. The question is too unrefined to do justice to the Church's historical reality. Therefore we must set aside from the outset any question such as "was there a primacy in our sense of the word at that time?" In particular, all kinds of thinking in categories of hierarchical subordination or superiority will lead us astray; such approaches are incapable of providing a correct view of the situation of the Roman church in the earliest period. The latter can only be perceived in the overall context of the ancient Church's struggle to locate a fixed point of unity. How were the standards for Church unity and the genuine tradition of Christ established? What was the significance of the Roman church in that context? We can discover, in essence, four stages or steps in development, although of course they overlap to some degree.

II. The Religious and Spiritual Significance of the Roman Church

The first stage (beginning about 100) was characterized by the general religious and spiritual significance of the Roman church, something not yet comprehended in a juridical sense. This high regard for the Roman church is certainly inseparable from the traditions of Peter and Paul, connected with the Romans' possession of the tombs of these two apostles. The esteem enjoyed by those two apostles and their prime importance for the New Testament tradition were transferred to the Roman community in a way we can scarcely understand. At a very early date, the Roman community responded to this universal religious status by a special sense of fraternal responsibility and concern for the other churches. This is attested, for example, by Bishop Dionysius of Corinth, who according to Eusebius wrote to the Romans in about 170, "From the start it has been your custom to treat all Christians with unfailing kindness, and to send contributions to many churches in every city."[4] The context shows that this refers primarily to material assistance to poorer churches and charitable gifts for Christians condemned to penal servitude in the mines, but clearly it refers also to consolation and spiritual advice, especially since Dionysius refers in the same context to the letter of Clement, which was read annually in the church at Corinth.

In fact, this "letter of Clement," written around 95, is the first document indicating that the Roman community felt responsible for other churches. Its name is a subsequent addition, of course: according to Hegesippus's list of bishops Clement was bishop of Rome at that time, the third in succession. However, he is not named as the author of the letter; instead, the true sender is the Roman community. We probably cannot say for certain that there was a bishop of Rome at that time. It seems likely that the Roman church was governed by a group of presbyters from whom there very quickly emerged a presider or "first among equals" whose name was remembered and who was subsequently described as "bishop" after the mid-second century.

The letter of Clement, then, is an admonitory letter from the Roman community to its sister church in Corinth, where the leaders of the community had been expelled in a kind of internal church revolution. In its content the letter is a unified instruction about order, humility, and subordination to those in office, and against the ambition and arrogance of some individuals, the latter being regarded as the worst of sins. The letter takes an authoritative tone throughout, even speaking in the name of God:

> But if some be disobedient to the words which have been spoken by him [i.e., God] through us [the Roman community!], let them know that they will entangle themselves in transgression and no little danger . . . you will give us joy and gladness, if you are obedient to the things which we have written through the Holy Spirit . . . .[5]

But it would be going too far to deduce from this that the Roman church had formal authority or precedence over other churches, as was too hastily done by Roman Catholics in the past. First, even if this admonition calls on the authority of God and the assistance of the Holy Spirit, it remains within the context of the universal fraternal solidarity of Christian churches, even though it is spoken to a sister church that had gone astray. We have the parallel example of Dionysius of Corinth, mentioned earlier, who circulated his own very firm letters of instruction and admonition to the sister churches in Sparta, Athens, Nicomedia, Gortyna, Amastris, and Cnossos.[6] Certainly there is an interesting difference between the two cases, as is obvious from Eusebius's account: while other churches are admonished, the church at Rome is only praised. And even if the letter of Clement remains within the context of universal fraternal correction, one may ask whether every community could speak in the same tone, especially toward an important church like that in Corinth with its proud claim to apostolic origin.

A distinction similar to that in the letters of Dionysius can be found sixty years earlier in the letter to the Romans written by Ignatius of Antioch (ca. 110). Whereas he urges the other communities to preserve unity, especially with the bishop ("Do nothing without the bishop"), and warns them against heresies, his letter to the Romans has a completely different tone. It contains no admonitions, no instruction, only praise; this is the church that needs no instruction because it "taught others." The crucial introductory sentences read:

> Ignatius, who is also called Theophorus, to her who has obtained mercy in the greatness of the Most High Father, and of Jesus Christ his only Son; to the church beloved and enlightened by the will of him who has willed all things which are, according to the love of Jesus Christ, our God, which also has *the presidency in the country of the land of the Romans*, worthy of God, worthy of honor, worthy of blessing, worthy of praise, worthy of success, worthy in its holiness, and *preeminent in love*, having the law of Christ, named after the Father, which also I greet in the name of Jesus Christ, the Son of the Father . . . .[7]

Much ink has been spilled especially in attempts to explain the expression "preeminent in love" (προκαθημένη τῆς ἀγάπης). Roman Catholic authors have interpreted "love" as a synonym for Church community *(communio)* and deduced from this that Rome has a consti-tutionally guaranteed position as "presider within the covenant of love," or center of ecclesial communion. However, this kind of juridi-cal-constitutional interpretation can scarcely correspond to the ideas of Ignatius's contemporaries. On the Protestant side "preeminence in love" has been applied to the charitable activity of the Roman com-munity, which even at that time because of the presence of influential and well-to-do Christians was better placed than other local churches to help poorer communities. There is certainly merit in this interpreta-tion. It is in harmony with the text of Dionysius of Corinth quoted ear-lier, and it would also match the universal brotherly and sisterly responsibility and concern for other churches manifested by the Roman church, an essential element of which was material aid. But that assistance was spiritual as well as material. This is evident espe-cially from the overall tenor of the letter: The Roman church appears as the teacher of others and not, like them, in need of instruction. In the context of this letter "preeminence" seems to mean a kind of universal religious and spiritual significance, not to be identified with "presid-ing" in the legal sense.

A particularly important document for this question of the religious and spiritual significance of the Roman church is the Abercius inscrip-tion, the epitaph of a Christian from Asia Minor from about the year 200. In highly pictorial and poetic language rich in primitive Christian symbolism, the author writes:

> My name is Abercius. I am a disciple of the holy Shepherd who herds the flocks on the hills and plains, who has enormous eyes that penetrate everywhere [= Christ]. . . . To Rome he [the shepherd] sent me to be-hold an empire and to see a queen in a golden robe and golden shoes; I saw there a people with a shining seal. . . . Everywhere I found people who shared my beliefs; for Paul was my companion [probably the refer-ence is to the letters of Paul, which he may have taken as spiritual read-ing for his journey]. Faith led me everywhere and placed before me in every place a fish from the spring as my food, a very great and pure fish caught by a pure virgin; and this he gave to his friends as a meal forever, dispensing excellent wine, offering mixed wine and bread [the fish is Christ, born of a virgin, given to us in the Eucharist].[8]

The Roman church thus appears as a "queen in a golden robe" and "a people with a shining seal." It bears a religious halo within an obvious faith context, and at the mention of its name hearts beat faster.

Finally, worth noting as a late attestation of this universal religious reputation enjoyed by Rome is the Synod of Antioch (341) because that synod defended itself directly against the interference of Rome. It wrote that the Roman church is regarded as glorious by all because it is the site of the apostles' monuments and from the beginning has been the capital of devotion, even though the bearers of the faith came to her from the East.[9]

III. Rome as Privileged Locus of Tradition

A further development began toward the end of the second century, against the background of the conflicts with gnosticism and the resulting emphasis on *paradosis* (tradition) as the objective rule of faith. Gnosticism, in itself a very complicated movement, was characterized by, among other things, its appeal to a deeper insight in faith, accessible only to an elite of the cognoscenti, handed on in "secret traditions," and thus to that extent immune to historical mediation or scrutiny. The faith of ordinary Christians was regarded as merely the primitive first stage for beginners; only the cognoscenti, those who "possess knowledge," can enter the inner sanctuary.

In their debates with these movements, orthodox authors emphasize a tradition that is open to all, historically accessible, and comprehensible even for ordinary Christians. This accessibility is twofold: in sacred Scripture and in the apostolic succession of the episcopal office. The authentic writings of the New Testament were now gradually assembled to form a canon and distinguished from the "nonauthentic" traditions in the apocrypha. The composition of "lists of bishops" extending back to the apostles was an effective way of saying that this uninterrupted succession guarantees that the public tradition is true. There are thus no "secret traditions." Everything is carried on in the full light of day.

Again, as far as *paradosis* was concerned, not every church was of equal importance. Most important were the *sedes apostolicae*, the apostolic churches either founded by apostles or known as places where the apostles worked or where their tombs were located. In such places the connection with the origins was stronger; the tradition was more fully alive; contact with the apostles, a resource against heretics, was closer. These churches were seen as less in danger of falling prey to novelties. The apostolic churches included Antioch, Philippi, Ephesus, Corinth, Thessalonica, and, of course, Rome.

On the basis of this principle Rome did, in fact, acquire a certain advantage. There were no individual churches that could compete with Rome, for here were the tombs of two apostles each of whom was more important for the New Testament tradition than all others. At most, John the beloved disciple could be mentioned alongside Peter and Paul (and we will see that at one point Ephesus asserted its equality with

Rome by appealing to his name). Even if there was no claim to a direct succession from Peter, it was clear that the authority of the chief apostle, the rock on whom the Church was built and to whom the power of the keys had been given, had to rub off on the church at Rome.

Added to this was the special reverence of early Christians for the martyrdom of Peter and Paul and its significance for the charism of the Roman community. In the definitive testimony to faith of their martyrdom, the two κορύφαοι [heads, leaders], Peter and Paul, had simultaneously handed on their faith as an enduring heritage for the Roman church *(paradosis)* and endowed it with that faith forever. Their witness to the faith, made perfect in the shedding of their blood, was handed on in the *paradosis;* their martyrdom remained present in the witness of the Roman church.[10] Thus, for example, the letter of the Synod of Arles (314) to Bishop Sylvester of Rome said of the Roman bishops: "[in them] the apostles also have their seat from day to day and . . . their outpoured blood *(cruor)* bears continual witness to the glory of God."[11] If any church was proof against heretics, it had to be this one.

Finally, one other important factor should be noted: Rome was the only apostolic church in the West, that is, in the Latin regions. Hence the seat of its bishop very quickly became *the* "apostolic see" not only for Italy, but also for Gaul and North Africa.

This is by no means to say that the tradition of the Roman church was decisive alone or independently of others. But in the choir of the apostolic churches this one's voice was of special importance, and scarcely any other could equal it in significance.

1. Individual Witnesses

There is a much-quoted passage in the third book of Irenaeus of Lyons' *Adversus haereses* ("Against All Heresies"), written ca. 180–190. Its background is the struggle against the Gnostic heresy and the need for a rule of faith. Against the Gnostics and their secret traditions, Irenaeus appeals to the public tradition of the churches that is associated with the episcopal office. In his view the preservation, without adulteration, of the faith received from the apostles in opposition to novelties involved a close association of apostolic tradition *(paradosis)* with apostolic succession. The continuity of the episcopal office was a guarantee of the continuity of doctrine and its being passed on intact from the apostles.

The passage that is significant for our consideration reads:

> Since, however, it would be very tedious, in such a volume as this, to reckon up the successions of all the churches, we do put to confusion all those who, in whatever manner . . . assemble in unauthorized meetings . . . by indicating that tradition derived from the apostles, of the very

great, the very ancient, and universally known church founded and organized at Rome by the two most glorious apostles, Peter and Paul . . . .

Then comes the crucial statement:

> For it is a matter of necessity that every church should agree with this church, on account of its preeminent authority *(potentior principalitas)*, that is, the faithful everywhere, inasmuch as the apostolical tradition has been preserved continuously by those [faithful persons] who exist everywhere.[12]

Irenaeus continues by saying that even if there is dispute over a relatively trivial matter one should have recourse "to the most ancient churches with which the apostles held constant intercourse and learn from them what is certain and clear in regard to the present question."[13]

There are a number of problems surrounding the original meaning of the passage quoted above, occasioned in large part by the fact that we know only the Latin translation and not the Greek original of the text. We must always reckon with the possibility that the Latin text as we have it is corrupt. The principal problems are:

1. What is meant by *"this* church"? Could it refer to any apostolic church that was normative for other churches, with the Roman church cited only as an example? In that case, the original phrase would have to have been something equivalent to "such a church."

2. But if, as seems more probable in light of the surrounding text, Irenaeus was thinking of the Roman church, what does it mean that all others (or perhaps the other apostolic churches) "should agree [or be in accord] with this church [in matters of faith]"? Does this mean that the Roman church represents the authoritative *norm* of faith for all other churches? Or did Irenaeus mean to say "I have simply traced the list of Roman bishops as an *example*. It is, however, understood from the outset that every apostolic church offers the same teaching"? Then "should agree" would not be understood as a norm, but as an *a priori* necessity: it is sufficient to offer a test case on a single point.

3. This is connected to the question regarding the reference of the last clause, "inasmuch as the apostolical tradition has been preserved continuously by those [faithful persons] who exist everywhere." Does this mean the Roman church, or every apostolic church?

4. Finally, what is the meaning of "those who exist everywhere"? It is possible that this means that Christians from all over the empire come together in the church at Rome, and they

exercise a corrective function in maintaining orthodoxy! But that would introduce a foreign element that does not fit within the train of Irenaeus's thought, because he sees the guarantee of truth here in purely vertical terms, as a connection to the apostles, and not horizontally in the agreement (or mutual correction) of all the churches.

There is no convincing solution that takes care of all the difficulties. However we interpret the passage, we probably cannot deny that it implies that the Roman *paradosis* had a certain qualified authoritative character, for

> 1. Even if the text is probably speaking of an a priori agreement, it is not illustrated by just any example, but by something very specific, the *potentior principalitas* of Rome: That which is the universal tradition of all the churches can be more clearly and reliably demonstrated by looking to that of Rome.

> 2. Also noteworthy is the multiplication of laudatory terms applied to the Roman church ("the very great, the very ancient, and universally known church founded and organized at Rome by the two most glorious apostles, Peter and Paul"), indicating that it is more than mere example.

> 3. We note further that Irenaeus apparently knows only the list of Roman bishops, or presumes it is the only one known to his readers. It appears that the list was familiar not only in Rome but also in the churches in Gaul, even though they had been founded from the East and not from Rome.

> 4. The Jewish Christian Hegesippus also attests, in this same period, that apparently as far as the apostolic tradition was concerned the Roman example could not be arbitrarily replaced by that of Corinth or Ephesus. His interest was the same as that of Irenaeus: preparing lists of bishops to counter the Gnostics. He wanted to say, "See, we stand in the unbroken line of continuity from the apostles!" And even though he came from the East he showed a special interest in the Roman list of bishops, which he researched in the archives at Rome.[14]

Another significant text, also against gnostic heretics, comes from Tertullian (ca. 200):

> Come now, you who would indulge a better curiosity, if you would apply it to the business of your salvation, run over the apostolic churches, in which the very thrones of the apostles are still preeminent in their places, in which their own authentic writings are read . . .

Achaia is very near you [in which] you find Corinth. Since you are not far from Macedonia, you have Philippi; [and there too] you have the Thessalonians. Since you are able to cross to Asia [Minor], you get Ephesus. Since, moreover, you are close upon Italy, you have Rome, from which there comes even into our own [i.e., the North Africans'] hands the very authority [of apostles themselves]. How happy is its church, on which apostles poured forth all their doctrine along with their blood! where Peter endures a passion like his Lord's! where Paul wins his crown in a death like John's [being beheaded like John the Baptist]! where the Apostle John was first plunged, unhurt, into boiling oil, and thence remitted to his island-exile![15]

At first glance it seems that Rome is simply placed on the same level as the other apostolic churches; it is merely the one nearest to the West, that is, to North Africa, and therefore "responsible" for that region. And yet it is again striking that when Tertullian begins to speak of Rome he suddenly abandons his prosaic style and waxes lyrical. The Roman church seems to be surrounded by a special nimbus, or to enjoy a more than ordinary status. Its universal spiritual importance also makes it extraordinarily authoritative for the true faith.

2. Acceptance of Responsibility for the Whole Church

It is within this context that we can discover, beginning in the late second century, the first attempts on the part of the Roman church to assume responsibility for the whole Church. We can observe on the one hand that these first initiatives encountered resistance and ended in failure. Rome did not succeed in maintaining its position against the contrary opinion and praxis of a significant portion of the Church. The two most important controversies of this type were the disputes over the feast of Easter and heretical baptism. Each marks a stage in Rome's sense of authority and at the same time reveals the initial resistance of other churches to the Roman claim.

In the case of Easter the question was whether the feast should always be celebrated on a Sunday. The "Quartodecimanians" (from *quartodecimus*, hence "fourteeners") followed Jewish custom in celebrating Easter on the fourteenth of Nisan, that is, at the first full moon after the beginning of spring, no matter what day of the week it was. That was the more ancient Jewish Christian custom. It was opposed to the "dominical" custom (from *dominica*, "Sunday") originating in the Gentile regions, which called for the celebration of Easter every year on the Sunday following the spring full moon. Until the end of the second century the two customs were carried on side by side in mutual toleration. Thus Irenaeus of Lyons[16] reports that Polycarp of Smyrna came to visit

Bishop Anicetus at Rome in about 160 and discussed the date of Easter with him. Polycarp upheld the quartodecimanian custom, referring to John and the other apostles, while Anicetus appealed to the customs of the "presbyters before him" to which he felt himself bound. In any case neither was able to convince the other. In spite of their differences, however, they continued in communion with one another.

Quartodecimanian practice was followed especially in the churches of Asia Minor, but at the end of the century, around 195, conflict arose, probably because Quartodecimanians arrived at Rome and attempted to introduce their dating of Easter in contravention of Roman custom. Synods were then held (in Palestine under the bishops of Caesarea and Jerusalem, in Italy under Victor of Rome, in Gaul, Pontus, and Osrhoene, as well as in Asia under Polycrates of Ephesus). These were probably called at the initiative of Victor of Rome, a fact directly attested by Bishop Polycrates of Ephesus, who according to Eusebius[17] wrote to Victor, "I could have mentioned the bishops who are with me and whom I summoned in response to your request." The letters from these synods were written to Rome (or at least Rome was among the addressees); at any rate Eusebius found them in the Roman archives. This is the first known case of a universal Church initiative coming from a bishop of Rome, or, to put it another way, it is the first occasion when Rome assumed responsibility for the whole Church. It may also be the beginning of the institution of the synod.

All these synods except that for the province of Asia under Polycrates opted for the dominical practice. Bishop Victor of Rome probably contended that the Roman tradition possessed special authority because it was legitimated by two apostles, Peter *and* Paul. In any case, Bishop Polycrates of Ephesus responded that the province of Asia could also appeal to two apostles,[18] namely Philip, who was supposed to be buried in Hierapolis, and John the beloved disciple in Ephesus. At that, Victor excommunicated the entire Church in Asia Minor.

The unheard-of severity of this measure drew sharp protests from many bishops. They called on Victor to "turn his mind to the things that make for peace and for unity and love" and sought to mediate the dispute. Prominent among them was Irenaeus of Lyons, who pointed to the example of Polycarp and Anicetus thirty years earlier, which had shown that there was room in the Church for both practices. These bishops preferred the dominical custom, but saw nothing in the question that was worth dividing the Church over. Eusebius tells us only of the efforts of these bishops on behalf of peace; we do not know the concrete details of how the controversy played itself out. At any rate there was no enduring breach of communion between Rome and the Churches of Asia Minor.

In the controversy over baptism by heretics some sixty years later (255–256) we can clearly discern a further step in Rome's perception of its primacy. Now the bishop of Rome no longer appealed merely to the legitimation of Roman tradition by Peter and Paul, but also considered himself the successor of Peter and the possessor of sovereign authority according to Matthew 16:18. This dispute revolved around the question whether those who had grown up in a heretical sect and then joined the catholic Church had to be rebaptized. Was baptism by heretics valid? Roman practice for decades had tended to regard heretics' baptism as valid. Those who entered the Great Church did not need to be baptized again; they only received imposition of hands from the bishop as a sign of ecclesial communion and the conferral of the Holy Spirit.

However, the practice of the churches of North Africa was different, and at that time of Asia Minor as well. Cyprian of Carthage made himself spokesman for those churches with the strong support of a synod of eighty-five North African bishops. Cyprian advocated the principle "outside the Church there is no salvation" in the harshest sense: An individual or a Church that did not possess the Holy Spirit could not confer the Spirit through baptism. On this point Cyprian was the superior theologian by the standards of argumentation of the time; he presented the stronger and more persuasive argument on the subject. Stephen of Rome, in opposing him, employed a kind of traditionalist appeal to Roman customs and traditions (*nihil innovetur nisi quod traditum est* [nothing should be introduced that was not handed down]).[19] But Cyprian argued that purely traditional arguments must give way to "reason." When Paul corrected Peter in Antioch, the latter did not appeal to his authority and say that "he held the primacy." Instead, he yielded to the better arguments.[20] A genuinely theological basis for the Roman point of view would only be supplied a century and a half later by Augustine.

In the course of this controversy Stephen must have claimed to be the successor of Peter in the sense of Matthew 16:18. This is the first known instance in which Matthew 16:18 was applied to the bishop of Rome. We learn of it in a letter from Firmilian of Caesarea (in Asia Minor) to Cyprian. Most accounts of the incident make it seem that this claim was rejected as unjustified and presumptuous, but such an assertion calls for some correction and attention to the precise context. Firmilian's letter[21] is a sustained polemic against Stephen and his arguments in favor of the validity of heretics' baptism. The seventeenth chapter contains the expressions "who contends that he has the succession from Peter, on whom the foundations of the Church were established" and "who claims that through succession he has the see of Peter," both directed against the Roman bishop. These claims are rejected, but not formally because in principle no individual bishop, not even the bishop of Rome, can make such a claim. Instead, the appeal to Matthew 16:18 is said to be unjustified in this instance because Stephen, by recognizing heretics' baptism, is "introduc[ing] many other rocks," that is, he is betraying the unity of the Church and thus acting contrary to the sense of Matthew 16:18 (and thus of the Petrine succession).

Firmilian himself had already cited Matthew 16:18-19 in his own six-teenth chapter ("whatever you bind on earth will be bound in heaven, and whatever you loose on earth will be loosed in heaven") in order to exclude any possibility of salvation and valid baptism outside the visi-ble Church order. Thus, according to Firmilian, Stephen could not rightly appeal to the Petrine succession in the sense of Matthew 16:18-19 because he also acknowledged the ecclesial character of heretical groups and thus acted contrary to the unity of the Church and the in-ternal sense of any possible Petrine succession. At the risk of being anachronistic, we might say that formally these arguments are very similar to those advanced by Lefèbvre against the popes since Vatican II. This does not mean, of course, that Stephen's claims were accepted in principle. We will return later to Cyprian's position on that question.

Despite the acerbity of Cyprian's polemic against Stephen, we should not fail to observe that the former's posture toward Rome is purely defensive. He does not excommunicate the bishop of Rome. Instead he writes to Stephen that he does not desire to impose his own position on anyone because every bishop is independent in the gov-erning of his church and is answerable to God alone.[22] This is remark-able in itself because it was not merely a question of different Church practices, as had been the case with the dispute over the date of Easter. Instead, what was at issue was the validity of baptism. Nevertheless, Cyprian did not break relations with Rome even when Stephen re-fused to receive his emissaries, neither admitting them to the Eucharistic celebration nor permitting them to be housed and cared for by the Roman community. Only under the next bishop of Rome and through the mediation of Bishop Dionysius of Alexandria was ecclesial communion between Rome and Carthage restored.

3. But in the Long Run . . .

We have seen in the cases of the dispute over the date of Easter and the controversy concerning baptism by heretics that an official word from Rome was by no means sufficient to bring either of these matters to a definitive conclusion, and yet in the long run the Roman position on both these questions was ultimately victorious. Nor are these excep-tional cases. In almost all the major controversies of the first centuries,

Rome established a position at a relatively early date that was then adopted and accepted by the entire Church, although often through a very long process and sometimes with certain modifications. The same is true of the great theological conflicts that began in the fourth century. For the first several centuries we should mention, in addition to the debate on the date of Easter and the conflict over heretics' baptism, two important processes of clarification in which Rome played a decisive part.

The first of these, occurring in the second century, was the establishment of the canon of books in the New Testament. It would of course be an exaggeration to say that the other churches accepted the canon used by the Roman church. On one point at least it was the East, and not the West, that won out, namely the acceptance of the Letter to the Hebrews, which for a long time was rejected in the West. Nevertheless, in this extended process of canon formation the Roman church enjoyed a certain advantage; its list of books was fixed earliest and approximates most closely the canon finally adopted. This is not surprising if we recall that the construction of a canon was also a measure for combating Gnosticism. The apostolic succession of bishops and the establishment of a canon of Scripture were two sides of the same coin: the fixing of the genuine, authentic tradition of the Church to put a stop to the unrestrained growth of special and secret traditions to which the Gnostics appealed. The establishment of the canon of apostolic writings was also done by recourse to the Church's apostolic tradition. Here the Roman tradition had a certain advantage, as we have seen.

Another process of clarification, this time in the third century, involved the question of penance. When we hear about ancient Christian penitential practices, we are shocked by their barbaric harshness: those guilty of serious sins were subjected to years of penance before finally being absolved and readmitted to the Eucharist. Nevertheless, the question with which the Church struggled in the third century was not whether these penances were too severe. Instead, the problem was: if I take the radical nature of baptism seriously, if in it I have died to sin once for all, and yet I fall away from faith, can I in any way hope to receive forgiveness from God?

In fact, the third-century Church made the important decision that *all* sins, even murder, adultery, and apostasy, could be forgiven once after baptism through the Church's penitential process. Rome again played a highly significant role in this development because these questions were first debated within the Roman community. The issue became acute especially after 250 under Bishop Cornelius during the Decian persecution, the first general and systematic persecution of Christians in the Roman Empire. Many Christians, perhaps most of them, weakened under persecution; they denied their faith or at least, by bribing officials, they obtained certificates *(libelli)* attesting that they had offered sacrifice. Bishop Cornelius admitted these Christians to penance even though the result was a schism in the Roman community (that of Novatian). Against all rigorism and any idea of a Church of the pure in which the worst sinners, at least, would have no place, the long, difficult, and complicated process of clarification within the Church established the fundamental rule that the Church must also be a Church for sinners and the weak, and its primary obligation as Church is to represent the mercy of God toward sinners.

Of course, in none of these processes of clarification was Rome the only player. In the penitential debates, for example, Cyprian pulled powerfully on the same rope with Rome. Nevertheless, there is no avoiding the question: How is it that in fact Rome always took the right side from the very beginning, even though it by no means had the better theologians or the better theology? The better theologians were in the Greek-speaking East or, as far as the Latin regions are concerned, in North Africa from the third century onward. The Roman presbyters were regarded as generally having good common sense in practical questions, but rather narrow-minded in other respects and not gifted with lively intellects. Great minds had a hard time in that community, where a rather traditionalist spirit with little patience for speculation seemed to dominate. The fact that in the long run Rome's position prevailed could be explained in different ways. Perhaps the weight of Rome's authority ultimately contributed to the decision of the Church. Or we might suspect that the experience of finding Rome always on the right side strengthened Rome's authority in hindsight and deepened the conviction that the Roman Church was proof against heresies. Probably both factors played a part and were mutually supportive.

In the dialogues of Anselm of Havelberg, written around 1150, Anselm's Greek conversation partner Nicetas attributes the fact that Rome, unlike the Churches of the East, remained untainted by heresy to a lack of intellectual sophistication and sensitivity to problems *(nimia negligentia investigandae fidei)*. On the other hand, the many heresies in the East were the obverse of an attitude of questioning and probing and the practice of intellectual debate.[23] On the positive side one could call this attitude of Rome, which has remained a constant throughout almost the whole history of the Church at least since the dispute over the date of Easter and the conflict over heretics' baptism, adherence to tradition. The Roman church was not directly involved in the intellectual controversies of the East. It took note of them and tried to establish a position, not always successfully because it did not always comprehend the fine points of the controversy. But it always kept its pivot leg firmly planted in tradition and not in speculation. To this the sober Latin spirit, more inclined to the positive than the negative, probably contributed a good deal. The proper theological answer was not always given in Rome, and yet the Roman church, with its traditional stance, strengthened resistance against heresy. As a result of this experience the conviction grew that the true faith was preserved in Rome more than anywhere else. This, of course, was a process that extended over many centuries.

IV. Rome as Center of *Communio*

The next stage of development began slowly in the third century and reached an acute stage in the fourth.

1. *The Early Church as* Communio ecclesiarum

The key to the ancient Church's self-understanding is the word *communio* [communion]. It encompasses varied dimensions: first of all, the *communio* is the local church as a community of believers with the bishop as its center. Beyond that, it is the community of faith uniting the churches with one another. This includes not only Eucharistic communion but also the very important element of communication. Bishops informed each other about important events: they notified each other of their election and sent word when they condemned and excommunicated heretics so that a heretic excluded from one church would not obtain access to another. Part of this *communio* of local churches in themselves and with one another was that when bishops were elected the choice by the local church and the final decision of the neighboring bishops were coordinated elements. Another expression of this communion was the "communion letters" or "peace letters" bishops wrote for travelers or Christians moving from place to place. Anyone who could present such a communion letter was accepted into the new community as a Christian and a member of the *catholica*; he or she could participate in the Eucharistic celebration and had a claim to Christian hospitality, which meant being housed and cared for at community expense. Only bishops could write such communion letters valid for the entire Church; presbyters could address them only to the churches in their immediate vicinity. For this purpose the bishops kept lists of all, or most, of the orthodox bishops with whom they were in communion.

Of course it was impossible for every bishop to keep all the other bishops constantly informed. Consequently the bishops in places that were crossroads of travel and commerce played a key role as hubs of communion. For example, the bishops of North Africa maintained communion with the whole Church through the bishop of Carthage, and the Egyptian bishops through the see of Alexandria. Rome thus communicated and corresponded directly with Carthage and Alexandria, and they in turn kept in touch with their provincial bishops.

To begin with this system was based on equality. But when communion was disrupted in some way—when, for example, two bishops in a single community quarreled over the episcopal see, or when bishops from different communities mutually "excommunicated" one another, where did true communion rest?

The first answer was that the true communion is "catholic," that is, universal. A local church whose communion was restricted to a single region or state did not count. It is characteristic of genuine communion that it extends throughout the whole world.

But how was that to be determined? The initial means, from the end of the second century onward, were regional episcopal synods. These synods were firmly convinced that they taught the truth and the genuine apostolic tradition. There was no need as yet for a higher authority; it was only the appearance of the Arian controversy in the fourth century that would bring to light the inadequacy of the synods. In the interest of communion these synods exchanged word of their decisions with other churches, especially the most important ones. The communication was often accompanied by a request that the other church join in the decision, but this was not regarded as a ratification by a higher authority even though such an affirmation from other churches, especially that of Rome, lent a certain added authority to such synods by making clear that the decree of the synod was a decision of the universal Church.

In this way, by the third century at least the three "principal churches" of Rome, Alexandria, and Antioch had acquired a kind of normative status. Important Church matters were often dealt with "at the highest level," that is, by these three. They were the three most important "nodal points" of communion. What was special about Rome's position?

2. From the Third Century Onward: Rome's Prominence within the Solidarity of the Whole Church

We can see that the practical significance of Rome increased throughout the third century, partly as a result of the growth of the Roman community. By the middle of the third century it is estimated to have numbered thirty thousand members, or at least five percent of the city's population. It had about fifty presbyters and more than one hundred other clergy. Its care for the poor and its provision for poorer churches throughout the Roman Empire were considered exemplary, and its internal life was well organized. In addition, the Roman community was no longer an outsider geographically: it was not the last outpost of a purely Greek Church, but the center of a new Latin Christendom. Now there were Christian congregations in North Africa with Carthage as their center, and others as far away as Spain and Gaul. In church conflicts the parties increasingly turned to Rome, especially if the decision in their own communities had gone against them. These included bishops driven from office and people condemned as heretics. That did not mean, of course, that they always accepted Rome's decision if it was not in their favor. But it was always important to be acknowledged at Rome. Being in communion with Rome was worth something and bore some weight in cases of conflict.

To what extent was this due simply to the position of Rome as the imperial capital and therefore a natural focal point, and to what extent was it because Rome enjoyed apostolic rank as the city of Peter and Paul and the place of their martyrdom? We must probably say that the two were mutually influential, a situation echoed in Irenaeus's reference to "those who exist everywhere." But whenever explicit reasons were given, it was Rome's apostolic rank that mattered most.

Rome's key position was not yet something set apart from general Church solidarity, within which Rome of course had a special responsibility. An interesting example is the case of Bishop Marcian of Arles in 255. He had permanently excommunicated members of his community who had denied their faith under persecution and would not even admit them to ecclesial penance. Moved by this incredible severity, Bishop Cyprian of Carthage, holder of the foremost episcopal see in North Africa, turned to Bishop Stephen of Rome with the request that he write to Gaul asking that Marcian be deposed and another bishop elected to replace him. He should then inform Cyprian of the name of the new bishop so that the North African episcopate would know with whom they were to maintain communion.

At first glance this looks like an unmistakable attestation of primacy. But when we hear the reasons Cyprian gave for the necessity of the Roman bishop's intervention we must be more cautious. He wrote:

> For that reason therefore, dearly beloved Brother, is the large body of bishops joined by the bond of mutual concord and the chain of unity so that, if anyone of our college should attempt to engage in heresy and wound and lay waste the flock of Christ, the others, as useful and merciful shepherds, should assist and should assemble the sheep of the Lord into the flock.[24]

He continues with other metaphors and imagery, concluding: "for although we shepherds are many, yet we feed one flock."[25]

Cyprian thus appeals simply to the mutual solidarity of *all* bishops and their responsibility for the *whole* Church: no bishop can simply practice an ivory tower policy and focus solely on his own church while other churches are being destroyed by their own bishops. He does not rely on any specific responsibility of Stephen as primate. Correspondingly, Bishop Faustinus of Lyons, the most important bishop in the vicinity of Arles, had previously written to Stephen and to Cyprian—in other words, to *both* the leading bishops in the Latin region. When Stephen did not react, he wrote to Cyprian again, asking him to renew his appeal to Stephen. Throughout this it is noteworthy that it was Stephen who was supposed to act; Cyprian himself did not write to Gaul. Apparently Stephen's word carried more weight, and although he had no superior status in law, it seems that he did possess greater authority.

It is especially through the letters of Cyprian that we can observe a certain wavering in the status of the Roman church. A few years earlier, when Cornelius was elected bishop of Rome, Cyprian spoke of the Roman church as the "matrix and root of the catholic Church;" he addressed a letter to the newly elected bishop there, assuring him that "all our colleagues . . . firmly approve and maintain you and your communion, that is, the unity and also the charity of the catholic Church."[26] Elsewhere he speaks of the Roman church as the *cathedra Petri* (chair of Peter) and "the principal church whence sacerdotal unity has sprung" (*ecclesia principalis unde unitas sacerdotalis exorta est*).[27] This is said in connection with North African schismatics who had elected an antibishop against Cyprian and were now daring to turn to the *cathedra Petri*, not considering that these are the Romans whose faith was praised in the preaching of the apostle (Paul) and to whom the *perfidia* could not have access. The issue here was the

> acknowledgment of a higher authority belonging to Peter's successors that cannot be adequately described in juridical terms. In principle, the Roman bishop had no greater authority than any other bishop, but in the hierarchy of authorities, his decision took the foremost place.[28]

On the other hand, Cyprian regarded every bishop as the successor of Peter, holder of the keys to the kingdom of heaven and possessor of the power to bind and loose. For him, Peter embodied the original unity of the Church and the episcopal office, but in principle these were also present in every bishop.

For Cyprian, responsibility for the whole Church and the solidarity of all bishops could also, if necessary, be turned *against* Rome. There is a striking example of this from the same period involving two Spanish bishops, Basilides and Martial. During the persecution they had not sacrificed to the idols, but like many other Christians they had bribed officials to obtain "certificates of sacrifice" *(libelli)*. As a result, they had lost credibility in their congregations and had been expelled. Nevertheless (in Cyprian's opinion by misrepresenting the facts) they succeeded in obtaining recognition from Stephen of Rome. Cyprian reacted immediately by calling an African synod to warn the two communities to reject Stephen's decision and refuse to readmit the two bishops.[29] Unfortunately we do not know how the matter was resolved.

We may thus summarize the essential information from the third century by saying that the Roman community was held in high esteem, but its status was not yet distinguished from the solidarity of the whole Church in which all the churches are responsible for one another. The Roman church held a preeminent place within the overall framework of universal Christian solidarity and episcopal collegiality.

The question that naturally follows is: What happens if this universal ecclesial unity and solidarity is no longer palpable? What is to be done when deep divisions not only afflict individual churches, but draw the entire Church into tribulation, when synods stand in opposition to one another and one synod seeks to annul what the others have decreed? What should happen when a solution could no longer be effected by the local church? That was the situation in the fourth century. However, by that time some significant turning points already lay in the past.

3. Turning Point: Constantine

What was the significance of the "Constantinian shift" for the Roman primacy? Its first result was to limit the primacy's growth and neutralize its influence in the East. From then on there was continual tension with the imperial Church headed by the emperor and its structures whenever the bishop of Rome attempted to enter into discussion of the affairs of the Church in the eastern half of the empire. And when Constantine founded a "new Rome" in 330, he created a city that would also rapidly enter into competition with the old Rome in Church affairs. This was all the more true because Constantinople was the first "completely Christian" major city; it contained no temples, only churches; in old Rome the ancient temples continued for centuries to give the city its character.

On the other hand, the decision to transfer the imperial capital from Rome to Constantinople was a kind of liberation for the bishop of Rome. With the imperial presence removed to Constantinople, he found it easier to expand his ecclesiastical authority in the West. He thus escaped the danger of becoming a "court bishop," something that very often (although by no means always!) befell the patriarch of Constantinople. One, at least, of the factors producing the dualism of spiritual and temporal power and the specifically western notion of Church independence was the removal of the seat of empire to the East.

In the period between 300 and 450 the structures of the Church underwent the following development: The communion of the churches that had previously functioned in very fluid fashion (through regional synods and principal churches as hubs of communion with Rome wielding the primary religious influence) was now more formally institutionalized. Over the episcopal sees now appeared the provincial Churches, with a metropolitan at the top, as the next-highest level of authority; for the most part the Church provinces were identical with the imperial provinces. It was in the provincial Churches that what we today call "episcopal collegiality" first fully emerged. Controlling episcopal elections, or even the nomination of bishops, became the right of the bishops of the same province, or even the metropolitan. If a bishop had to be deposed because of heresy or other failure in office, the duty fell to the provincial synod, which was also responsible in general for questions of faith and the condemnation of heretics.

Above the metropolitan organization, the bishops of the three principal churches of Rome, Alexandria, and Antioch, joined near the end of the fourth century by the bishop of Constantinople, began to exercise a kind of supervisory function over the larger regions under their influence; beginning in the fifth century these bishops were called "patriarchs." Alexandria was the first to achieve such a central position, thanks to its natural location as the only major city in a region that was otherwise almost entirely rural; it was followed by Antioch and then by Rome, which at first was responsible only for central and southern Italy.

This institutionalizing of communion in fixed forms and areas of responsibility, a situation encouraged by the state, of course brought with it the risk of provincialism and regional autonomy, especially in the case of the patriarchates. Alongside and above the latter, the universal Church was no longer so concretely visible.

4. The Arian Controversy and Bishop Julius of Rome: The Universal Church Closes Ranks against Regional Autonomy

The danger of regionalism was heightened by a crisis in the fourth century that threatened the very existence of the Church. It was connected with "Arianism," the doctrine proposed by the presbyter Arius of Alexandria and condemned by the first ecumenical council at Nicea in

325. Arius, in order to profess that God is absolutely one, regarded the divine Logos not as truly God, but only God's "external aspect" or the "mediator of creation." The controversy over this doctrine was by no means resolved by the Council of Nicea, of course. It lasted more than half a century longer.

In the first phase of the conflict the storm over the Nicene formula of faith, the *homoousios* ("of one being" with the Father) had not yet blown up. In the beginning everything revolved around a personal and political vendetta between Athanasius of Alexandria and Eustatius of Antioch, the bishops of the two sees that represented the most important pillars of Nicea. Now synods supported by the state authorities met and deposed both bishops; noteworthy among them was a synod at Tyre in 335. In the eyes of the earlier Church the next highest court that could depose a bishop was the synod of neighboring bishops. This time, however, the conflict was too immense for that institution to handle, as other synods decided in favor of Athanasius and his supporters. Especially significant among these was a synod at Rome in 341 to which the deposed bishops, especially Athanasius, had turned for help.

The problem then was: If one synod annuls what another has decreed, which action is valid? As the controversy swung back and forth some overall positions crystallized. The eastern bishops, especially at the Synod of Antioch in 341, advocated the autonomy in principle of every synod: the decree of Tyre was final and could not be annulled, and no bishop or presbyter condemned by a synod could appeal to any other synod. The ultimate consequence of this position, of course, was that every church was autonomous or autocephalous, but the practical result was the principle of the imperial state Church.

Opposed to this was the position of Rome favoring a hierarchy of synods. Not all synods are equal, and the lesser can be annulled by the greater. Here an openness to the whole Church was defended against an attempt to regionalize the conflict, and the participation of the whole Church was emphasized at a moment when the empire was politically divided between East and West and the anti-Athanasians were enjoying the support of the eastern emperor.

A key position may be ascribed to the letter written by Bishop Julius I of Rome to accompany the communications of the Roman synod of 341 to the eastern bishops. It represents a new stage in the Roman idea of primacy:

> If, as you say, there has been an offense, judgment should have been pronounced according to the ecclesiastical canon, and not as has happened. It should have been addressed to all of us so that what was right could have been determined by all. This matter concerned bishops, and not just any churches, but those that were governed by the apostles themselves.

> Why, in particular, did you not write to us about the Alexandrian church? Do you not know that the customary law was to write to us first and to start from that point in determining what is right? If you had something to bring forward against the bishop of Alexandria, this church should have been informed. But now those people, having proceeded without informing us and going ahead just as they please, want us to agree with them without our having investigated these offenses. These were by no means the instructions of Paul or the things the Fathers handed down to us. This is a foreign form, a new custom. What I am writing is for the good of all; please receive it with open minds. For what we received from the blessed apostle Peter, that I make known to you.[30]

The question so often posed, and receiving such different answers at different times, is: What is at issue here, "collegiality" or "primacy"? The right answer can only be: both, for the two are inseparable! To begin with, Julius insists on the participation of the West in dialogue and action, and thus on the principle of universal Church communion against a regional isolation and segregation he calls a "new form." In this context he again emphasizes the special bond among the principal churches, which must participate in any case involving one of their own bishops. Rome must be brought into the case especially because it involves Alexandria. "So that what was right could have been determined by all" means collegial decision at the level of *communio*, and especially a discussion and agreement among the principal churches. But it is especially evident from the last sentences that Julius is writing out of a special awareness of his responsibility, and not from a strictly juridical point of view as holder of the see of Peter and protector of the heritage of Peter and Paul. On the basis of the Petrine and Pauline commission, the Roman bishop has a moral sense of responsibility for ecclesiastical communion. What is at stake, then, is his concern for communion based on his special, apostolic (Petrine and Pauline) responsibility.

5. The Synod of Sardica: Rome Assumes the Task of Supervision

The response to Bishop Julius's call for participation by the whole Church led to the calling of a general council, the first since Nicea. It was convoked by both emperors and met at Sardica, present-day Sofia, in 342. The council collapsed at the very beginning. First the eastern, anti-Athanasian bishops demanded that Athanasius and the other bishops should not be allowed to take part, but their demand was rejected. They insisted particularly on the autonomy of East and West, asserting that the West should not interfere in eastern disputes and vice versa. Finally they excused themselves, saying that they had just received news of a victory by their eastern emperor over the Persians and they felt obligated to celebrate it in their own congregations.

The West continued to meet alone. One result of their deliberations was that, in light of their experience that synods were no longer sufficient to deal with ecclesiastical conflicts, they made the first attempt to establish a legal basis for Rome's responsibility to maintain communion among the bishops. At the initiative of Bishop Ossius of Cordoba it was decreed that bishops who were deposed by a synod could appeal to the bishop of Rome. If he judged that the synod's decision was incorrect he could order a new hearing before the bishops of the neighboring province; if the deposed bishop so desired, Roman presbyters could also take part. This synod was then to review the case.[31] Strictly speaking, Rome is not yet established as a genuine court of appeal because it is not the Roman bishop himself who makes a new decision in the case. Rome is only a reviewing authority to see to it that the appeal (to a different synod) is carried out.

Noteworthy in this is the reason given for the Roman bishop's being entrusted with this kind of supervisory function: *Petri memoriam honoremus* (out of respect to the memory of [the apostle] Peter). This is typical of the contemporary state of historical awareness. The religious authority that accrues to the Roman church as the church of Peter is very general in nature. This ascribed religious authority makes it legitimate for the Roman church to accept the new legal obligation that has become necessary because of ecclesiastical conflicts.

The immediate historical results of Sardica should be distinguished from the longer term effects. Its decisions were not immediately carried out even in the West, let alone the East. The Canons of Sardica, falsely dubbed "Nicean" in Rome from the early fifth century onward, were the initial cells that would slowly germinate throughout almost a thousand years to bloom around 1200 under Innocent III: they were the germs of Rome's exclusive juridical competence in *causae maiores,* that is, in everything having to do with bishoprics or bishops (removal, translation to another diocese, resignation, and so on).

It is true that later, when the development of the primacy had gone far beyond Sardica and the "Pseudo-Isidorean Decretals" in the ninth century had introduced a great many more direct rights of interference by the apostolic see, Sardica was adduced to establish a concept of primacy that leaned more toward subsidiarity and was structured more within the synodal system. After the eleventh century it was practically forgotten. Its fuzzy reasoning in comparison to later theories of primacy, its statement that it was creating a new right (rather than recognizing an existing right resting on Christ's institution), and finally the fact that we never hear of a single appeal based on its principles—

all these factors made Sardica appear to be a most inappropriate witness to the tradition. It was rediscovered in the seventeenth century and acquired greater significance because Pseudo-Isidore had been discovered to be inauthentic. This reevaluation of its status is evident in the work of Robert Bellarmine, who even thought of Sardica as an ecumenical council. At the same time, however, Gallican authors depended on Sardica for their more subsidiary view of primacy.[32]

6. Rome as Refuge in Critical Situations

The further course of the Arian controversy seems to present the picture of a conflict in which Rome by no means prevailed; in fact, it appears that Rome did not even make an energetic and deliberate attempt to counteract the increasing deviation from Nicea. The Roman bishops Julius and his successor Liberius (352–366) did at first belong to the small group of those who remained true to Athanasius. Over time this certainly contributed to the strengthening of Rome's authority, especially in the East, but we can by no means speak of anything like success at first. Even the Roman church had its weak moments: Bishop Liberius, under imperial pressure (he was separated from his community, sent into exile, and replaced by an antibishop) accepted a formula of faith that, while not expressly denying the formula of Nicea, deviated from and practically abandoned it. Liberius also broke communion with Athanasius.

Nevertheless, in the long run the Arian controversy served to strengthen the position of Rome. The decisive factor here was that Rome of all the principal churches most clearly held the lead in strength, stability, and clarity when, after about the year 370, Arianism was overthrown in the East and a theologically mangled Church faced the necessity of restoring communion, consolidating its relations, and fixing its consensus in creedal formulas. Rome, in contrast to the shattered East, represented the communion of the entire Latin West. It is understandable that in this situation it was important to the most diverse groups that they achieve communion with and recognition from Rome. Thus Rome became in fact the center around which unity was established.

As would frequently be the case in centuries to come, the expectation of finding assistance in Rome far exceeded the ability of Rome to meet that expectation. Rome often lacked both competence and adequate information about the difficult problems of the East, nor did it have any real ability to carry through on its decisions. The Church Father Basil had something to say about that: he found that Rome too readily gave letters of communion to bishops even if they were separated from each other.[33] He complained especially about the Roman bishop Damasus, calling him proud and arrogant, handing down judgments from his high horse without really understanding the complicated relationships in the East: "What help is there for us from Western superciliousness?"[34]

In fact it was this very Damasus (366–384) who introduced a new and lordly style that was called "dictation, not dealing."[35] He got his way most obviously at a synod of 153 bishops at Antioch in 379, which accepted the conditions for communion he dictated and adopted the formula of faith he devised. Of course Rome did not always determine the conditions of communion so directly. But on the whole the result of these conflicts was that communion with Rome acquired an immense importance, so that when crises arose or parties were at odds they repeatedly turned to Rome and placed great value on being in communion with it. The view that Rome was the center of communion was accepted almost everywhere in the western Church by the fifth century. For someone like Jerome or Ambrose of Milan, communion with Rome was the same as communion with the *catholica*.

The mind of the East was not so clearly settled. But in the East as well the experience of the Arian controversy and its outcome had established a way of thinking that became quite clear in the imperial laws of 380 by which Emperor Theodosius made Christianity the state religion and at the same time used his power to put an end to controversies over matters of belief. He decreed that the faith preached to the Romans by St. Peter and now proclaimed by Damasus of Rome and Peter of Alexandria should be the accepted rule of faith for the entire empire. On the one hand, Rome alone did not establish the norm, but rather Rome and Alexandria, the primary sees in West and East. On the other hand we should note that the source of that faith was St. Peter and his preaching in Rome. There was, then, a certain difference in rank: Rome is the original source.

It remained true, nevertheless, that the Roman church not only exercised no leadership in the East in normal times, but also that serious ecclesiastical divisions and conflicts could by no means be quickly resolved by appeal to Rome. It does seem, however, that in crisis situations a tradition was created, beginning with Athanasius and growing in importance throughout the fifth century, especially in the wake of the "robber synod" at Ephesus in 449, whereby in emergencies it became customary to turn to Rome and expect to receive aid and support from there. This was again and again crucial when bishops were expelled or "heretical" teachings were imposed through imperial pressure. Rome was not merely regarded as the higher court in a strictly legal sense. These cries for help could be seen, in the first instance, more as extra-legal appeals to a court with higher religious authority that is called upon to act in Christian solidarity when ecclesiastical order is disturbed. The Roman bishop was not really expected to apply authoritative measures since he was in no position to take such actions in the East, especially against imperial power; instead, the hope was that he would give aid in the form of moral expressions of solidarity and by issuing warnings, writing to other bishops, and requesting new councils. It also happened that letters were sent to all the important sees in the West at the same time; so when Patriarch John Chrysostom was banished from Constantinople in 404 he wrote to the bishops of Rome, Milan, and Aquileia.[36]

These instances primarily concerned the "communion of the West." On the other hand, the boundaries between such cases and genuine appeals to a "higher court" were fluid, at least in cases like those of Patriarch Flavian of Constantinople and Bishops Eusebius of Dorylaeum and Theodoret of Cyrus after the "robber synod" in Ephesus in 449. Moreover, Rome was regarded by these appellants as the city of Saints Peter and Paul; its religious aura blended with their hopes for concrete help. This is clearest in the case of Theodoret. He wrote that the renown of Rome was due not only to its political status but also and primarily to its faith, as recorded in Romans 1:8 ("your faith is proclaimed throughout the world"), and to its possession of the tombs of Peter and Paul. He continues with a comparison that was very popular in the East: Peter and Paul, like the sun, rose in the East and set in the West; from there they now give light to the whole world, making illustrious the chair of the bishop of Rome.[37] In short, Rome was seen as a religious authority beyond all law. In emergencies people expected it to assume a special responsibility for the oppressed and the afflicted.

V. From Center of *Communio* to Leadership of the Whole Church

The next developments began in the second half of the fourth century and were confined to the West. With few exceptions, these ideas were not developed in the East to the same degree.

1. Further Development of the Roman Concept of Primacy

Beginning in the second half of the fourth century there was a remarkable development of the concept of primacy, especially under Popes Damasus (366–384), Siricius (384–399), Innocent I (402–417), and above all Leo I, the Great (440–461), the initial high point of the papacy in Christian antiquity. The title "pope" itself first appears in the fourth century, initially for a number of individual bishops including the bishop of Alexandria; it has been reserved for the bishop of Rome since the fifth century.

This development was characterized in the first place by the concentration of the general complex of ideas surrounding the Roman church, based on the special reverence reserved for Peter and Paul, and now extended along one specific line, namely the Petrine succession of the Roman bishops. This first appeared in the mid-third century with Stephen, but now it became the central and directing idea in the concept of primacy. In the pope, Peter himself is present; indeed, Peter lives on in him. Leo I's conception of papal primacy revolved around two central ideas: the pope is both the "heir of Peter" within the meaning of Roman law and therefore the possessor of his power of the keys, and he is Peter's "vicar" or "representative" as Peter is vicar of Christ. The title "vicar of Peter" would over the course of centuries become the core of papal self-understanding. However, well into the second Christian millennium Roman tradition established the significance of Rome by reference to both the "leaders [κορύφαιοι]," Peter *and* Paul, the Christian counterparts of Romulus and Remus.

In addition, the Petrine succession was more expressly made the content of the papal claim to leadership over the whole Church. The core concepts were now *sollicitudo omnium ecclesiarum* (care for all the churches: cf. 2 Cor 11:28) and the idea of the Roman church as *caput* (head), to which the other churches were related as members. Rome was now to a much greater degree an active institution that intervened everywhere, and no longer simply the fixed center of communion. Authority to make binding decisions for individual churches was now claimed more explicitly, by reference especially to Matthew 16:18-20. As far as the image of Peter was concerned, emphasis was now placed on the motif of Peter as lawgiver *(Petrus legislator)*. Artistic representations of Peter showed him as a second Moses: just as Moses was the lawgiver of the old covenant, Peter now gives to all nations the tables of the law of the new covenant. Thus in the mosaic in the apse of the old Roman Basilica of St. Peter, the apostle is shown receiving from Christ the tables of the law of the New Testament.

An important milestone in the development of the genuine authority of Rome to make new laws was the appearance of the "first papal decretals," a response by Pope Siricius to questions posed by the Spanish bishop Himerius of Tarragona in 385; by papal request he was to make this response known to all the Spanish bishops.[38] The style, to begin with, is striking. It is no longer the kind of fraternal admonition, however urgent and often authoritative, that appears in earlier documents from the Roman bishops. Instead, we find here the commanding style of the imperial court. Equally striking is the claim it enunciates. According to this, Himerius had written to the Roman Church as the "head of [his] body,"[39] and instructions from the apostolic see were not to be ignored by any bishop; in the pope, Peter is present in both a mystical and juridical manner: "We bear the burdens of all who are oppressed; or rather the holy apostle Peter bears them in us; we, the heirs of his stewardship, trust that he protects and preserves us in all things."[40]

Before this, only synods could create new law in the Church. Now papal writings were placed *de facto* on the same level as synodal law. It is true that at this point, and for centuries afterward, the accent is more on witnessing to law than on making it. The Roman bishop responds as the witness to a privileged tradition, and with regard to difficult questions of Christian life or Church discipline he communicates the Roman church's position, that is, the tradition handed on to it by Peter. For the western churches this rested on the assertion (first made in 416 by Innocent I, but historically false) that all the churches of the West were founded directly or indirectly by Peter or his successors, since no other apostles had been active there. It was therefore fitting "that they follow the usage of the Roman church from which they undoubtedly take their origin."[41] It is true that Rome was more modest in its dealings with the East. Here even Leo the Great made no claim to be able to make laws; in the East the pope is only *custos canonum*, the guardian of the conciliar canons. In the East the Petrine office had primarily a conservative function, acting against the continual appearance of new creeds that were always trying to overturn the old, and maintaining the dogmatic and disciplinary decrees of the councils.

Beginning with the last third of the fourth century a feeling emerged that the Roman bishop had a position independent of and superior to councils. From the Roman council of 382 onward it was taken for granted that the Roman church outranked other Churches not by conciliar decree, but by divine institution. Since a Roman synod in 371 or 372, it had been emphasized that councils, no matter how large their attendance, were invalid without the assent of the Roman bishop. The concrete background for this was the double synod of Seleucia and Rimini in 359–360 that under imperial pressure had adopted an ambiguous formula that even Arians could accept. It was the conciliar confusion of the fourth century that made this claim appear plausible and made it necessary to draw some distinction between "authentic" and "false" councils. Councils as such had proved to be rather unreliable institutions. In this situation Rome became, as we will see more clearly from the fifth century onward, a guarantor of a "line of continuity." This came to mean that councils once acknowledged were valid, and their decrees were to be maintained in perpetuity; all others were rejected.

2. *Background:* Roma christiana

We can best understand the background of this development by considering the earliest artistic portrait in a Roman church (not including catacombs), the apse mosaic in Santa Pudentiana from the end of the fourth century. Christ is enthroned and flanked by the apostles Peter and Paul clad in the togas of Roman senators. This is a vivid symbol of the "baptism" of ancient Rome that was in progress!

Only at that time, in the fourth and fifth centuries, did the Christianization of the city of Rome succeed on a grand scale. The Roman senatorial nobility in particular had remained until that period one of the last bastions of paganism. From the end of the fourth century onward they increasingly turned to Christianity. The result was a combination and fusion of the most portentous historical consequence. Until this time the *city* of Rome had been "Babylon" for the Christians, and even in the fourth century Rome was a less Christian city than Constantinople or Alexandria. A vast gulf yawned between the *church* of Rome, that is, the Rome of Peter and Paul, and *political* Rome. Now the spirit of *Roma aeterna,* Rome the *caput mundi,* the city that gave the world its laws, was joined to the Rome of the apostles. Now the two currents flowed together into one, and the unique character of ancient Rome was communicated to the ecclesial, papal Rome and recast the primacy as well. The Roman nobility brought its way of thinking with it: especially its ideas of order and of law, its charism of leadership, its talent for reconciling opposites, its sober feeling for what is practical as well as its sense of power: in short, everything that had made Rome capable of world domination.

So it happened that out of the whole traditional complex of ideas bound up with the ecclesial idea of Rome especially those things were retained that could be translated into the context of law: Peter as lawgiver; the pope as the continuing embodiment of Peter and the heir and possessor of his power, holding the *plenitudo potestatis,* the supreme leadership over all the churches. These elements, of course, were still further expanded. The result was an important shift of emphasis as regards primacy: The church of *tradition,* whose connection to its origins was particularly strong (Irenaeus), became the church of the *capital city* that extends its laws to the whole world. The Rome of *paradosis* that witnesses became the Rome that made law and commanded. The fusion between the political Rome as *caput orbis* and Christian Rome as site of the martyrdom of Peter and Paul is clearly evident in a sermon of Leo the Great for the feast of Peter and Paul in 441. For Leo, the Christian importance of Rome was based on its character as capital of the empire but surpasses it as Christian universalism presupposes and surpasses the universalism of the Roman Empire; for it was through Peter and Paul that "you [Rome], who have been the teacher of error, became the pupil of truth." These two κορύφαιοι (leaders), as the new founders of Rome, take the place of Romulus and Remus who contaminated the origins of the city by fratricide:

> It is they who have brought you to your glory as a holy race, a chosen people, a priestly city and kingdom; through the holy see of Peter you have become the crown of the world and by divine religion you preside more widely than once by political dominion.

Divine providence has used the political unity of all people in the Roman Empire to prepare for the religious unity of all humanity in the Christian religion. Peter was sent to Rome "so that the light of truth revealed for the salvation of all peoples may radiate more efficaciously from the head through the whole body of the world."[42]

3. To What Extent Was the Roman Claim Recognized?

In the West as in the East, papal leadership was far more a program than a reality. The "western patriarchy" embracing Illyricum and Greece as well was by no means a Church ruled from Rome, but a very loose-knit and heterogeneous entity. The maximum of Roman attachment was approached when the bishop of Rome was queried and his advice followed on Church affairs, mostly practical matters such as administration of the sacraments, Christian morality, penitential practices and Church order; his instructions were later recorded in collections of laws. In addition, the pope could make decisions regarding Church organization in the provincial Churches. For the most part, however, reality fell far short of Roman ambitions. In Spain, southern Gaul, and North Africa dogmatic decisions were still made on matters of faith and heretics were condemned without any reference to Rome.

Three particular zones of Roman influence can be discerned:

> 1. The closest thing to a genuine papal government of the Church was to be found in *Italia suburbica,* that is, in central and southern Italy and the Italian islands. Here the bishop of Rome had a position comparable to that of the patriarchs of Alexandria and Antioch in their own regions. These areas also constituted a single Church province in which the pope was the metropolitan.

> 2. Next came the Churches with relatively close ties to Rome, including *Italia annonaria,* or northern Italy, an important source of grain for the capital city. It contained the Church provinces of Milan and Aquileia. It is true that for a time Milan enjoyed a status

almost equal to that of Rome, thanks to its position as residence of the western emperor and still more to the reputation of its bishop, Ambrose (374–397). As a result, questions and appeals for help from the East, Gaul, or North Africa were sometimes sent to Rome and Milan simultaneously. This case shows that the acknowledgment of particular Church centers was still in flux and was largely dependent on personalities. This second sphere of Roman influence also included Gaul, Illyricum, and Greece, all of which belonged to the Roman patriarchy until 733. The zone thus described is characterized by the fact that relatively frequent inquiries about problems of Church order and morality were directed to Rome; they were often answered in circular letters to the bishops of whole provinces or several provinces together. The metropolitans of Thessalonica and Arles had been "apostolic vicars" of the pope for Greece-Illyrica and Gaul since the reigns of Popes Siricius (384–399) and Zosimus (417–418); they were commissioned by the pope to administer justice in those regions. Their office should not be confused with that of the "apostolic vicars" appointed for the Diaspora and missionary regions since the seventeenth century.

3. Spain and North Africa were much more loosely connected to Rome. Spain maintained very sporadic contacts with the Roman center, but the North African Church, if only because of its theological importance, kept up a much more lively exchange while preserving its independence. It combined a marked self-confidence with a strong organizational cohesion approached by no other Church in the Latin region. Fundamental decisions about questions of faith and discipline were made by the North African plenary council in Carthage, with the bishop of Carthage having the highest rank. The North African Church regarded Rome, the only apostolic church in the Latin region, as the *sedes apostolica* pure and simple. The Roman tradition was especially important in questions of faith. Still, the Roman church was far more like an older sister than a mother.

The scope and geographical horizon of the papal "care for all the churches" and the varying importance attached to these regions are reflected in papal letters. Of one hundred seventy-nine letters addressed to bishops or other important Church figures that have come down to us from Siricius to Leo I (384–461) more than half, or ninety-two, were sent to the East, but almost all of those were connected with the conflict over John Chrysostom or the councils of Ephesus I (431), Ephesus II (449), and Chalcedon (451). Fourteen went to *Italia suburbicaria*, nine to *Italia annonaria*, twenty-three to Illyricum and Greece, twenty-five to

Gaul, but no more than three to Spain and thirteen to North Africa, most of these last related to the Pelagian controversy, which we will discuss next.

In the case of North Africa it is interesting to note the attitude of a self-confident and organizationally intact Church toward Rome. The saying of Bishop Augustine of Hippo (396–430), *Roma locuta, causa finita* ("Rome has spoken, the matter is settled") was quoted repeatedly. However, the quotation is really a bold reshaping of the words of that Church Father taken quite out of context.

Concretely the issue was the teaching of Pelagius, an ascetic from Britain who lived in Rome. Pelagius took a stand against permissive and minimalist Christianity that shrank from the moral seriousness of Christian discipleship and used human incapacity and trust in grace alone to excuse personal sloth. He therefore emphasized an ethical Christianity of works and moral challenge for which grace was primarily an incentive to action; human beings remain capable of choosing between good and evil by their own power. This teaching was condemned by two North African councils in Carthage and Mileve in 416. But since Pelagius lived in Rome, and Rome was the center of the Pelagian movement, it seemed appropriate to inform Pope Innocent I of the decision. Ultimately, the struggle against Pelagianism could only be carried on with the cooperation of Rome. The pope finally responded in 417, accepting the decisions of the two councils. Augustine then wrote: "In this matter, two councils have already sent letters to the apostolic see, and from thence rescripts have come back. The matter is settled *(causa finita est)*; if only the heresy would cease!"[43]

Both the context of this statement and its continuity with the rest of Augustine's thought permit no interpretation other than that Rome's verdict alone is not decisive; rather, it disposes of all doubt *after* all that has preceded it. This is because there remains no other ecclesiastical authority of any consequence to which the Pelagians can appeal, and in particular the very authority from which they could most readily have expected a favorable decision, namely Rome, has clearly ruled against them!

In general, Augustine attributes a relatively substantial weight of authority to the Roman church in questions of faith but does not consider that it has a superior teaching office. It has *auctoritas* but not *potestas* over the Church in North Africa. The very councils mentioned above give a clear picture of the way the Africans, including Augustine, regarded Rome's teaching authority. They sent their records to Rome not to obtain formal confirmation, but because they acknowledged that the Roman church, with its traditions, had a greater *auctoritas* in matters of faith; therefore they desired to have a Roman decision united with their own.[44] This is especially obvious in a letter from Augustine writing for five bishops; we are not, he said, pouring

> our little trickle back into your ample fountain to increase it, but . . . we wish to be reassured by you that this trickle of ours, however scant, flows from the same fountainhead as your abundant stream, and we desire the consolation of your writings, drawn from our common share of the one grace.[45]

Every word of this should be noted: The Roman church is not the source of the African Church, for both, in parallel streams, flow from the river of the same tradition, even though the river is fuller in the Roman church. Rome thus has a relatively greater and more weighty authority, and that is why the African Church seeks a verdict from Rome.

Nevertheless, Pope Innocent I's answer[46] clearly indicates the difference between Roman and African opinions in this matter, for he interprets the African bishops' inquiry as a request for approval. He speaks of *all* streams flowing from the Roman church as their source—thus no longer in the sense of parallel currents, but in terms of one-sided dependence on Rome—and he emphasizes that questions of faith can be definitively settled *only* by Rome. Rome alone is thus the ultimate normative authority in matters of faith.

In reality, of course, the *causa* was by no means settled, for under Zosimus, the next pope, the Pelagians succeeded in obtaining a hearing at Rome and defending their orthodoxy. Augustine did not wait for Rome's decision; in 418 he called another council at Carthage that solemnly condemned particular Pelagian doctrines. The decree was simply communicated to Rome, and the pope confirmed the council's decisions.

The African Church was even more determined to defend its jurisdictional autonomy. Councils at Carthage in 419 and 424 forbade any appeals to Rome. The background of these actions was the case of a priest named Apiarius, who had been excommunicated by his own bishop and then received a favorable judgment at Rome (probably because the authorities there were ignorant of the situation). The North Africans reacted by providing a court of appeal even for ordinary presbyters from their own bishop's verdict to the North African council at Carthage. That appeared to satisfy the requirements of justice. In turn they took a firm stand against Roman intervention, where people acting at a distance were almost certain to make wrong decisions, if only because it was impossible to bring the witnesses necessary for such a judicial proceeding from North Africa to Rome. Moreover, it was unthinkable that God would give the spirit of right judgment to a single individual, the Roman bishop, and withhold it from an entire council of bishops.[47] Therefore the North African bishops forbade any "ultra-marine" appeals. In contrast to Sardica, they applied this prohibition even to bishops. This particular decision had been preceded by a similar case involving a bishop who had fallen out with his congregation but was protected by Rome; at that, even Augustine of Hippo threatened to resign. From now on, the only court of appeal was to be the North African council at Carthage. This case was to be brought up repeatedly in future as an example of resistance by the episcopate of a national Church against Roman centralism.

Of course, as time went on the African Church's ties to Rome grew stronger. A major factor was the period of Vandal domination (429–533), an entire century of persecution of catholic Christians during which the African Church depended on the assistance of Rome. But even in the sixth-century incident involving Vigilius the African Church still manifested its sense of independence from Rome.

4. Theological Assessment of the Development of the Idea of Primacy in the First Five Centuries

In any case it is clear that Roman primacy was not a given from the outset; it underwent a long process of development whose initial phases extended well into the fifth century. The question is then: Can we reasonably say of this historically developed papacy that it was instituted by Christ and therefore must always continue to exist? This seems a more radical question than the similar challenges posed to other Church offices (e.g., the episcopate) or the sacraments because in the case of the papal office the initial process lasted much longer and clearly extended beyond the "apostolic" era of the Church, however one might wish to define that time period. In the case of the episcopal office, or the threefold office of bishop, priest, and deacon, the fundamental process of formation was completed at least by the end of the second century. For papal primacy the process lasted another two or three centuries.

The first answer can only be that recognition of the need for an enduring Petrine office as a guarantor of unity presupposes the historical necessity of a multitude of experiences that build on one another and could not be completed in one or two centuries. That need is unrelated to the greater efficiency of a community with a unified head to coordinate its activities. In fact, until the modern era the Roman church constituted such a coordinating center only to a very limited degree, and not at all before the eleventh century, if only because very few popes pursued a consistent and active ecclesiastical policy; their actions were mainly reactions.

The need for an office that guaranteed unity presented itself on other than technical or rational grounds, but this presupposes a long period of development. If we do not understand the institution of the Church by Jesus Christ in an unhistorical sense, but rather in such a way that an awareness of what is essential and enduring in the Church develops only as a result of historical challenges and experiences, we cannot reasonably expect to discover a "primacy from the very beginning" in the sense of a primacy of teaching and jurisdiction as defined by Vatican I.

Instead, without doing violence to history we may interpret this process in terms of theology and salvation history somewhat as follows: Only in the course of history does the Church learn how to preserve both its connection with its historical origin (apostolicity), and at the same time and closely united with that origin its present unity as a visible community of faith and a society in communion (community of the body of Christ). When threatened by heresies, the Church learns that it draws its life from recollection of its apostolic origins. It realizes that tie to its origins in a twofold manner: through the canon of sacred Scripture, which is thus clearly distinguished from the "inauthentic" writings, and through the continuity and "apostolic succession" of office, primarily that of bishops. In both of these the Church's apostolic origins are present. But in this not all churches are equally important. The "apostolic" churches have the greatest importance, because there the connection to the origins is somehow more tangible.

In a further process, the Church learns through the experience of schisms that it needs an enduring center of unity. But because the Church cannot "create" its essential elements, but lives its life as a Church founded by Jesus and endowed with certain gifts and traditions, it cannot produce such a center of unity out of nothing. It must seek within its apostolic traditions for such a point of unity. An artificially created center of unity devised for practical reasons could, of course, have a certain usefulness as an administrative clearinghouse and center for arbitration of disputes, but in times of real crisis and when the faith is in danger there is no guarantee that the Church can maintain itself in truth purely by relying on such a manufactured office of unity. In effect, the Christian imperial throne from Constantine onward was such an "artificially manufactured," humanly devised center, and it is a prime illustration of the problems involved. The Church must therefore seek within its own tradition to see whether it does not possess at least the elements of such a center. In the course of that search it discovers the Roman church, which has an advantage over all the other "apostolic" churches in its ties to the beginning by the fact that it is associated with Peter and Paul, and therefore has a *potentior principalitas.*

The next element that comes into view against this background of experience of the need for an office that endows the Church with unity and preserves it as one is the biblical Peter as primitive image and model of such unity. Now the Church understands that the words of Jesus to Peter had significance for the entire Church as well. The Petrine office is thus the link between two elements: the apostolic (the Church's attachment to its origins because it descends from Peter) and the catholic (the Church's universality in space because it serves present and enduring unity).[48]

The two elements—the concrete historical demand elicited by current need and a diligent search within the tradition—must coalesce. The synod of Sardica is an especially vivid illustration of the interplay of the two. On the one hand, there was a current need for an office of arbitration and appeal in a situation in which synods met sequentially and annulled each other's actions. The search for an existing tradition, still very tentative and clumsy, found its expression in the reasoning *Petri memoriam honoremus.* In other words the Church of Peter, to which special honor is due because of its apostolic rank, should be the one to assume a function that has proved itself necessary in present circumstances.

What kind of theological assessment should be given to the way in which this development was shaped by a Roman and imperial environment, circumstances that marked the papacy from the fourth century onward? It is certainly not wrong to see a "secularization" of primacy in this sense as a partial aspect of a Church that adopted secular and political models step by step with the Christianization of the masses. Is it not true that the special character of ecclesial authority was obscured, above all, when the papacy adopted the characteristics of Roman public officialdom? No matter how valid it is to see here one of the more unfortunate aspects of "inculturation" (the obverse of which is always a blurring of what is specifically Christian), in historical perspective this cannot be the sole answer. We could sharpen the point by asking whether the specific charism of the Roman Church does not consist at least in part in its refusal to suppress or ignore the problems of institutionalization and power as if they were foreign to the gospel—especially since the problem of power continually arises in the Church, whether in the form of dominance over the Church exercised by the Christian emperors or in the established Churches of the Reformation. The concrete legal and institutional shape of primacy, with all its claims to power, may well be the precondition and the price to be paid, in a real Church of sinners and even "sinful structures," so that the universal Church may remain a concrete and not an abstract reality, one that cannot be absorbed into the state or national order but instead preserves its own independence.

NOTES

[1]*1 Clement* 5–6.

[2]For more detail, see among others Karl Baus, *From the Apostolic Community to Constantine*, vol. 1 of Hubert Jedin and John Dolan, eds., *Handbook of Church History* (New York: Herder & Herder, 1965) 115–18.

[3]Eusebius, *Hist. eccl.* 2.25.

[4]Eusebius, *Hist. eccl.* 4.23.

[5]*1 Clement* 59, 63.

[6]Eusebius, *Hist. eccl.* 4.23.

[7]Ignatius, *Rom.* 3.1.

[8]The German text is found in *LThK* (1st ed. 1930) 25; see also H. Grotz, "Die Stellung der Römischen Kirche anhand frühchristlicher Quellen," *AHP* 13 (1975) 47.

[9]Sozomen, *Church History* 3.8.5 (*PG* 67.1054A/B).

[10]J.M.R. Tillard has described this easily forgotten aspect in his *The Bishop of Rome*, trans. John de Satgé (Wilmington: Michael Glazier, 1983).

[11]G. D. Mansi, *Sacrorum Conciliorum Nova et Amplissima Collectio* (Arnhem and Leipzig: Welter, 1927) 2:469C.

[12]*Adv. haer.* 3.3.1-2; see number 1 in "Texts," p. 184.

[13]Ibid., 3.4.1.

[14]Eusebius, *Hist. eccl.* 4.22.

[15]*De praescriptione haereticorum* 36.1–4. Translation by Peter Holmes, in Alexander Roberts and James Donaldson, eds., *The Ante-Nicene Fathers* (New York: Charles Scribner's Sons, 1908) 3:260.

[16]As quoted by Eusebius, *Hist. eccl.* 5.24.

[17]*Hist. eccl.* 5.24.

[18]"For in Asia great luminaries sleep who shall rise again on the day of the Lord's advent" (Eusebius, *Hist. eccl.* 5.24).

[19]*Saint Cyprian, Letters*, translated by Rose Bernard Donna, C.S.J. The Fathers of the Church, vol. 51 (Washington: Catholic University of America Press, 1964) 73.13.

[20]Cyprian, *Letters*, 71.3.

[21]Cyprian, *Letters*, 75.

[22]Cyprian, *Letters*, 75.

[23]*Dialogues* 3.11 (*PL* 188.1223–24).

[24]Cyprian, *Letters* 68.3.

[25]Ibid., 68.4.

[26]Cyprian, *Letters*, 48.3.

[27]Cyprian, *Letters*, 59.14.

[28]Myron Wojtowytsch, *Papsttum und Konzile von den Anfängen bis zu Leo I. (440–461). Studien zur Entstehung der Überordnung des Papstes über Konzile* (Stuttgart: Hiersemann, 1981) 392.

[29]Cyprian, *Letters* 67.

[30]Athanasius, *Apologia contra Arianos* 35 (*PG* 25.308A/B).

[31]See number 2 in "Texts," p. 185.

[32]For the history of the reception of Sardica, see H. J. Sieben, "Sanctissimi Petri apostoli memoriam honoremus. Die Sardicensischen Appellationskanones im Wandel der Geschichte," *ThPh* 58 (1983) 501–34.

[33]Letter 129.3 (*PG* 32.561).

[34]Letter 239.2 (*PG* 32.893B).

[35]E. Caspar, *Geschichte des Papsttums von den Anfängen bis zur Höhe der Weltherrschaft* (Tübingen, 1930) 1:227.

[36]*PG* 47.11–12.
[37]Theodoret of Cyrus, *Letters.* SC 111. Letter 113, 56–58.
[38]*PL* 13.1131–47.
[39]Ibid., 1146A.
[40]Ibid., 1133A.
[41]*PL* 20.552B.
[42]*PL* 54.422–24.
[43]*PL* 38.734.
[44]CSEL 44.655, 667–68.
[45]Ibid., 688.
[46]Ibid., 701–3.
[47]CCL 149.170–71.
[48]On this, see the very notable remarks of Rudolf Pesch, *Simon-Petrus. Geschichte und geschichtliche Bedeutung des ersten Jüngers Jesu Christi* (Stuttgart, 1980) 163–70.

SELECTED BIBLIOGRAPHY

Grotz, Hans. "Die Stellung der Römischen Kirche anhand frühchristlicher Quellen," *AHP* 13 (1975) 7–64.

Joannou, Perikles Pierre. *Die Ostkirche und die Cathedra Petri im 4. Jahrhundert* (Stuttgart, 1972); but see also the critique by W. de Vries, "Die Ostkirche und die Cathedra Petri," *Orientalia Christiana Periodica* 40 (1974) 114–44.

Marschall, Werner. *Karthago und Rom. Die Stellung der nordafrikanischen Kirche zum Apostolischen Stuhl in Rom* (Stuttgart: Hiersemann, 1971).

Pesch, Rudolf. *Simon-Petrus. Geschichte und geschichtliche Bedeutung des ersten Jüngers Jesu Christi* (Stuttgart, 1980).

Pietri, Charles. *Roma christiana. Recherches sur l'église de Rome, son organisation, sa politique, son idéologie de Miltiade à Sixte III (311–440).* 2 vols. (Rome, 1976).

Stockmeier, Peter. "Römische Kirche und Petrusamt anhand frühchristlicher Zeugnisse," *AHP* 14 (1976) 357–72 (with a critique of Grotz).

Twomey, Vincent. *Apostolikos Thronos. The Primacy of Rome as Reflected in the Church History of Eusebius and the Historico-apologetic Writings of Saint Athanasius the Great.* Münsterische Beiträge zur Theologie 49 (Münster: Aschendorff, 1982); see also the critical review by H. J. Sieben in *ThPh* 58 (1983) 257–60.

Wojtowytsch, Myron. *Papsttum und Konzile von den Anfängen bis zu Leo I. (440–461). Studien zur Entstehung der Überordnung des Papstes über Konzile* (Stuttgart: Hiersemann, 1981); see also the critical review by St. O. Horn in *AHC* 17 (1985) 9–17.

PART TWO:
DIFFERENCES IN THE UNIFYING FUNCTION
OF PAPAL PRIMACY IN EAST AND WEST

In the five hundred years from the fifth to the tenth centuries the role of Rome was very different in the Byzantine "imperial Church" and in the West, which after the tribal migrations of the fifth century consisted of a group of independent Germanic kingdoms. Until the eighth century, except for the period between 476 and 536 when it was ruled by Odoacer and the Ostrogoths, Rome belonged to the empire governed from Constantinople. The pope was a subject of the emperor, and from the sixth to the eighth century the Roman bishop elected by the clergy and people of Rome had to be confirmed by the emperor in Constantinople before he could be consecrated. But in the eighth century the West attained a decided measure of self-confidence and asserted itself as a new and independent cultural entity separate from the Mediterranean world. The latter, in turn, was sundered by the Arab invasions between 640 and 711. As is quite obvious, for example, in the *Libri Carolini* of Charlemagne (ca. 790) this self-confidence was identified with a particular attachment to Rome: The West desired to be "more Roman" than the Greek world. But at the same time it rejected the reality that still constituted, even for Rome, the basis for an ecumenical council: the pentarchy of the five patriarchates that, in turn, represented the *oikoumene* of the Mediterranean world.

I. Primacy and Imperial Church Structures, 400–900

For five hundred years the role of Rome in the imperial Church was determined essentially by the relationships among three entities: the ecumenical councils, the patriarchates, and the imperial establishment. The essential features of this set of relationships developed in the middle years of the fifth century, with the events of the years 449–451 the crucial turning point.

1. The Test Case: The Councils of Ephesus II (449) and Chalcedon (451)

For the ecumenical councils, as for all matters that had to be settled at the highest levels, the "patriarchates" came increasingly to be the most important entities. The terms "patriarch" and "patriarchate" emerged in the fifth century and became fixed usage in the sixth. They originated in the triad of principal churches at Rome, Alexandria, and Antioch. The sixth canon of the Council of Nicea (325) explicitly confirmed the "ancient custom" that these three bishops were to have ecclesial jurisdiction (not specifically defined) over their own regions. The significance of Alexandria, the second see, was enhanced still further by the fourth-century struggle with Arianism, but gradually a fourth ecclesial see emerged as foremost, namely Constantinople, the new imperial capital, which claimed and exercised ecclesial governance over the three eparchies of Thrace (with its capital at Heraclea), Asia (with its seat at Ephesus), and Pontus (headed by Caesarea)—in other words, the Anatolian peninsula and the territories that are now eastern Bulgaria and European Turkey. The contest between Alexandria and Constantinople for preeminence in the East was inevitable; it was to be a constant element in ecclesial conflicts throughout the first half of the fifth century.

The confrontation between these two sees rapidly became intertwined with theological debates revolving around the relationship between unity and plurality in Christ. The unitive Christology of Alexandria (*logos-sarx* Christology) sought to find a consistent and complete way of describing the unity of the incarnate Word, and thus of the divine Logos, as a subject acting in the flesh, while the distinguishing Christology of Antioch (*logos-anthropos* Christology) took its theological starting point from the autonomy of Jesus' humanity.

These discussions were further overshadowed by a traditional principle that had been worked out in the struggles with Arianism in the fourth century. In the wake of those conflicts the creed formulated at Nicea in 325 had acquired *the* foremost place, so much so that it had come to embody the traditional faith as such. Nicea was not seen as one council among others, but as a "super council." Other councils did not stand alongside and equal to Nicea; they had to be measured against it as a pure and unsurpassable norm. The task of other councils was the "actualization of Nicea," that is, they were not to propose new creeds or definitions, but to test disputed texts and statements against the Nicene creed and determine whether they agreed with it or not.

Of course, applying this principle of "Nicea alone" to every new question was asking too much of it; the real result was a one-sided affirmation of Alexandrian unitive Christology because the Nicene creed gave a more explicit statement of the unity of the Son as subject (he is one in being with the Father, was born and suffered, etc.) than of the non-identity of divinity and humanity in Christ. Under the banner of the absolute validity of Nicea the first great victory of Alexandrian unitive Christology over Antiochene distinguishing Christology—or of Alexandria in the person of Cyril, in alliance with Rome in the person of Celestine, against Constantinople as represented by Nestorius—was won at the Council of Ephesus in 431. But the principle of "Nicea alone" was carried to an extreme by Dioscorus of Alexandria at the second council of Ephesus (later called the "synod of thieves") in 449. The expression "robber synod" is a bad translation of Pope Leo I's judgment on the council *(latrocinium, non concilium):* a better rendering would be "gangster synod." The issue was a debate over the teaching of Abbot Eutyches of Constantinople. He denied that Christ was "in two natures" and only considered the formula "from two natures" valid. Pregnant with future consequences was the fact that at this council Dioscorus ruptured the traditional alliance between Rome and Alexandria, and as a result destroyed the unity of the ancient triad of Rome, Alexandria, and Antioch. He succeeded in posing an open challenge to Rome by refusing to allow the Roman legates to read to the council the letter of Pope Leo ("Tome of Leo") emphasizing the duality of natures; he then excommunicated the bishop of Rome.

When a loud opposition broke out in the council and the Roman deacon and later pope Hilary, who did not know Greek, hurled his "contradicitur" into the assembly, Dioscorus had the doors of the church where the council was meeting thrown open: Soldiers, rampaging monks, and a screaming crowd rushed in. Thus the resistance was beaten down and Patriarch Flavian of Constantinople was deposed.

For the first time in history the question of the relationship between an ecumenical council and the bishop of Rome had been sharply and unavoidably posed. This council was held not only without Rome, but unmistakably against Rome. However, it was closely connected with the traditionalist principle of "Nicea alone." Equally unavoidable, therefore, was the conflict between the Roman claim to be able to renew the traditional faith in each new age through teaching documents like the Tome of Leo and the attempt to preserve the identity of the Church and its faith by clinging rigidly and unconditionally to an absolutely fixed line of tradition.

When the succession of a new emperor made it possible to hold a new council in cooperation with Rome, it was obvious that these problems would have to be dealt with. The council met at Chalcedon in 451. For the Roman delegate Lucentius, Dioscorus' crime was that he had "dared to hold a council without the authority of the apostolic see, something that has never happened before and should never happen."[1] He was not referring to the calling of the council as such, because it had been done by agreement with Rome and Roman delegates had been sent; he was thinking of the council's actions, especially preventing the reading of Leo's letter. At any rate this central point, that Dioscorus had made a frontal attack on Rome's authority, was incorporated into a letter from the council fathers to the emperor, Marcian. They wrote that Dioscorus had "barked at the apostolic see itself" and "even attempted" to excommunicate Leo.[2]

Leo's letter of instruction was accepted by the fathers of the council with the well-known shouts, "Peter has spoken through Leo," "This is our faith," "Leo and Cyril teach the same thing."[3] This last statement was intended to prevent Cyril from being co-opted by the supporters of Dioscorus and Eutyches and to emphasize the continuity between Ephesus I and the purposes of Alexandrian Christology, while also giving special weight to the Tome of Leo. Breaches of tradition must be avoided although, or precisely because, the previous development had not moved in a straight line. The question whether "Peter has spoken through Leo" meant that for most of the council fathers the letter of Leo had formal or merely material authority is, in this either-or form, too simply put. Certainly one cannot read out of it an unconditional formal authority, and definitely not an "infallibility" of papal teaching documents. Leo's letter was by no means accepted without discussion of its content, and it created serious difficulties for some individual fathers. This, in fact, was not contrary to Leo's instructions, which called for agreement based on discussion and accommodation among the fathers. It is true that he did not consider the rejection of his letter a possible solution, but that was because he was convinced that he was clearly teaching the traditional faith. Nevertheless, that acceptance should not be understood as if it had nothing to do with the Roman *cathedra* as such. As is clear from the council's allocution to Emperor Marcian, Leo was always regarded as the holder of the chair of Peter, and his instructional letter was seen as the *kerygma* of the chair of Peter.[4] Rome was regarded as the church in which the charism of the apostle Peter is always present; in this letter it had fulfilled its obligation in model fashion. For Leo as for most of the council fathers the intimate connection between Peter's confession of Christ and Christ's saying about Peter as the rock (Matt 16:13-19) was vital: Through Leo, Peter had again given his testimony to Jesus as Son of God and truly human.

In spite of their conviction that Leo's letter agreed with the tradition, most of the fathers continued to insist on the traditionalist principle that "Nicea alone suffices." Consequently, they did not want any new formula of faith or at most an expandable compromise formula that would leave open the crucial question ("in two natures" or "from two natures"). In the complicated interplay of those days it was primarily the Roman delegates who forced a decision and so broke the deadlock. They threatened to break up the council by leaving and continuing it in Italy. Their pressure—combined with the continued insistence of the principal emissaries of the emperor that a new formula of faith should be devised—proved to be decisive and led to a change in the council's direction that would have major historical consequences. While the delegates from Rome simply wanted a conciliar affirmation of Leo's letter, the actual result was an independent conciliar definition that even more emphatically supported the aims of Alexandrian unitive Christology. But without Leo's letter and the deliberate political pressure of the Roman delegates the council would certainly have taken a different direction. In fact, Chalcedon was the key to Roman primacy in the East. In essence it was only through the Petrine office, or at least not without it, that it was possible to overcome the traditionalist principle of absolutizing Nicea, which would essentially have immobilized the Church.

Still, from another point of view Chalcedon itself marked a victory for the principle of an imperial established Church over the Petrine principle: the crucial factor here was the famous Canon 28. It required that the bishop of "new Rome" (Constantinople), because of the political importance of his city, should have the same "prerogatives" as the bishop of the old Rome, and hence should be second in rank (after the bishop of Rome). The bishop of Constantinople thus moved ahead of the bishop of Alexandria. It is not clear to what extent the canon was directed solely against Alexandria and to what extent it was aimed at the Roman primacy. At least indirectly and as a result the latter was also threatened, especially because the canon's prescription was founded not on the apostolic rank of the cities, but solely on their political importance. In any case, Leo protested this demand and upheld the apostolic and Petrine principle of Church structure over the political and imperial. Apostolic foundation, not the political importance of a city, should determine its ecclesial rank. Rome had received its ecclesial dignity from Peter and Paul, not from its status as the imperial capital (which in Leo's time was merely an ideal). Moreover, for Leo the second and third positions were also eternally fixed. Alexandria followed Rome, and then came Antioch. For this ranking Leo referred first of all to the unchanging validity of the canon of Nicea, and then to a theory that first appeared at a Roman synod in 382 and appears to have been developed primarily to fend off the claims of Constantinople. This was the thesis of three Petrine sees. It posited that Alexandria and Antioch should enjoy a special status in the Church, after Rome, because they all were traceable to Peter in a special way: Peter worked in Antioch (according to Gal 2:11), and Alexandria was brought within the Petrine tradition by the presence of Peter's disciple Mark, who was supposed to have worked in Alexandria (although it seems that this tradition only appeared at the beginning of the fourth century).

2. The Constellations of Authority after Chalcedon

The status of Roman primacy in the East during the centuries immediately after Chalcedon was determined to a very great degree by the decisions made before that council, the results of the council itself, and some problems that followed in its wake.

1. The undisputed organizational bond of the imperial Church was the imperial throne itself. This was clear already from the fact that the council was called by the emperor and to a great extent directed by him or his representatives; for the most part he determined, at least factually, the direction they would pursue. In general, this organizational leadership was not contested even by the papacy, but the emperor seldom restricted himself to that sphere of ecclesial leadership. One particular line of conflict was pre-programmed in the constellation of authority after Chalcedon. An essential constant in Byzantine religious policy was concern for the religious unity of the empire. However, this aim could not be accomplished simply by suppressing the opponents of Chalcedon. (These people are usually called "Monophysites," that is, those who confessed only one, divine nature in Christ, although the description is not really accurate. It would be better to see them as "traditionalists" upholding the principle of "Nicea alone.") Those opponents dominated the whole of Egypt as well as parts of Syria. The religious conflict between the Monophysites and the rest of the population of the empire was a threat to imperial unity, all the more because it was increasingly combined with national tensions: The Monophysites represented the non-hellenized eastern peoples against the ruling Greeks. When there were military invasions, including those of the Persians in 614 and the Arabs in 639, the Monophysites tended to join the conquerors and greet them as liberators. Therefore for reasons of imperial policy Constantinople was always interested in forging a religious compromise with the Monophysites; this, however, implied a weakening or abandonment of Chalcedon and its confession of the full doctrine of two natures in Christ. The popes were forced to present themselves as the saviors of

Chalcedon and uncompromising defenders of the truth against the tendency to make compromises for political reasons. This experience could only strengthen the authority of Rome, even in the East, as the haven of orthodoxy and the rock on which the true faith rested, especially for those who had resisted the imperial religious policy for decades and now discovered what it would mean for them if the Church's primary see refused to back down. Because, in addition, hopes for a union with the Monophysites constantly collapsed when the latter refused to be won over, the result was a twofold schism: ultimately it appeared that a restoration of ecclesial peace with Rome was also a requirement of imperial policy. In the end, and gradually in the East as well, especially in the later battles over iconoclasm, this led to a more profound awareness of the independence of the Church from the state.

On the other side, Rome was thus forced to uphold against the imperial establishment the principle of independent Church power, especially in the field of dogma, but also in Church discipline and law. A classic instance of this was the letter of Pope Gelasius to Emperor Anastasios in 494, on the "two powers that rule this world: the sanctified authority of the bishops and the royal power." The East also had a doctrine of two powers, but while for Gelasius dogma and law were clearly subject to Church authority, it appears that Emperor Justinian, for example, restricted the episcopal office more to the cultic sphere and the "service of prayer." He ascribed to himself the "most devoted care for true dogma" and for "fidelity to the traditions of the faith." He definitely did not say what Gelasius had so strongly emphasized, namely that this obligation, which certainly belonged to the emperor, was fulfilled by his listening to the bishops in this regard.

In all the major ecclesial conflicts from the fifth to the ninth century without exception the turn of the tide was always the result of a shift of power in Constantinople. Only then would a council be called in which Rome participated in order, for example, to annul an earlier council that had made a contrary decision. At first glance, therefore, it seems that decisions were purely the result of shifting power factors. But that is only the superficial aspect. In reality, in each case the Church in the East had been divided; Rome would be called on, sooner or later, to take a position. If Rome supported the opposing front in the East, it was not defeated. It could also happen that Rome had scarcely any choice but to sanction the results of the power struggle in Constantinople. But even then it appears that Constantinople needed Rome for a complete resolution of its own conflicts, because there would be no peace as long as there was an opposition that could appeal to Rome. In most cases Rome was able to take an independent position, but it was by no means victorious at the outset; instead, it strengthened the opposition in the East and thus prevented a contrary decision. In any event it repeatedly appeared that the East could not achieve peace on its own and depended on Rome and the communion of the West in order to obtain it. A political reversal was thus usually the result of the experience that the previous religious policy had not brought peace. The solution was a council with Roman participation that could restore unity.

These constellations usually resulted in an augmenting of Roman authority only for the moment, and not in the long run. This appears to have occurred, on the one hand, because in normal times the apparently natural union of Church and empire worked against an awareness of the need for a purely ecclesial and apostolic center of unity. On the other hand, it was also the result of the fact that the serious problems of the East were often more than the popes could handle. Rome quite often interfered in these problems with a very rigid and principle-bound outlook and without much skill or sensitivity; this gave rise to a kind of Byzantine allergy against the "barbaric West" and its attempts to intervene.

2. The relationship between Rome and the patriarchates was affected in particular by Canon 28 of Chalcedon. Rome's opposition to the canon was a complete failure as was its objection three centuries later to the separation of Greece and Illyricum. Here it was strikingly clear that Rome could not have its way in questions of Church organization in the East, at least not as long as the common interests of the Byzantine Church were against it. In spite of Roman resistance, Constantinople became the second see, if only because the patriarchs of Antioch and especially Alexandria were weakened by the dominance of monophysitism in their regions. It is true that in times of tension Rome continually repeated its protest against the ecclesial rank of Constantinople (for the last time in the eleventh century under Leo IX), and recalled the unalterable and eternal ordering of Rome, Alexandria, and Antioch. But that did not change the reality, and when otherwise good relations with Constantinople were in place or had been restored, Rome abandoned its protests and at least kept silence about Constantinople and its rank.

So developed, from the sixth century onward, a pentarchy of five patriarchates; in order, they were Rome, Constantinople, Alexandria, Antioch, and Jerusalem. After Constantinople III (680–681) a council was regarded as ecumenical if representatives of all five patriarchates took part. In the later period (eighth and ninth centuries) the pentarchy was increasingly idealized: The five patriarchs were the five pillars on which the Church is built; the infallibility of the Church rests on them because all five together cannot err; even if four should fall away from the true faith, the fifth will remain orthodox and will bring the others back.[5] They were regarded as the true successors of the apostles. Thus Theodore of Studios wrote (ca. 800) that according to Matthew 18:18 ecclesial authority belongs to "the apostles and their successors":

> And who are their successors? The one who sits on the seat at Rome and is the first; the one who sits on the seat at Constantinople and is the second; and after them, those at Alexandria, Antioch, and Jerusalem. This is the fivefold authority of the Church. Theirs is the right of decision over divine teaching. The emperor and the secular authority are obliged to help them and to confirm their decisions.[6]

Now, differently from Canon 28 of Chalcedon, the argument for the pentarchy is framed in apostolic and not in political and imperial terms. Even Constantinople finally achieved apostolic status. First its origins were traced to John the beloved disciple: Constantinople, as the new capital of Asia, was the successor of Ephesus and inherited its status. Later, and with more success after the tenth century, the Johannine rationale was replaced by the legend of Andrew, the brother of Simon Peter, as the true founder of Constantinople.

Within this pentarchy, Rome certainly had the undisputed first place. But if we ask whether Rome was seen merely as first among equals or first in a series, or whether it had a qualitatively different and more prominent function, the eastern witnesses cannot be summarized under a single heading. There were variations according to time and interest. The relationship of equality between the bishop of Rome and the other patriarchs was more common than any kind of subordination. When ecclesial peace was restored after schisms, the key was usually communion with all five patriarchs, not with Rome alone. The Roman interpretation of the pentarchy was offered in the second half of the ninth century by Anastasius Bibliothecarius: the thrones of the patriarchs are the five senses of the Church, and the Roman seat embodies the sense of sight because it perceives more clearly and is more in communion with the others.[7] But in the East also there were statements, as we will see especially in the context of the iconoclastic conflict, that indicate a clear gradation between Rome and the "other patriarchs."

3. As regards the position of Rome at the ecumenical councils after Chalcedon, there were variations in detail that will be described in their historical context in the next chapter. There is a certain undeniable and constantly recurring tension between the Roman conception of that relationship and the ideas of a majority of the eastern council fathers. At Constantinople III (680–681) and Nicea II (787) the popes, like Leo at

Chalcedon, pointed the way for the council through dogmatic letters. They did not expect their decisions to be accepted by the councils without discussion, and they always acknowledged the councils' independent authority. By no means were they seen as merely mouthpieces of papal authority; they had a weight of their own, especially as a manifestation of the horizontal consensus of the whole Church. Nevertheless, they excluded any rejection of their own dogmatic decisions by the councils. As is clear from Pope Agatho's letter to Emperor Constantine IV on the occasion of the Third Council of Constantinople,[8] the basis of that assurance was not the awareness of any papal magisterial infallibility in the later sense. It was, instead, the infallibility of the apostolic tradition of the Roman church stemming from Peter which made it impossible for that church, unlike the church of Constantinople, to fall into error. Because of that assurance, it was no longer necessary for a council "to discuss something that is uncertain, but only to define it more completely and to proclaim it as certain and unchangeable."[9]

As far as the conciliar fathers were concerned, their attitudes toward these Roman instructional letters were not always the same. Apart from the special case of Constantinople II in 553, the general synods accepted the content of the Roman teachings and sometimes, especially at Constantinople III, they were profuse in their praise of them. The fathers of that council received the letter of Pope Agatho as "written by the highest divine summit of the apostles."[10] The final acclamation read:

> The supreme prince of the apostles struggled with us; his emulator and the successor to his chair is on our side and has explained to us through a letter the mystery of the divine incarnation. The ancient city of Rome has brought forth a confession written by God and has caused day to dawn in the West for this dogma. It appeared in paper and ink, and Peter spoke through Agatho.[11]

Of course, in order not to overinterpret such hymns of praise one should note what immediately follows:

> and with the almighty who rules with you, O most devout emperor, you decide, because you are appointed by God.

This is followed by still more flowery encomia of the emperor, in the course of which Matthew 16:18 is even applied to the empire:

> Rejoice, O city of Zion, summit of the world and the empire! Constantine ornamented you with purple and crowned you with faith . . . and the gates of hell shall not prevail against your orthodox empire.[12]

Obviously, in such cases one cannot give equal weight to every word, but it is undeniably true that such words of praise express a special religious regard for the Roman church that elevates it above all other churches. The confession of the true faith is always seen as related to the special apostolic and Petrine origins of the Roman see. This is very clear from the text of the council just quoted. Of course, for most of the council fathers it was probably in essence a kind of spiritual and charismatic leadership founded on the charism of Peter but to be tested in each individual case.

Rome was clearly aware from the beginning of the fifth century onward that a council was only valid if it was in union with the bishop of Rome, and the same awareness existed for most of the eastern council fathers as well. But the basis for this special importance of Rome is not always clear. The participation of Rome's delegates was always regarded as extremely important and usually as necessary for the additional reason that they represented the entire West. Before the iconoclastic conflict in the eighth century there was no clear criterion in the East to determine why and under what conditions a council is ecumenical, especially when there is serious doubt, and even after that conflict there are only traces of such a determination. This was connected with the fact that the councils were all imperial councils supported by the unity of Church and empire. Ultimately, valid councils were those acknowledged by the empire. Only when that unity became problematic or the imperial office proved ineffective, as in the matter of iconoclasm, did other criteria, such as union with Rome, achieve importance.

3. Church Unity: Rifts and Restorations

Concretely, there were five major conflicts between 451 and 900 in which Church unity was ruptured and again restored. Each of them brought about shifts in the relationship between the Church and contemporary political entities.

1. The first confrontation was the so-called Acacian schism (484–519). Because the monophysite movement continued to grow after Chalcedon and could not be suppressed, the emperor urged Patriarch Acacius of Constantinople to agree to a formula of union with the monophysites (the "Henoticon") which, although not materially heretical, still avoided any reference to Chalcedon or use of its definition. It made use of the well-known principle of "Nicea alone," alongside which "there is no other definition of faith." The Henoticon led the pope to excommunicate the patriarch, beginning a schism of thirty-five years between East and West. The papal situation was made easier by the fact that in this very period the popes were not subjects of the emperor because Rome was ruled by Odoacer (476–493) and then by the Ostrogoths (493–536)—Arians, but tolerant rulers. The great "magna

carta of western Church freedom," the letter of Pope Gelasius to Emperor Anastatios in 494, could only have been written under such circumstances.

For political reasons, and because the union with the Monophysites was unsuccessful, Emperor Justin I again renounced the Henoticon and restored ecclesial union with Rome. Pope Hormisdas now seized the opportunity not only to achieve a renewed recognition of Chalcedon, but to force the East to acknowledge the formal principle that the guarantee of the true faith was only to be found in union with the Roman church. This "Hormisdas formula," signed in 519 by the emperor, the patriarch, and some two hundred bishops, asserts that what is promised in Matthew 16:18 has been confirmed by historical experience: in the apostolic sea "the catholic religion has always been preserved intact." In communion with it is "the complete and true steadfastness of the Christian religion" (*integra et vera christianae religionis . . . soliditas*).[13] This formula clearly expresses the Roman position: Rome is the only ultimate norm for ecclesial communion and the true faith.

Formulae such as this were forced down the throats of the heads of the eastern Church in times of weakness. The extent to which they really penetrated the eastern perception of the Church's reality is another question entirely. It cannot be denied that the Roman claims were not only known in the East but were quite often accepted. For the emperor Justinian himself (527–565) the bishop of Rome was the head of all churches and bishops and was ultimately responsible for the entire sphere of ecclesial order and doctrine, no matter how striking the contrast between that and the emperor's own behavior. Certainly one element in this was that the emperor was attempting to reconstitute the whole Roman Empire in the West, and Rome fit well within his overall concept as the ecclesial capital; but that could only happen if such a conception was not perceived in the East as something foreign. On the other hand, this kind of attachment to Rome almost never proved to be an unfailing security in the East against Church schisms.

2. The next controversy, the "three chapters" dispute, led to an unexampled low point in papal authority not only in the East but even more in the West. The historical background was that Rome had been under Byzantine rule since 536. For more than two centuries the popes were subject to the emperor in Constantinople. During that period the pope elected by the clergy and people of Rome had to be confirmed by the emperor as well; only after receiving that confirmation could he be consecrated.

The "three chapters" affair had to do with the emperor Justinian's attempt to achieve union with the Monophysites by arranging for the condemnation after the fact of three theologians (Theodore of Mopsuestia, Theodoret of Cyrus, and Ibas of Edessa), or rather their writings. All of them had belonged to the Antiochene wing. Justinian thought he would not be able to cleanse the Council of Chalcedon from the Monophysites' charge that it had been a "Nestorian" synod as long as these three theologians, each of them a thorn in the side of the Monophysites, were recognized as orthodox. Of course, he had to win over the pope to this way of thinking. Pope Vigilius (537–555), who had very little backbone in conflict situations, first gave way and condemned the three chapters in his *Iudicatum* of 548. Faced with a storm of protest in the West, where the pope was accused of betraying Chalcedon, he made an about-face and retracted his condemnation (*Constitutum*, 553). The emperor in turn called a council at Constantinople (the Second Council of Constantinople, 553) made up only of opponents of the three chapters. It not only condemned those three chapters but even excommunicated the pope. This was a unique case of an ecumenical council setting itself clearly against the pope and yet not suffering the fate of Ephesus II. Instead, over time it was accepted and even recognized as valid by the pope. The council got around the papal opposition by referring to Matthew 18:20 ("Where two or three are gathered in my name . . ."): no individual could therefore forestall the decision of the universal Church.[14] This kind of argument was invalid, of course, because the pope was not alone; the entire West was behind him, and yet it was not represented at the council. Broken in spirit, Vigilius capitulated after the end of the council and assented to its condemnation of the three chapters.

The result was a schism in the West, where the pope was accused of having surrendered Chalcedon. A North African synod of bishops excommunicated the pope, and the ecclesial provinces of Milan and Aquileia broke communion with Rome. (Milan returned to communion only after fifty years; for Aquileia the breach lasted one hundred and fifty years, until 700). The bishops of Gaul also raised objections. The Spanish Church did not separate from Rome, but throughout the early Middle Ages it refused to recognize this council. The authority of the papacy in the West had suffered a severe blow with regard to dogma as well. The shock still echoed half a century later in a letter written by the Irish missionary Columbanus to Pope Boniface IV on his arrival in Italy. It is a rather peculiar letter, concealing blunt criticism behind a deliberately jocular humility. Columbanus describes himself as a "strange bird" *(rara avis)* and addresses the pope as *pulcherrimo omnium totius Europae* (most beautiful of all Europeans). He goes on inventing pompous titles like this, saying that he writes as "a peasant to a cultivated man" *(agrestis urbano)* and so on. But the crisis of authority in Rome resulting from Vigilius' actions is bluntly described: "It is sad when the catholic faith is not preserved by the apostolic see." Central to the letter is his demand that the pope be watchful: *"Vigila,"* he writes imploringly, with a clever play on words, "see that it doesn't turn out for you as it did for Vigilius, *qui non vigilavit."* If he is not alert,

> the lower orders will rightly oppose you and break ecclesial communion with you until all is forgotten. If these things are all too true and no invention, the normal situation of the Church will be reversed. Your children will become the head, but you—how painful it is to say—will become the tail of the Church; therefore your judges will be those who have always preserved the catholic faith, whoever they may be, even the youngest, for then they will be the orthodox and true catholics since they have never accepted or defended heretics or those suspected of heresy, but have remained zealous for the true faith.[15]

Vigilius' successors found themselves in a very unenviable position; they were stuck between the chairs. In the West it was not as important to impose Constantinople II as it was to defend themselves and the council with difficulty against the charge of heresy and to emphasize that Chalcedon had not been abandoned. This was not accomplished without some interpretations that watered down and minimized the importance of Constantinople II. However, the problem posed for the papacy by that council has not really been resolved to this day.

3. The third dispute occupied the entire seventh century; the controversial teaching this time was called "monothelitism." The formula affirming that there was only "one will" in Christ (i.e., only the divine will) or "one power of action" was supposed to provide another avenue to reunion with the monophysites. This was under the emperor Heraclius I (610–641). Pope Honorius I (625–638) accepted such a formula in 634 in his letters to Patriarch Sergius of Constantinople, or at least he claimed to see some sense in it. For that, the third Council of Constantinople (680–681) condemned him, half a century later, as a heretic. This "matter of Honorius" was forgotten in the Middle Ages (which certainly believed in the possibility of a "heretical pope," but adduced other supposed examples). Rediscovered in modern times, it was brought forward at Vatican I (1869–1870) as one of the principal historical arguments against papal infallibility. In reality, a minimum of historical interpretation shows how impossible it is to seriously assert that Honorius proposed a heretical monothelitism as magisterial teaching. He did not really understand the theological question; he was not on the same intellectual level as the Greeks and thought in terms of a kind of naive biblicism, supposing that by going back to the simple words of sacred Scripture he could calm the opponents, mini-

mize their differences, and achieve a pastoral solution. He deliberately avoided taking a solid doctrinal stance or making a final decision. The real problem was not Honorius (in whose case the infallibilists at Vatican I generally had the stronger arguments), but Constantinople III, for it is an undisputed fact that must be maintained against all attempts to water it down that the council and the subsequent popes clearly condemned Honorius as a heretic. In other words, they were absolutely convinced that a pope could fall into heresy.[16]

Rome's real dogmatic statement of position against monothelitism was prepared by Pope Martin I (649–653) and the Lateran Synod of 649. It undoubtedly led to a strengthening of Rome's reputation among those struggling against monothelitism in the East, including Maximus the Confessor, who hymnically praised the Roman church as the standard of the true faith and genuine communion.[17]

The Third Council of Constantinople (680–681) set the seal on this development by proclaiming belief in a divine and human will in Christ to be the consequence of the two-nature doctrine of Chalcedon. It is true that this took place against the background of a situation fundamentally altered by the Arab conquests (beginning around 640). Egypt and Syria had now been lost to the Arabs, hence union with the Monophysites was no longer the most urgent internal political problem for the Byzantine Empire. The council itself represented another high point of Roman authority in the East, but this contrasted with the condemnation of Honorius, an event that seems to have been interpreted in the West in such a way that the faith of the Roman church founded on the Petrine tradition remained intact despite the failure of an individual pope. In any case even for most of the eastern council fathers, no matter what the internal relationships between proclamation of the true faith and Petrine origins in the Roman church, nothing automatically excluded the possibility of failure on the part of an individual Roman bishop; hence the situation could be understood in much the same way in the East as well. Heresy was an individual, personal event and was not incompatible with the standing and special charism of the see.[18]

That papal authority also had very narrow limits was evident ten years later at the so-called "Trullan Synod" (692), a council in Constantinople that made some important regulations for the eastern Church without the participation of papal representatives. Especially as a result of imperial attempts to force the pope to observe its regulations even in the West it led to serious confrontations with Rome, although the dispute was later resolved.

4. The next phase of conflict was the iconoclastic controversy (730–843). The battle against religious images carried on by the emperors

Leo III and Constantine V aroused opposition from the outset at Rome, which defended the practice of veneration of images. Since Rome still nominally belonged to the Byzantine Empire but in fact the locally powerful people were allied with the pope, the emperor could not proceed against the pope himself. Instead, in 733 he removed Illyricum and Greece, as well as lower Italy and Sicily, which were still under Byzantine jurisdiction, from the Roman patriarchate and placed them under the patriarch of Constantinople. This action could not be reversed, in spite of all papal efforts from that time until the Fourth Council of Constantinople (869–870), not even when peace was otherwise restored to the Church. Even the eastern Church leaders who were otherwise partisans of Rome did not think of acceding to Roman claims in this matter.

Iconoclasm was sanctioned by a council at Hiereia near Constantinople in 754, but it is important to note that this took place in a different context. Byzantium and the Byzantine imperial Church, now restricted by the Arab conquests to Greece and Anatolia, were no longer the sole representatives of the Eastern Church. The council at Hiereia was restricted to the patriarchate of Constantinople. Resistance came not only from Rome and the West, but also from the eastern patriarchs now under Arab rule (for example, John of Damascus). In this context the pentarchy acquired a new value for those who supported the veneration of images. Emphasis on it now had somewhat the same function as Rome's prior insistence on the threefold patriarchy and its protest against the pentarchy: namely as a critique of the state and a defense of the independence and universality of the Church. It was now equivalent to saying: The Church is not identical with the Byzantine Empire and Constantinople; only in the five patriarchates does the universality of the Church drawn from all the regions of the world find expression. At the same time we can observe that Rome acquired more influence within the pentarchy especially for the principal defenders of the veneration of images.

This was not yet true in the first phase of the struggle. John of Damascus could still speak of Peter, in the midst of the iconoclastic conflict, without thinking of him as anything more than a heavenly advocate in the present storm.[19] But it appears more or less obviously in the general atmosphere surrounding the second Council of Nicea (787), which united with the pope in dogmatically sanctioning the veneration of images, as well as in the later struggles and very prominently in the works of the monk Theodore of Studios.[20]

What is especially important about Nicea II is the reasoning it put forward to show why Hiereia (754) was not a valid council. This was formulated by the Roman delegate John the Deacon and accepted by the council. Hiereia was invalid because neither the Roman pope nor the bishops around him cooperated in it, either through delegates or letter, which is the law of councils. But even the patriarchs of the East, from Alexandria, Antioch, and the Holy City [Jerusalem] did not approve it.[21]

One should note the gradations here: On the one hand, as regards the council it is an issue of the entire pentarchy: not merely Rome, but also "the other patriarchs." But Rome is also singled out. It must "cooperate," the other patriarchs "approve." It plays an active role of synergy (*synergeia*), while that of the others is more receptive. The "law" (*nomos*) of councils probably refers to the reasons approved at Chalcedon to explain the invalidity of the "robbers synod," and perhaps also to the factual position of Rome and the papal instructional letters to Ephesus I, Chalcedon, and Constantinople III. In addition, it is possible that the tradition of Julius' letter of 341 played a part. There the Roman bishop had written that it was "customary law" (also) to write to Rome, and to deviate from this was a "new custom." This formulation was reproduced in the Greek histories of the Church written circa 440 to 450 by Socrates and Sozomen in such a way that Julius appears not to have been invited to the council, and this was "against the law," while it was in fact contrary to the canons to make a decision for the churches without the Roman bishop,[22] or else it was a "holy law" that anything decided contrary to the pope was invalid.[23] This strand of tradition was apparently combined here with the actual experience of the importance of Rome at earlier councils (except for Constantinople II), and not least with the significance of this rule for the iconoclastic controversy.

This internal hierarchy is found in other witnesses as well, and at Nicea II. In each case it is said that Rome, especially, must be present; then follow the other patriarchs. In similar fashion, Patriarch Nicephoros of Constantinople later established the validity of Nicea II and the invalidity of Hiereia:

> Without them [the Romans] no dogma can receive definitive approbation . . . for they preside over the episcopal office and they have received this dignity from the two leading apostles.

Then follows the note that the other patriarchal thrones also participated.[24]

The "other patriarchs" evidently represent the universality of the Church and its manifold and yet harmonious testimony to the faith. But Rome appears to have a singular position: its cooperation is simply irreplaceable, while the others are mentioned more as a collective or group; it appears that everything does not depend so unequivocally on each individual patriarch.[25]

Nicea II was the last ecumenical council recognized by both the Catholic and Orthodox Churches. However, it must be said that this council held in union with Rome did not really put an end to the eastern iconoclastic conflict, to say nothing of the fact that it was not recognized in Charlemagne's empire. Iconoclasm triumphed again. The final "victory for orthodoxy" and the restoration of the images was achieved only in 843 after the installation of the new emperor, Michael III. At that point, Rome was no longer a participant.

5. The last of these conflicts was the primarily inter-Byzantine quarrel between Photius and Ignatius, rivals for the patriarchal throne of Constantinople. From 860 to 880 this conflict split the imperial Church into two camps. Its background, apart from personal power struggles, lay in the clash of different mentalities and intellectual currents in the wake of the iconoclastic controversy. Rome was approached by both sides. Pope Nicholas I, ignorant of the underlying conflicts, decided against Photius and for Ignatius. However, Photius was supported by Emperor Michael III; he in turn deposed the Roman bishop in 867. The shift occurred under the new emperor, Basil I, who withdrew his support from Photius. A council was held at Constantinople in 869–870 at which Roman delegates participated. (It has been counted in the West since the eleventh and twelfth centuries as ecumenical and called the "Fourth Council of Constantinople.") That council deposed Photius and reinstated Ignatius.

Nevertheless, since Photius had excommunicated the pope, Rome again sought to make use of the occasion to effect a general ecclesiological housecleaning. If they wished to be restored to their offices, the bishops who supported Photius had to sign a *libellus satisfactionis* consisting of the very slightly altered Hormisdas formula of 519. However, the remarkable events that followed showed how little internal acceptance these statements found within the Byzantine Church. Bishops complained to the emperor that he was permitting the church of Constantinople to be subjected to the Roman church as a maidservant to her mistress. The signed copies of the *libellus satisfactionis* suddenly disappeared from the apartments of the papal delegates: the servants assigned there had stolen them, of course on orders from higher up. The delegates then threatened to depart immediately and so break up the council, at which point the documents were "accidentally" found again! The head of the Roman delegation, Anastatius Bibliothecarius, took this as a warning and had copies made of all the conciliar documents. The benefits were apparent after the close of the council. On the homeward journey the ship bearing the Roman delegates was attacked by pirates in the Adriatic. The pirates seemed especially interested in the papers: they returned all the delegates' personal belongings but kept the most important council documents—namely those that contained the acceptance of the Roman claims. But the pirates, or rather the emperor who had given them their orders, had not counted on the fact that Anastatius Bibliothecarius, who had sailed to Italy on a different ship, had kept copies of all the documents. Only because of his action did the papers survive to be read by us.

At any rate it was clear that this kind of surprise attack designed to force the Greek Church to recognize the claims of Rome would not gain true intellectual assent; instead, it provoked an underhanded reaction from the emperor. The internal disagreements in the council itself were expressed in Canon 21, which bore the features of a compromise between widely opposed positions: When a council is called and a complaint is made against the Roman church, it must be investigated "reverently and with appropriate respect," but it should not "thoughtlessly" (*audacter*) render a judgment against a pope.[26]

Certainly this by no means put an end to the conflict. Photius was reinstated after the death of Ignatius, and his complete rehabilitation and acknowledgment were accomplished, with Rome's cooperation, at a new Council of Constantinople in 879–880 with four times the attendance of the previous one. It is significant on the one hand that Pope John VIII was prepared to take into account the new realities in Constantinople, yet he insisted that the council of 869–870 should not be declared invalid. Therefore Photius had to be reinstalled and present himself as a repentant sinner asking forgiveness. It was important to John that legal continuity be maintained. In this, however, he was not successful. The council of ten years earlier was annulled and Photius was not reinstalled; instead, he was acknowledged as having been the genuine patriarch from the beginning. The delegates' task was to silence the last remnants of opposition by making clear that Rome was also behind Photius. The Roman see was still important for overcoming internal conflicts in the church of Constantinople, but its authority was no longer useful for anything more than sanctioning the outcome of the power struggles in the capital.

4. Did the East Ever Recognize a Roman Primacy?

Since the time of Paul VI many, including Cardinal Ratzinger, have repeatedly stated that as far as the Orthodox Churches are concerned the task at hand is to restore the unity that existed in the first millennium. The problem is only that such a unity in the first millennium is an equivocal concept. It looked very different in different eras and was very differently interpreted, not only in the West and East, but especially within the Eastern Church itself. One question not easily answered is: Did the Eastern Church as a whole ever recognize more than a "primacy of honor," whereby the Roman bishop was *primus inter pares* (first among equals) with respect to the other patriarchs, but not more?

Here the methodological crux is to make a correct assessment of the meaning of "more." If it is understood to mean a "primacy of jurisdiction" in the sense of a leadership of the Church that is somehow effective and applicable in normal times, the answer must certainly be negative. It is clear especially in the conflicts surrounding Canon 28 of Chalcedon and the allegiance of Illyricum that Rome was scarcely or not at all able to accomplish its aims in serious jurisdictional questions affecting the whole Church, especially when the emperor took the opposing side.

The answer would be different if we were to ask whether Rome was acknowledged as the ultimate norm of ecclesial communion. It would not be difficult to find a continuing series of witnesses in the Eastern Church throughout the centuries who give a clear acknowledgment of that principle, and who speak in one way or another of the Roman church, or even the Roman bishop, as the head or presider over all churches. This is, of course, especially true when leaders in the Eastern Church sought help at Rome, but by no means all the witnesses can be explained in terms of such interests.

On the other hand, there are also witnesses on the opposite side expressing a very different opinion. Often Rome is only the first see in the series of the patriarchs, but its preeminence does not seem to be qualitatively different from that of the other patriarchates. In the later theory of the pentarchy the issue is mainly that of harmony among the five patriarchs, and not simply union with Rome. Rome is especially important for communion, but it alone is not decisive. Of course, we have also seen that matters were different at Nicea II and generally among supporters of the veneration of images: In those cases Rome was not said to be on the same level with the other patriarchs, but had a special role. However, that was a particular line of development that did not continue in a consistent manner afterward. In general, then, the question of the ultimate center of Church unity was not posed in such well-defined terms because the East, unlike the West, subsisted on the basis of a union of Church and empire.

At the same time, there were moments when that unity was problematic, for example during the iconoclastic conflict. Especially in such periods even eastern authors later acknowledged as representatives of orthodox faith recognize that *controversies involving the whole Church, especially those having to do with matters of faith, can only be definitively resolved in union with the Roman see and not apart from it.*

Thus especially when the imperial throne was incapable of fully managing affairs the market value and theological status of the Roman see could rise remarkably, even among eastern authors. One example who could be cited is Theodore Abu Qurra, who wrote Arabic works in Syria around 800. For him, the Roman bishop is the successor of Peter, the rock of the Church; therefore he must call a council, for it cannot take place without him and he is its proper leader. But Abu Qurra no longer lived within the world of the imperial Church. The imperial throne no longer meant anything to him, and therefore the papacy had to take its place. In particular, he was engaged in a struggle against the Monophysites that required the development of a clear rule of faith and an unmistakable criterion for the formal legitimacy of councils. Imperial leadership was now an obstacle and a counterargument. Only in the papacy did he find the ultimate criterion for the legitimacy of councils.[27]

Certainly Abu Qurra, given his circumstances, is not representative, but he indicates a particular possibility and a consistent direction. The idea that differences that call the identity of the Church and its faith into question can only be definitively clarified in union with Rome (which certainly does not mean "only by Rome") is a conviction with a very broad tradition in the East. But this conviction is primarily found among authors who have since been regarded as pillars of "orthodoxy" among Roman Catholics as well as Orthodox—in other words, the conviction in itself played a part in the triumph of orthodoxy, and this conviction was expressed particularly in periods when the imperial office failed and was no longer available as a support for the Church. All this means that we must acknowledge that these "witnesses to primacy" are indeed significant as testimony to the *common* faith of East and West.

II. Primacy in the Emerging West

1. Primacy and the Autonomous Regional Churches in the Political and Ecclesiastical Context of the Early Middle Ages

The great migrations of the fifth century and their consequences resulted first of all in a weakening of Rome's position within the Western Church. For the period from 500 to 700 it may be said that on the whole the tendency to a stronger connection between the churches of the West and Rome, reaching its high point under Pope Leo the Great (440–461) did not continue. At first the development went in the opposite direction, namely toward more or less independent regional

Churches. They all acknowledged Rome as the center of communion and true faith, but they regulated their internal affairs independently and very seldom referred questions to Rome. As is evident from papal letters and the recipients to whom they were sent, the geographical horizon of Rome was shrinking even for Leo's immediate successors.

The immediate cause of this was the general cultural, political, and economic trend in the West: the collapse of the Roman state system put an end to easy travel on well-maintained routes; consequently, the lively economic and mercantile connections of the past were sadly reduced. The one world that the Roman Empire had produced dissolved into empires that had little contact with one another. Politically, culturally, and ecclesially, all these states had their own particular problems. Contacts became rare; people did not travel as they used to. Added to this, around the middle of the sixth century, was the steep decline in Roman authority as a result of the Vigilius case (described above), which contributed greatly to a loosening of the ties to Rome in northern Italy, Spain, and North Africa.

In detail, one may speak of six relatively independent ecclesial units in the West in the sixth and seventh centuries. Across the Mediterranean, the North African church led by Carthage, although weakened by a century of Vandal rule, still constituted a relatively independent and self-contained entity. The most internally self-subsistent and organizationally independent "regional Church" was the Visigothic church in Spain, which from the end of the sixth century onward was under royal leadership much as the imperial Church in the East was under imperial direction. Its supreme organ was the imperial councils of Toledo, called and directed by the king of the Visigoths just as the eastern imperial councils were called and led by the emperor. These national councils even issued dogmatic definitions without consulting the pope or even asking for confirmation afterward; the records were simply communicated to Rome in accord with the ancient Church custom of exchanging messages. Nothing at all was said about a request for confirmation. The "ecumenical" imperial councils in the East were either received independently (including Constantinople III in 684, received by the Fourteenth Council of Toledo), or else they were not received (one case being Constantinople II). The Visigothic church successfully defended itself against Roman attempts to correct the decrees of its councils. Contact with Rome was as loose as can be imagined; it reached a nadir in the seventh century, the rock bottom that marks the division between antiquity and the Middle Ages. It was a century during which the West as a whole, as well as Rome, reached its low point in education, theological education included, while at the same time Spain remained a last oasis of ancient learning and theological investigation. The rare contacts between the Visigothic church and Rome reveal a rather frosty and tense tone: on the Roman side we find carping and pedantry, on the Spanish side irony and parading of their theological superiority.

Relatively autonomous and from time to time separated from Rome because of the "three chapters" controversy were the provincial churches of Milan and Aquileia. The latter in particular sent missionaries into the Danube and Alpine regions as far as Bavaria. The Frankish church was under royal leadership from the time of the conversion of Clovis, king of the Franks, in about 500. As in the Visigothic kingdom, the king appointed the bishops and led the imperial councils. The collapse of any strong central power after the death of Dagobert I in 639, however, caused that Church to lose cohesive strength. It fell more and more under the centrifugal influence of the feudal nobility.

Most eccentric of all was the Irish church, which had developed its unique character during a century of relative isolation (ca. 450–550). Here we find the unique example of a Church that was led not by bishops, but by the abbots of monasteries. It was a Church with a powerful spiritual and missionary aura; above all it was this Church that, next to Rome, contributed most in the early Middle Ages to overcoming the isolation of the "regional churches" and shattering the "Gentile" boundaries.[28]

These churches sometimes adopted papal decisions as part of their own collections of laws, combining them with other legal traditions. They had their own liturgies, all in Latin of course, but taking divergent forms. Anything resembling papal governance of the Church could only be said to exist in the Roman provincial church, that is, in ancient *Italia suburbicaria* and the Italian islands.

2. German Inculturation: Roman Tradition as the Guarantor of "Correct" Church Procedures

The theological memorandum *Libri Carolini* (Caroline Books) prepared at the instruction of Charlemagne in about 790 reflects the pride of the Franks in being especially connected to Rome for half a century by their acceptance of the Roman liturgy, "so that those who are united in faith may also sing the psalms in the same way."[29] Here we find an entirely new religious mentality and thus a new kind of connection to Rome. This is the idea, based on archaic German thinking, that the Roman church and tradition guarantee "right" cultic and ritual actions that truly put human beings in touch with the divine power. This special ability of the Roman tradition in particular to mediate salvation and divine power was seen as deeply connected to the image of Peter as the heavenly gatekeeper.

The power of that image is evident from an odd occurrence at the synod of the kingdom of Northumbria held in 664 in the Abbey of Streaneshealh, now called Whitby (hence the name "Synod of Whitby"). The issue was a choice between the rival Irish and Roman dates for Easter.

To begin with, Wilfrid, speaking for the Roman side, appealed to Peter as the guarantor of the Roman tradition, while on the other side Abbot Colman of Lindisfarne appealed to the apostle John. That argument can, of course, be deprived of its force because the issue was no longer the same as in the ancient Christian dispute over the dating of Easter. The Irish were not Quartodecimanians; they celebrated Easter only on Sunday, but sometimes the date varied by a week. In effect, the Irish could appeal only to the authority of St. Columba, who had vigorously defended the Irish custom.

The Roman party first objected that the Church throughout the world was on their side, encompassing Italy, Gaul, Spain, and North Africa, while the other side could only count the two remotest islands on the edge of the world, and not all of them! But King Oswiu made the decisive move, and in typically Germanic fashion. He had heard of Peter's prerogatives according to Matthew 16:18, and he asked the representatives of the Irish side whether they could establish that a similar power had been given to St. Columba. Of course they had to say they could not. That settled it as far as the king was concerned:

> Then, I tell you, since [Peter] is the doorkeeper I will not contradict him; but I intend to obey his commands in everything to the best of my knowledge and ability, otherwise when I come to the gates of the kingdom of heaven there may be no one to open them because the one who on your own showing holds the keys has turned his back on me.[30]

What was behind this decision? We could interpret it to mean that just as the German princes chose the stronger and more powerful god, the decision was made here in favor of Peter because as the gatekeeper of heaven he was "more powerful" than St. Columba. Still further, and more portentous: the whole thing looks like a duel between two saints carried on by their earthly representatives. In fact, it was the image of Peter as the powerful "gatekeeper of heaven" that fascinated archaic Germanic sensibilities. The image, and the veneration of Peter, was by no means an invention of the Germans, but it appears to have appealed to them in a powerful way. We find here a revision of the Petrine traditions in their transfer to the Germans similar to what we have already seen happening in the fourth and fifth centuries with the conversion of the Roman nobility: while the latter were impressed by the juridical aspect (Peter as the one who brings the law), here Peter is seen as the powerful keeper of heaven who brings others into the place of salvation.

Although there is undoubtedly a power motive based on an archaic and magical mindset at work here, there is something else behind this and many similar decisions: namely the desire, articulated in early medieval categories in terms of powerful patron saints, to get closer to a unified Church, to belong primarily to the one universal Church and not to some other individual church. Veneration of Peter and Paul thus stands for the unity of the Church. The Anglo-Saxon church in particular was a very young Church without its own traditions and history, very different from the churches of Gaul, Spain, or even North Africa, all of them rich in tradition. This new church therefore found its identity especially by associating itself with Rome and with Peter.

This in turn, however, was closely connected with that Church's origins in the fateful decision of Pope Gregory the Great (590–604) in 596 to send forty monks from St. Andrew's Abbey in Rome as missionaries to the Anglo-Saxons. Rome, previously the fixed center of Christian unity, thus became active in mission for the first time, although it is true that Gregory I was not especially venerated at Rome for a long time to come, and the subsequent popes did not pursue his new directions. But by his action he established the new Anglo-Saxon church's special attachment to Rome. It is evident in the growth of veneration for Peter and especially in pilgrimages to Rome. These latter were not a new thing, for from the third century onward the holy places in Rome were visited especially by pilgrims from the East, but they now swelled to a torrent. Rome became a kind of holy city and goal of pilgrimage in a way that only Jerusalem and the holy land had been before. In Rome, at the tomb of St. Peter, people venerated the center of Church unity; they wanted to be as close to it as possible, perhaps even die there. Four Anglo-Saxon kings in the seventh and eighth centuries humbly resigned their thrones and went on pilgrimage to Rome to end their lives there. The figure in the foreground, of course, was certainly not the pope (going to Rome "to see the pope" is a relatively new phenomenon beginning in the nineteenth century!) but Peter, and the tombs of the two apostles.

This Roman connection was further evident from the fact that beginning in 601 both Anglo-Saxon metropolitans (at Canterbury and York) received the pallium from the pope as a sign of their status as metropolitans. This is a band of white wool that has rested on the tomb of Peter; hence it is a kind of "second-class relic." Boniface tried to introduce the same custom to the Frankish Empire, but that took a long time to accomplish. Apparently every new metropolitan was required after the beginning of the ninth century to receive the pallium in Rome; he had to make his profession of faith there and was not permitted to consecrate any suffragan bishops before receiving the pallium. Little notice was taken of this, however, especially in the kingdom of the West Franks, and it was only put into effect after the middle of the eleventh century. After that the pallium was increasingly understood to be the genuine sign of the conferral of office. This in turn, with other factors, contributed to the idea that the status of a metropolitan and ultimately all supra-diocesan authority in the Church was a participation in the authority of St. Peter, at whose tomb the sign of archiepiscopal status had been blessed.

This connection of the Anglo-Saxon Church to Rome was expanded to the continent and throughout the Frankish kingdoms after the end of the seventh century by the Anglo-Saxon missionaries (beginning in 690 with Willibrord, the "apostle of Frisia," and intensified by Wynfrith, later known as Boniface, who acted after 719 as the "ambassador of St. Peter"). These missionaries began by asking the pope to authorize their mission. Their first concern was to act primarily in the spirit of Church unity and to derive their mission from that unity; ultimately it was Peter himself whom Boniface saw as sending him. A close connection to Rome, quite apart from its practical uses, had for these missionaries a spiritual and religious dimension: they worked and strove in the spirit of unity, and Peter was its symbol.

Boniface in particular continually asked the pope's direction on serious matters. But it is important to understand the nature of this Roman connection. What was at stake was the *Roman tradition* as norm not only of faith, but also of Church life as a whole; it was a question of Roman praxis in faith, law, and liturgy. Boniface did not so much ask the pope to make new decisions as seek to know how the Roman church did things or what the Roman church taught (*qualiter teneat vel doceat haec sancta Romana ecclesia*). [31] Here the pope is primarily the authentic witness to the Roman tradition. By holding fast to Rome, Boniface is close to the apostles, especially St. Peter. Boniface, as a man of the early Middle Ages, did not distinguish between the necessity for Church unity and the things in which variety and difference should exist. For him, as for most people of his time, unity involved everything. It was always a question of the right tradition for the sake of the unity of Christian life in dogma, law, liturgy or morals: whether the issue was the validity of baptism, or whether the number of signs of the cross and blessings was to be the same as at Rome, or whether there should be only one chalice on the altar at the consecration, even to the question that apparently was the last straw for Pope Zacarias, because he wrote to Boniface:

You have asked how long it must be before one can eat bacon. The Fathers have given us no instructions in this matter. But since you ask, we advise you to eat it only when it has been dried in smoke or cooked over the fire. Still, anyone who wants to eat it raw should do so only after Easter [i. e., not during Lent].[32]

This orientation to "how the Roman church does it" was strengthened by Charlemagne (768–814) at the end of the eighth century. In particular, he began the adoption of the liturgy of the city of Rome throughout the Frankish Empire and so indirectly and gradually (especially in the eleventh century) throughout the entire Western Church. This imposition of uniformity was intended particularly to serve the interests of imperial unity; Charlemagne of all people would never have permitted a genuine Roman centralizing of Church government. He regarded the pope as a kind of worshiping high priest who, like Moses, raised his hands to heaven; meanwhile, the real government of the Church was in the hands of the king.[33] Rome, or rather the Roman tradition, was for him the standard *by* which to measure; but the one who did the measuring and shaping was the king. The pope, as authentic witness, gives information about the Roman tradition; to that extent he has a superior and unique authority. But he does not "rule" the Church. Thus for example in 785–786 Charlemagne had Pope Adrian I send him a Roman missal as a model (the so-called "Gregorian Sacramentary"), but he himself was the one who then prescribed the uniformity of the liturgy. The same was true of Church law, which was also modeled on the norms in use at Rome.

By present theological standards, then, one would not applaud this specific connection with Rome unreservedly. It appears to threaten a confusion with serious consequences: namely mistaking an accommodation to Roman customs for the necessary unity with Rome in faith and communion. Of course, we must say that such a distinction was seldom or never made even by the popes after Innocent I.

One striking exception to this was Pope Gregory the Great, who wrote in 601 to Archbishop Augustine of Canterbury that he should not necessarily introduce the Roman liturgy among the Anglo-Saxons, but should choose whatever he found best from Rome, Gaul, or elsewhere.[34]

But historically speaking what was demanded by this "necessary unity" and what ought to be maintained as legitimate pluralism were quite relative from time to time and were always contentious questions. This is clear especially in the case of the ancient Christian dispute about the date of Easter: what Victor of Rome then regarded as a danger to Christian unity was defended by Irenaeus as legitimate pluralism. For the Venerable Bede, the Irish dating of Easter was heresy, and when because of the different dates in Northumbria the king was already celebrating Easter while the queen, who came from Kent (which had received a Roman mission), was still fasting together with her courtiers,[35] for Bede this represented something utterly inadmissible because it meant that the fundamental community of Christian celebration and ritual had been lost.

As far as Boniface is concerned, we need to remember the context within which he so persistently demanded that everything be done "as the Roman church does it." For him, the Frankish church seemed to have grown wild to a shocking degree and become "Germanized" to the point that it was hardly recognizable; in other words, here inculturation had taken place at the expense of Christian substance. He saw the possibility of achieving order and reform only in the closest possible relationship with the center of unity and its tradition, in a movement that was centripetal rather than centrifugal, not in further accommodation to what was Germanic, but in a return to what was Roman. Finally, we need to consider that without Boniface there probably would have been no unified western culture. The West as a unit with a common history only began to exist in the eighth century on the unified basis of Roman liturgy, Roman canon law, and Benedictine monasticism.

3. Primacy and the Collapse of Episcopal-Synodal Structures

At the same time a multitude of factors converged to promote a Church structure in the West that would result in the collapse of the old communities of bishops and episcopal synods, which to this point had existed on the basis of their own rights and by no means through delegation of authority from Rome; in the end only the papacy remained above the individual bishops as an independent ecclesial authority.

The Church historian Ignaz von Döllinger, who opposed papal infallibility at the time of Vatican I, wrote as "Janus" of one great "fall" of the papacy into sin, namely the ninth-century "False Decretals" attributed to Isidore of Seville. Up to that time papal primacy had of course developed through the years, but this marked a break in the continuity and the beginning of the "more artificial and sickly than sound and natural extension of the primacy until it became a papacy." Now the papacy began, like a cancerous tumor, to destroy the natural and organic order of the Church by its rank and diseased growth.[36] Döllinger's point of view was nothing new. Beginning in the sixteenth century, when the inauthenticity of the False Decretals was first demonstrated by Protestant authors (definitively by 1628), even Gallican and episcopalist authors taking part in discussions within the

Catholic Church have repeatedly advanced this argument. For "Febronius" in 1763, the False Decretals were the original sin of the primacy and the true internal caesura in its history.

The document now known as the False Decretals was a collection of Church laws supposedly prepared by one Isidore Mercator. It contains a series of forged papal letters along with some that are authentic. It did not originate at Rome, nor was its original purpose the strengthening of Roman authority. Instead, it was written in France around 850, in the ecclesial province of Rheims. In order to understand its background, we have to take a look at the development of the institution of metropolitans in the early Church.

The ancient Church system of establishing provincial churches under a metropolitan was the primary form of episcopal collegiality and the next level of authority above individual bishops. However, in the early Middle Ages it had largely disappeared, especially in the Frankish Empire. The early medieval state or regional churches, including the Visigothic and Frankish, were headed by the king and held regional synods under royal direction. In the Frankish Empire these also disappeared, and every kind of synodal activity was snuffed out. Boniface's reform endeavored to renew the ancient Church order, including the system of metropolitans and the synods. Charlemagne then effectively restored the power of the metropolitans in his empire, but in reality what he created was not exactly equivalent to the metropolitan groupings in the ancient Church. In them, the chief emphasis was on collegiality, as in the present-day episcopal conferences. Their principal organ was not the metropolitan, but the provincial synod. The metropolitan was essentially a *primus inter pares*, much like the president of an episcopal conference today.

But the restoration of the metropolitan system in the Carolingian Empire did not succeed in reviving the ancient spirit along with the old structures. What was now created tended rather to create a superior status for the metropolitan over the bishops. This is easily understood. Charlemagne wanted an obedient and tightly organized imperial Church. The new ecclesial provinces he established were intended primarily to make possible a more efficient control of the episcopate through the metropolitans as supervisory instruments. Synodal activity was supposed to take place at the imperial level. At the provincial level a more centralized structure was created. Of course, this created a potential for opposition from the suffragans that (in line with a law of power relations that we encounter again and again in history), especially when the secular power failed to provide support or was too weak to do so, could join with the Roman central authority and bolster it against excessively powerful metropolitans.

This was the very opposition behind the False Decretals. They were prepared around 850 in the ecclesial province of Rheims within the group of suffragan bishops under Archbishop Hincmar of Rheims. Hincmar advocated strong authority for metropolitans, in opposition to Pope Nicholas I (858–867), and proposed that when bishops were put on trial Rome should have only a subsidiary right of intervention, bound by synodal action, in the original sense of the Canons of Sardica. Rome should not be a court of appeal, but only a court of review entitled to initiate a new trial in the province. Pope Nicholas, however, believed on the basis of the other interpretation of Sardica that had long been accepted at Rome that he had an independent right to depose and reinstate bishops. He achieved some remarkable victories in such cases. On his own authority he reinstated the deposed Bishop Rothard of Soissons and was even successful in deposing archbishops Gunther of Cologne and Teutgaud of Trier, who had acceded to the will of King Lothar in the matter of his marriage.

Thus the immediate intent of the False Decretals was not the strengthening of Roman authority. Instead, they made use of the acknowledged authority of Rome in order to break the much closer and more dangerous authority of the metropolitans. To that extent they are first of all a testimony to the degree to which the position of Rome was already acknowledged as a matter of course: For even, or especially, in a forged document one appeals to notions of law that already seem at least plausible in order to support one's own doubtful claims.

The following were the most important demands raised by the False Decretals:

> 1. In the trial of a bishop, he must have the right to appeal to Rome at every stage of the process, not merely after the verdict has been reached. Thus Rome is now the proper court of appeal; it is no longer limited to seeing that a new synodal process is initiated. This effectively prepared the way for the principle that the deposition of bishops is a right properly belonging to Rome. Thus another step had been taken toward the independent responsibility of Rome for all *causae maiores,* a principle that would only be fully realized in the high Middle Ages.

> 2. All councils and synods receive their legal authority through being confirmed by the apostolic see. This principle certainly had significant ecclesiological consequences. It meant that synods were no longer independent manifestations of episcopal collegiality (as they had been from the beginning) acquiring their authority from that very fact. Instead, only the apostolic see possessed authority in its own right.

On the whole, the False Decretals represented an important step toward the point at which supra-diocesan structures, which previously had had independent authority in their own right, were more fully bound by papal authority. This applied to synods as well as to the authority of the metropolitans. Of course, this new step was not immediately and fully accomplished in reality.

It is certain that a decade or two later Pope Nicholas I knew the False Decretals and made use of them (for example, in his conflict with Patriarch Photius). He himself innocently believed that they were genuine, although we may suppose that he would have viewed them with a more critical eye if the forgeries had happened to be contrary to his own claims. On the other hand, the false Isidore had at that time not attained his greatest hour; that came only in the eleventh century with the Gregorian reform. The fundamental principles of the Decretals were by no means accepted everywhere at first. We may consider, for example, the "Rheims upheavals" around the end of the millennium, when at the Synod of Verzy (991) Bishop Arnulf of Orléans, supported by the majority of the bishops and employing the sharpest kind of attacks on the Rome of his time, rejected out of hand any suggestion of permitting Rome to intervene in the matter of the deposition of the archbishop of Rheims.[37] This and other similar cases show that the majority of bishops still thought in pre-Isidorean terms.

It is true that before this the False Decretals had already contributed to the gradual weakening of the idea of episcopal collegiality. First of all, they promoted the idea that the special position of the metropolitans flowed from the plenary power of the papacy and rested on papal delegation; the giving of the pallium to metropolitans worked along the same lines. This conception was first fully expressed in a Salzburg forgery written around 970–980: the popes "install archbishops to represent them in the Churches."[38] Here the issue was the securing of the rights of the metropolitan of Salzburg, so the plausibility of the notion is presumed. The ancient Church's idea that groups of metropolitans and especially provincial synods are the original expression of episcopal collegiality and therefore exist in their own right is now replaced by a vertical notion: in themselves all bishops are equal except the pope; when one of them has an outstanding function, or if there is any kind of authority at all over individual bishops, including that of a synod, it can only come from the pope. If one were to ask whence the metropolitan receives this extraordinary authority, the only recourse would be to papal authority; the answer that he receives it from his fellow bishops would seem remote because episcopal collegiality was no longer a living reality.

We must say, of course, that it was not Rome that had destroyed collegiality in the first place. It was rather the reverse: Because the ancient episcopal collegial structures no longer existed or had ceased to function, because royal control of the Churches had replaced them and episcopal cooperation now existed only in the form of an imperial episcopate surrounding the king, there was an inner necessity in the development that tended toward papal centralism. Döllinger's diagnosis was thus incorrect insofar as it was not the primacy that was the tumor destroying the Church's synodal organism. Instead it was the reality of the individual churches and the royal Church—in short, the embeddedness of the Church in the power structure. The excessive growth of the primacy was in great part the result of the non-functioning of other Church structures, and not simply of a Roman will to power. Although that, like everything else that is human, is always present in the Church, it is of little use as a historical explanation.

Something similar can be said of another development, namely that new dioceses could only be established by Rome. Originally the establishment of a new diocese was primarily the responsibility of the neighboring bishops, and ultimately of the metropolitans or provincial synods. The founding of new dioceses was thus the expression of independent episcopal collegiality. In the early Middle Ages dioceses were established by the rulers within whose territory they were located. Charlemagne founded new dioceses in Saxony after 800 (Osnabrück, Münster, Paderborn, Bremen, Minden, and Verden) independently and without the participation of the pope. It is true that from the time of the Anglo-Saxon mission in the seventh century onward the pope was responsible for the establishment of new ecclesial provinces in the West. But the idea that the canonical establishment of new dioceses required Roman authority probably had its roots at least partly in the new missionary dioceses in the North and East that extended beyond Christian kingdoms into pagan territory. The first examples of these were the Danish dioceses of Schleswig, Rippon, and Aarhus around 950, and then the archdiocese of Magdeburg and its suffragan dioceses for the Slavic regions in 968. Thus from the tenth century onward new dioceses could not be founded without papal authorization. Of course this did not mean that a right formerly belonging to the king was suddenly transferred to the pope. There was always cooperation between the pope and the king, although it is true that the weight of authority was shifting in favor of the pope.

Finally, one factor in this development that should not be underestimated was the fact that the two Churches in the West with the strongest internal autonomy, the best-developed self-confidence, and the best-functioning episcopal-synodal structures (the Church of North Africa and that of the Visigoths in Spain) were eliminated by the Arab conquests. (Carthage fell in 697 and the empire of the Visigoths collapsed in 711.) This was also a precondition for the ultimate success of an exclusively "Roman" influence throughout the West.

4. Prima sedes a nemine iudicatur: *The Development and Limitations of a Principle*

The principle that *prima sedes a nemine iudicatur,* "the principal see [Rome] is judged by no one" (which effectively means "can be judged by no one") became in the course of the centuries a succinct way of saying that there can be no court above the pope that can condemn him, depose him, or set aside his decisions. In this sense the principle has developed an enormous influence, especially since the eleventh century. But it was known and effective long before that. It acquired a secular and political sense for the first time in the year 800 during the investigation that Charlemagne initiated because of the complaints brought before him by the Roman opponents of Leo III: It is also impossible for the pope to be judged and sentenced by any earthly court, including that of the emperor.

In this succinct phrasing the principle can be traced back to the Symmachian forgeries, written in about 500. Their setting was the period of Ostrogoth domination. Pope Symmachus, politically a supporter of the Arian Ostrogoth king Theodoric, faced strong ecclesiastical opposition within the Roman clergy, whose orientation was to Byzantium, and he was about to be deposed by a synod. The forgers hoped that this principle could be used to prevent his deposition; they referred to supposed cases around the year 300 when the deposition of a pope was averted because of this principle. Of course it was only this bold formulation that was new, not the content. It appears very clearly in two letters of Pope Gelasius I from 493[39] and 495[40] in the context of the Acacian schism. According to the canons, everyone can appeal to the pope, but there is no appeal beyond him, "and thus he judges the whole Church and himself stands before no tribunal, and no judgment can be passed on his judgment, nor can his decision be abrogated."[41] But it was through the Symmachian forgeries that the principle entered the legal canon; it was this formulation, and not that of Gelasius, that made history, but only slowly and by roundabout ways. It was apparently not until the ninth century that the principle became a fixed element in the legal traditions of Rome, possibly under Frankish influence.

This principle was, in essence, a necessary conclusion if the Roman bishop was the center of ecclesial communion and union with him was the ultimate criterion in times of schism. But for the principle to be at all viable and not to be breached in critical situations it required some structural underpinnings that did not exist before the high Middle

Ages. Among these was some legal criterion for situations in which there were double elections and two Roman bishops stood opposed to one another: how was it possible to determine which of the two was the legitimate bishop? Apart from actual acceptance by the Church, however, there was no such criterion until the third Lateran Council in 1179, for with regard to the election of the bishop of Rome there was neither a clearly delimited electorate (although, according to the decree on papal elections of 1059 the leading role was to be taken by the cardinal bishops) nor a set majority. As a result, there were schisms lasting for years—two in the twelfth century alone, from 1130 to 1138 and from 1159 to 1177—that split the West and could not be resolved by any unobjectionable legal criterion. Only in 1179 was a two-thirds majority of all the cardinals made the rule for papal elections.

In addition, the principle *prima sedes a nemine iudicatur* was full of loopholes in practice, because under varying circumstances the legitimacy of a pope could be attacked on other grounds than a legally doubtful election. Heresy was a special case: a pope who became a heretic was no longer a legitimate pope; he no longer needed to be judged by human beings, because "those who do not believe are condemned already" (John 3:18). The heresy of a pope was acknowledged at Rome at least from the ninth century onward as an exception to the principle *prima sedes a nemine iudicatur.* The same was true of the acquisition of the office through simony, whether in the form of money or other use of favors; this was an accusation that could easily be brought forward, especially in turbulent times, and usually not without foundation in fact. Simony, however, was practically regarded as heresy.

Another objection that might be raised against a pope was that he had previously been the bishop of another diocese, and therefore was committing adultery in the sense that a "spiritual marriage" existed between a bishop and his church. This was the undoing of Pope Formosus (891–896), previously the bishop of Porto, after his death: in a gruesome "court of the dead" his successor Stephen VI had his corpse dug up, dressed in papal robes, tried, stripped, and finally thrown into the Tiber. The discussion over the validity of Formosus' consecrations went on for decades; a number of his successors declared that all of them were invalid. Obviously uncanonical or criminal behavior, whether real or supposed, could very easily become grounds for challenging a pontificate. All of this offered, in particular, the constant opportunity to call the authenticity of the current pope into question when the popes were playthings of factions among the Roman nobility, mixed up in the power struggles of the Roman upper classes, and in almost every case owed their offices to shady dealings. That, in fact, was the situation throughout the so-called *saeculum ob-*

scurum ("dark century"), the period from 896 to 996, and for some time afterward.

In such periods, the principle *prima sedes a nemine iudicatur* easily became pure fiction. Consequently, from the eighth to the eleventh century, for the reasons mentioned, there were repeated depositions of popes. The dismissal of John XII by a synod under the patronage of Otto the Great in 963 was the most spectacular of these, but not the only one; this time it involved a pope who had been acknowledged by the Church without objection for eight years. Formally such a deposition, or the decision that the person in question had been a usurper from the beginning, would have to have been carried out by the Roman church, that is, a synod of the Roman clergy, or else by a more or less numerous group of neighboring bishops. In fact, it was a power issue: who could call the synod, who controlled it, who could promulgate its decisions, and who could prevent the opposing party from issuing propaganda of its own? From Otto the Great onward that person was usually the emperor, and especially rulers like Otto III (983–1002) and Henry III (1039–1056) to an even greater degree put an end to chaotic situations in Rome and thus performed a service on behalf of Church unity in their own time that was beyond the capabilities of the contemporary papacy.

NOTES

[1] *ACO* II.3.1.40.
[2] *ACO* II.3.2.(98), 83–84.
[3] *ACO* II.1.2.81.
[4] *ACO* II.2.3.(20), 113.31–38.
[5] These are the words of the imperial representative Baanes at the Council of Constantinople in 869–870 (Mansi 16.140–41).
[6] *PG* 99.1417.
[7] Mansi 16.7; *MGH* Ep. 7.409.4–10.
[8] Mansi 11.234–58.
[9] Ibid., 294D/E.
[10] Ibid., 684.
[11] Ibid., 666.
[12] Ibid., 668.
[13] *DS* 171–172.
[14] *ACO* IV.1.209.
[15] Ep. 5: *PL* 80.274–284; *MGH* Ep. III.170–77.
[16] On this, see G. Kreuzer, *Die Honoriusfrage im Mittelalter und in der Neuzeit* (Stuttgart, 1975).
[17] *PG* 91.137–38; Mansi 10.691–92.
[18] For this subject in detail, see P. Conte, "Il significato del primato papale nei padri del VI concilio ecumenico," *AHP* 15 (1977) 106–11.
[19] J. Gouillard, "L'Église d'Orient et la primauté Romaine au temps de l'iconclasme," *Istina* 21 (1976) 25–54, at 30.

[20]Ibid., 46–53.

[21]Mansi 13.208–9; on this, cf. V. Peri, "La synergie entre le pape et le concile oe-cuménique. Note d'histoire sur l'ecclésiologie traditionelle de l'Église indivise," *Irenikon* 56 (1983) 163–93 (on this text at pp. 168ff.).

[22]Socrates, *History* 2.17 (*PG* 67.220A).

[23]Sozomen, *History* 3.10.1 (*PG* 67.1057A/B).

[24]*PG* 100.597A/B.

[25]Cf. especially Mansi 12.1134.

[26]*PL* 129.160A; *DS* 664.

[27]For Theodore, see H. J. Sieben, *Die Konzilsidee der Alten Kirche* (Paderborn, 1979) 169–91, esp. 177.

[28]On this, see especially W. H. Fritz, "Universalis gentium confessio. Formeln, Träger und Wege universalmissionarischen Denkens im 7. Jahrhundert," *Frühmittelalterliche Studien* 3 (1969) 78–130.

[29]". . . ut non esset dispar ordo psallendi, quibus erat compar ordo credendi" (*Libri Carolini* 1.6: *MGH* Concilia II suppl., 21).

[30]Bede [the Venerable], *The Ecclesiastical History of the English People*, ed. Judith McClure and Roger Collins (Oxford and New York: Oxford University Press, 1994) 3.25.

[31]The quotation is from the response of Pope Gregory II on November 22, 726. See *Briefe des Bonifatius* (Darmstadt: Wissenschaftliche Buchgesellschaft, 1968) no. 26, p. 91. Cf. T. Schieffer, *Winfrid-Bonifatius und die christliche Grundlegung Europas* (Freiburg, 1954) 135: "Here the pope was addressed in terms of his special competence: not to 'rule,' but to speak definitively on the valid norms, the *antiquus mos ecclesiae.*"

[32]Letter 87, November 4, 751: ibid., 299.

[33]*MGH*, Ep. IV, 137–38.

[34]Bede, *History* 1.27.2.

[35]Ibid., 3.25.

[36]Janus (pseud.), *Der Papst und das Concil.*

[37]Text in *MGH* Scriptores III.671–76.

[38]*MGH* Scriptores VII.404.

[39]To his legate, Faustus, in Constantinople (*PL* 59.28B).

[40]To the bishops of Dardania (*PL* 59.66C).

[41]*PL* 59.28B.

SELECTED BIBLIOGRAPHY

Angenendt, Arnold, and Schieffer, Rudolf. *Roma—Caput et Fons. Zwei Vorträge über das päpstliche Rom zwischen Altertum und Mittelalter* (Opladen: Westdeutscher Verlag, 1989).

Conte, Pietro. "Il significato del primato papale nei padri del VI concilio ecumenico," *AHP* 15 (1977) 7–111.

Dvornik, Francis. *Byzantium and the Roman Primacy.* Translated by Edwin A. Quain (New York: Fordham University Press, 1966; 2nd printing with corrections 1979).

Fuhrmann, Horst. *Einfluß und Verbreitung der pseudo-isidorischen Fälschungen.* 3 vols. (Stuttgart, 1972–1974).

Horn, Stephan Otto. *Petrou Kathedra. Der Bischof von Rom und die Synoden von Ephesus (449) und Chalcedon* (Paderborn: Bonifatius-Druckerei, 1982).

Kempf, Friedrich. "Primatiale und episkopal-synodale Struktur der Kirche vor der gregorianischen Reform," *AHP* 16 (1978) 27–66.

Maccarrone, Michele, ed. *Il primato del vescovo di Roma nel primo millennio. Ricerche e testimonianze* (Vatican, 1991).

Sieben, H. J. *Die Konzilsidee der Alten Kirche* (Paderborn, Munich, Vienna, and Zurich: Schoningh, 1979).

Vacca, Salvatore. *Prima sedes a nemine iudicatur. Genesi e sviluppo storico del'assioma fino al decreto di Graziano.* Miscellanea Historiae Pontificiae 61 (Rome: Editrice Gregoriana, 1993).

Vries, Wilhelm de. *Rom und die Patriarchate des Ostens* (Freiburg: Alber, 1963).

_____. *Orient et Occident. Les structures ecclésiales vues dans l'histoire des sept premiers conciles oecuméniques* (Paris, 1974).

Zimmermann, Harald. *Papstabsetzungen des Mittelalters* (Graz, Vienna, Cologne, and Bohlau, 1968).

Part Three:
The Papacy as Head of the Medieval Church and Christianity

In the period between the reformed papacy and the eve of the Reformation (eleventh to fifteenth centuries) there occurred some crucial changes in the status of papal primacy within the Church. It became no longer simply the center of Church unity, the norm of true belief, and the measure of authentic apostolic tradition. Now, for the first time, the papacy became truly the head of the Church; from it went forth all important decisions, and within it all the functions of the life of the whole Church were coordinated. Now Rome raised (and enforced), to a far greater degree than before, the claim to play an active role in shaping the life of the Church and determining the way it should go—thus not merely by responding to questions or petitions, which until that time had constituted by far the greater part of papal activity outside the ecclesiastical province of Rome.

Now for the first time, beginning with the reform crises of the eleventh century, it began to be clearly sensed that the health of the entire body of the Church depended on Rome, the head. It was thus no longer sufficient to acknowledge simply that here the measure of sound teaching and the true tradition lay, in some sense, ready to hand, as was the case to a greater or lesser degree in the Carolingian period. Instead, the welfare of the Church depended on the decisions made in Rome. The active, and not merely passive role of Rome, and thus also the concentration of activity in the person of the pope, who must continually decide matters anew, was a natural result. The central concept was no longer simply the Roman church or Roman tradition, with the pope primarily the authentic speaker, witness and administrator of that tradition, and thus responsible more for giving witness than for making new judgments.

From that point of view, of course, Rome's failures and its inability to respond creatively to new historical demands had very different and ultimately catastrophic consequences for the Church. And when the head of the Church was itself torn apart and divided, as happened in the great schism in the late Middle Ages, the result was a much more dangerous crisis for the Church than the previous papal schisms, which had been decided within the Roman church or, on occasion, by the emperor as protector of the *Ecclesia Romana*. The fact that this crisis could no longer be resolved by the papacy, but only by a council, meant a decline in the authority of the papacy itself, which previously had attained a magnitude theretofore unequaled. This status of diminished authority was not fully restored until the nineteenth century.

At the same time, the papacy was at this period not only the head of the Church but also of "Christendom" (that is, the community of Christian nations). This position of leadership, which in fact extended beyond the ecclesiastical realm as such, is indicated, for example, by the Crusades, beginning at the end of the eleventh century, which were considered a common undertaking of Christendom invoked by the pope (the first in 1095 by Pope Urban II at the Council of Clermont). It was further indicated by the medieval councils, which in principle were "general assemblies of Christianity." Whereas the Church councils in the first Christian millennium had simply been assemblies of bishops, usually with the emperor presiding, the medieval councils, in contrast, were constituted as assemblies not only of the Church but of Christendom, presided over by the pope. Taking part in them were not only bishops, but also representatives of other Church institutions (abbots and members of cathedral chapters), as well as representatives of the civil rulers and of the universities—in other words, the individual "orders" of the Church. At the Fourth Lateran Council in 1215, where this new type of council emerged in its full breadth, the bishops were only about one third of those present; at councils in the late Middle Ages they were a still smaller percentage.

This development took place against a well-defined historical background. The increase in papal authority took place, in fact, not simply as a result of a Roman drive for power (no matter how undeniable that was!), but because the papacy proved itself capable of responding to particular historical demands and of recognizing the importance of certain significant developments.

I. The Historical Background

Which historical challenges were at stake? In simple terms these were the whole set of trends in the eleventh to thirteenth centuries that moved toward freeing the Church from its involvement in the medieval system of feudal government and society. Such protection against feudalism could most easily be provided by a central authority. Closely associated with this, however, was an increasing cohesion of Europe that can be observed at a great many levels. This cohesion was the result of the monastic movements, travel (especially pilgrimage), and ultimately the rise of the universities and the increasing volume of business. It was not only the population of Europe that doubled between the beginning of the eleventh century and the end of the thirteenth; this new Europe also pursued a far greater degree of mutual communication. The papacy proved itself more adequate to the great variety of demands resulting from this situation than any other institution.

We may also consider this from another point of view: European society in the early Middle Ages was dominated to a great degree, in fact almost exclusively, by "vertical" relationships of a personal and mainly local nature (lords and vassals, manorial owners and serfs, etc.). What was now being inaugurated was a European society of "horizontal" relationships, mainly of a broader, non-local nature, which in turn frequently assumed communal or cooperative forms.[1] These included the clergy, which, beginning in the eleventh and twelfth centuries, was understood as an "order" or "status" in itself and not primarily as part of a family or a system of governance; included also were the new religious orders, and ultimately the cities and universities. What was crucial for the papacy was that it functioned to a great degree as a catalyst for these increasingly horizontal social relationships, encouraged them, and in turn derived more authority from them.

1. Libertas ecclesiae

The most important background for the new status of the papacy, beginning in the eleventh century, was the struggle for the *libertas ecclesiae*, the "freedom of the Church," and against the subordination of the Church to the rule of kings and nobility, visible both in the royal appointment of bishops and at lower levels of the Church in different localities. This very quickly developed into a struggle not merely against individual abuses, but as a profound conflict over the proper ordering of the world. In Gregory VII's battle with the German King Henry IV this culminated in the question whether the right ordering of Church and world is ultimately the responsibility of the papacy or of the sacred office of the ruler who enjoys a guarantee as "the anointed of the Lord" (i.e., the Lord Christ) and the "vicar of Christ." It was the common assumption of the supporters of Gregory and of Henry that both powers belonged to the Church. But who was the superior in announcing the will of God? For the Gregorians, obedience to Peter guaranteed the proper order of things according to God's will and the freedom of the Church from secular rule; the pope was superior to the king as the prophetic proclaimer of the divine will.

The Gregorian reform movement had no desire to strip the episcopacy of power in favor of an absolutist papacy. It desired, instead, to restore its dignity and freedom; its intent was also to restore the custom of election of bishops, not to replace royal appointment of bishops with papal appointment. It was quite clear that the episcopacy, especially as an imperial episcopacy centered on the emperor, constituted a lively unit. The successful attempt in the Gregorian period to release it, to some degree, from its connection to the secular authority revealed that the authority of an independent ecclesial collegiality was, in fact, weak. This was a factor demanding further Roman centralization, beginning in the twelfth century. The phenomenon was apparent in the growing avalanche of appeals to Rome coming from different parties within the Church, and the many judicial processes that threatened to engulf Rome. The pressure in this direction came much more strongly from the periphery than from the Roman center. More objectivity and justice were expected from the Roman curia than from local church authorities, which were by nature more dependent on the power centers of the particular place. A similar phenomenon appeared quite often in the election of bishops. The absence of any spirit of ecclesial community in local church institutions increasingly led to the transfer of decisions to Rome.

The "freedom of the Church" from the world was supposed to appear most concretely in monasticism: this was the rule of thumb that governed the origins and all the later reform movements of the monastic life. It was important at this point to note that, especially from the eleventh century onward, a compact existed between the papacy and the new monastic reform movements, a constellation that would repeat itself in the thirteenth century with the rise of the mendicant orders and again in the sixteenth with the Jesuits. These reformed monasteries and orders were freer and better shielded from cooptation by family interests or political power groups because they enjoyed papal protection. Previously the monasteries were entirely subject to episcopal supervision. There probably had been no special exemptions of monasteries from episcopal authority in the first millennium, although there were papal letters of protection, especially for Cluny and other monasteries of its type in the tenth century. After 1000, however, papal exemptions multiplied. In the Gregorian period the issue was not merely one of guaranteeing independence and monastic discipline. The papacy now not only provided protection but also received support. Reform movements like those of the Vallumbrosans in Italy and the Hirsauers in Germany that intervened actively in ecclesial-political struggles also became important reinforcements for the papacy.

2. The World of the Cities and the New Mobility

For the period beginning with the twelfth and thirteenth centuries we need to mention another important set of problems the papacy was in a better position to resolve than were other Church institutions, namely those of the new world of the cities and the bourgeoisie. Together with other factors of a more spiritual nature (including the increase of pilgrimages and the movements emphasizing poverty), these promoted a new kind of mobility. People growing up in cities were no longer confined within the narrow horizon of an earldom and the acquaintance of their closest neighbors. They began to travel and explore other cities. The cities, in turn, became spiritual centers, previously the role of monasteries and episcopal schools. Now arose the new universities, which acquired a sphere of influence beyond their particular region.

From an ecclesiastical point of view, the city found its profile, especially beginning with the thirteenth century, in the new mendicant orders, which combined two spiritual impulses. On the one hand, there was the new unrest that seized monasticism beginning with the eleventh century, and increasingly in the twelfth: the impetus to move out of the wealthy monasteries, away especially from the stable attachment of the Benedictines to a particular place (the *stabilitas loci*) and back to *peregrinatio*, ascetic homelessness and wandering for the sake of Christ; the *vita apostolica* as itinerant preaching without the shelter of a home to return to. In other words, there was the impulse to a radical following of Christ as a breaking away from all forms of security. On the other hand, the mendicant orders combined this with the new mobility associated with the cities, which became the homes and scenes of activity for the mendicants—the Franciscans and Dominicans as well as the Carmelites and the Augustinian hermits. Only in the cities could there be religious houses that sustained themselves not from their landed property, but by begging alms; in the countryside, governed by the feudal order, the only possible gifts were donations (of land) by the nobility. In the cities the religious orders also developed entirely new forms of community, more communally organized and centrally governed. It was thus possible for the new orders to release themselves from the local connections of the existing Benedictine form of monasticism.

The papacy was better able than bishops or other specialized Church institutions to deal with this mobile and differentiated world, which required a leadership and supervision that only Rome could offer. This began as early as the twelfth century with the encouragement of pilgrimages and the issuing of privileges and dispensations for orders of hospitalers and pilgrims' hospices and the building of bridges and pilgrimage roads.

The canonization of saints was now taken over by Rome. The first non-Roman saint to be canonized by a Roman synod was Ulrich of Augsburg in 993. In the eleventh and especially in the twelfth century Roman canonizations increased dramatically. Beginning with Pope Innocent III (1198–1216) canonization became a privilege restricted to the papacy.

New problems were presented especially by the universities with their more rational theology designed to analyze problems independently and no longer subject to tradition in the specific manner of the early Middle Ages. The episcopal magisterium was overmatched here, especially in the case of institutions of international reputation, as was the University of Paris in the second half of the thirteenth century. Ultimately the papacy also became the founder or accreditor of new universities. The first universities of the twelfth and thirteenth centuries, such as Bologna, Oxford, and Naples, had originated independently of the pope, but in 1231 the University of Paris became subject to papal protection. This example was increasingly imitated until ultimately universities began to seek papal confirmation as a general rule.

The same is true of the papal inquisition established in 1231. Precisely at this point it had become clear that the bishops, who until that time were responsible for taking action against heretics, were unable to deal with the problem of heretical groups, especially the Cathari. Here, to begin with, the Church was faced with the task first clearly discerned by Pope Innocent III (1198–1216) of making a definite determination in face of these new groups (often difficult to define) of the exact point at which the line between orthodoxy and "heresy" was crossed, and where instead a radical Christianity was being pursued in forms that might appear unconventional. An episcopal inquisition (the primary alternative at the time) was more likely than the papal inquisition to issue a blanket condemnation of everything new. By no means could a consistent strategy for combating the new heresies be developed on that basis.

Finally, the new mendicant orders played a highly significant role in the history of papal primacy. Their very existence within the Church was only possible because of the papacy, for itinerant preachers who were not bound for life to a particular monastery or subject to a bishop did not fit within the traditional notions of ecclesiastical order. These new orders could only be integrated within the overall governance of the Church by receiving a papal mission and license to preach. This occurred under Innocent III (1198–1216), who confirmed the missions of both Francis of Assisi and Dominic—an event of the greatest possible significance, for with it the papacy, from above, shattered the closed hierarchical order of the medieval Church. These mendicant orders were free because they were dependent on the highest Church authority. In this the papacy showed itself, institutionally as well, to be the empowerer of charismatic independence and internal mobility and of a missionary dynamic that ruptured the rigidity of local church structures.

This in turn had major consequences for the papacy itself. In the first place it meant a transition from the monastery to a non-localized association of individuals, because the spiritual home of the members of the new orders was not a local sanctuary, but the universal Church. The fact that in addition there were now priests whose only bishop was the pope had inevitable consequences for the awareness of an immediate papal jurisdictional authority that could touch each individual priest and believer, even avoiding the intervening levels of hierarchy. Here this immediate papal jurisdiction was experienced as both important and relevant for praxis, especially when it made possible a type of independence otherwise nonexistent. From that point of view it was natural for the theologians of the new mendicant orders to think more "papally." Added to this, the orders themselves experienced a new kind of international organization that was able to transfer members from one country to another, and for which there was no analogous secular institution. However, at the same time the result was, as Joseph Ratzinger emphasized,

> that the centralism first realized as a novelty within the order was at the same time transferred to the Church as a whole, which now for the first time was understood in the sense of a modern centralized state. With this, in fact, the primacy encountered something that is a matter of course for us today [1957!], but is by no means a necessary consequence of its nature: Now, for the first time, it was understood in terms of modern state centralism.[2]

3. The World of State Sovereignty and National Differentiation

Nevertheless, on the whole the papacy, from about the middle of the thirteenth century, was unable to meet the new historical developments with the same degree of creativity and thus to derive new authority from them. In contrast to its increasingly elevated claims stood the reality of a papacy that, especially after its victory over the Hohenstaufen Empire of Frederick II, fell more than before under the influence of constellations of political power and was less and less capable of maintaining a supranational position. This was already evident in the standoffs created by papal elections, often extending over a year or more and brought about by the terrible divisions among political parties in the college of cardinals.

The same situation was evident also from the fact that papal political ideology began to lose contact with reality, in part as early as the papacy of Innocent IV (1243–1254). From the time of Gregory VII, who had not only laid claim to the authority to depose secular rulers but had successfully exercised it, that same authority had revealed a tendency to hierocracy—that is, the rule of spiritual over temporal power. Nevertheless, as Kempf emphasizes against Ullmann (I think rightly),[3] it is not permissible to speak of a single hierocratic line extending from that point to Boniface VIII (1294–1303) and his bull *Unam sanctam* of 1302. Even someone like Innocent III (1198–1216) was simply close to the line. It was only later, and most fully in *Unam sanctam*, that it was argued, starting from a seamless understanding of the Church as a unit and leading the *reductio ad unum* to its ultimate consequence, that the one Church could not be like a deformed child with two heads. It was said to be a "Manichean" error to admit that there could be two principles within the Church that were not ultimately reducible to one. If, then, the Church had two swords, a temporal and a spiritual, the one must be subject and obedient to the other.[4]

Added to this was the gradually emerging phenomenon of "national" divisions in the Europe of the fourteenth and fifteenth centuries, as well as the transition to communal forms of self-government in the cities, universities, and supralocal leagues, and the rise of representative bodies through which the population of a country related to their ruler (for example, the councils of the different social orders in the large cities). In the face of a papacy that asserted a seamless claim to authority, but on the other hand (as in the Avignon papacy and the division of Europe by the great papal schism beginning in 1378) failed to maintain itself against the new, particularistic powers, thus becoming a prisoner of their interests and destroying the very unity of the Church, the "conciliarist" movement demanded that the crisis be resolved on the basis of a genuine "representation" of the Church, namely in council.

II. Stages of the Concept of Papal Primacy

1. Gregory VII (1073–1085) and the Reformers of His Period

The new interpretation of primacy of the eleventh century "Gregorian reformers" and of Pope Gregory VII himself was not primarily juridical in nature, but more spiritual or even mystical. It was a particular type of spiritual "feeling for the Church," drawing sustenance primarily from union with Rome and deriving its spiritual power from that union. The Roman church is *mater omnium ecclesiarum* (mother of all churches); it is *cardo, fons et origo* (hinge, source, and origin), *vertex et fundamentum* (pinnacle and foundation). The health of the whole body of the Church depends on its head, the Roman church; if everything is well there, the life of the Church blossoms; if it lies low, the whole body is sick: thus we read as early as 1053–1054 in the work *De sancta Romana ecclesia* by Cardinal Humbert of Silva Candida. What is new here is not the set of individual elements, terms, and associations, but their ordering and the overall conception. Their very concentration and complexity yields a new, comprehensive picture in which the Roman church is no longer merely the center and bond of unity, but the very source and origin of all churches. Primacy has become the central point for understanding what the Church is, and at the same time the source of the Church's entire life. Ideas of this type were certainly present in their initial stages in the work of Innocent I and Leo I, and more powerfully in that of Nicholas I, but now they were developed with much greater consistency.

This is especially evident in Gregory VII's conception of papal primacy. An aggressive and compact expression of his consciousness of his papal power appears in his *Dictatus papae (DP)* of 1075. This document became a virtually unrivaled symbol of a papacy whose claim to sovereign power caused it, practically speaking, to appear as a replacement for Christ. In fact, it inevitably produces this impression on the reader.[5] The underlying tone of the entire document emerges in the statement that the pope alone can do everything in the Church; without him, nothing can be validly or legally done; there appear to be absolutely no limits to papal authority.

It is true that this document must be interpreted within the overall context of Gregory VII's thought and actions.[6] Gregory was still far from regarding the bishops as mere representatives of the pope, or from seeing himself in absolutist terms as authorized to exercise sovereign disregard for Church laws and the rights of others. The sentences in *DP* that hint at this (especially numbers 3, 7, and 25) do sound quite revolutionary, but in the overall context of his thought they must be interpreted with much greater moderation. If Gregory in his actual behavior as well as in *DP* did really exercise his papal power in a brusque manner and acted especially against bishops with a severity theretofore unheard of, it was because he was convinced that the traditional Church order had been grossly distorted, and that his office obliged him to use all available means to restore the true tradition (which was not identical with actual practice *[consuetudo]*).

Dictatus papae was a collection of brief, individual theses of widely differing significance without any systematic order. The origin and purpose of the document have been and continue to be disputed by scholars. Probably these are outline headings or superscriptions for a planned collection of scriptural passages, writings of the Fathers, and other witnesses to the tradition. *DP* itself was not incorporated into the Church's law, but it does to a great extent raise points that, from that time onward, were pressed as legal issues by other means.

Most of these statements do not deal with laws or rights that are really new, but are concerned to formulate what already exists or has resulted from a long development. Among these, for example, is the responsibility of the pope for *causae maiores* (no. 21), and his sole right to depose and reinstate bishops (no. 3), or, on the other hand, to transfer them to other sees (no. 13). The demand that *causae maiores* should be brought before the apostolic see was already a familiar topic. The expression appears for the first time in 401 in a letter from Pope Innocent I to Bishop Victricius of Rouen.[7] At that time the pope founded this demand on a decision "of the synod," which according to the context should mean the Council of Nicea, but really refers to the Council of Sardica.

There was never a determination or definition of what precisely are the *causae maiores* that should be brought before the apostolic see. In general the expression was understood to mean everything having to do with the deposition (later also the resignation or translation) of bishops. Gregory claimed for himself the right to depose bishops even "without a synodal assembly" (no. 25). In fact, of course, such events were exceptional even for Gregory apart from a synod, and obviously bishops continued, as in the past, to be deposed only as punishment, and never merely for reasons of convenience.[8] Also by no means new were the sole papal authority for establishing dioceses (no. 7), the statement that the pope cannot be judged by anyone and his sentences cannot be reconsidered by anyone (nos. 18 and 19), the freedom of the Roman church from error (no. 22)—not yet a statement of the personal infallibility of the pope, but to be understood within the traditional framework of the tradition of Peter rightly understood and handed on intact. When it was expressly stated that the pope can establish new laws "according to the need of the time" (no. 7), this was always to be understood within the context of the conservative early medieval conception of law according to which laws (whether in Church or state) are not made, but are transmitted or discovered. This is by no means, as yet, the opinion that would come to prevail from the thirteenth century onward, in which "divine" and "human" laws are neatly divided, with the former remaining unchangeable while the latter are entirely within the disposition of the pope. For Gregory the traditional law, as "the tradition," was still a unity; it was to be preserved and at most— this is the sense of the "new laws according to the need of the time"— put into effect as the times required, and sensibly applied or protected. Papal jurisprudence was primarily the identification and definition of the true and genuine tradition of the Church over against the possible infiltration of an improper *consuetudo* as represented, for example, by lay investiture.

It is true that the statements that the pope can depose emperors (no. 12) or release subjects from their oaths to wicked princes (no. 27) are new. This right, exercised by Gregory in 1076 and again in 1080 against Henry IV (who, however, was at that time only a Roman king and not yet emperor), was not claimed again until 1245 when Pope Innocent IV invoked it against the Hohenstaufen emperor Frederick II.

The peculiar statement about the "holiness" of the papal office, by which the Roman pontiff "indubitably becomes holy through the merits of Blessed Peter" (no. 23) has been given widely differing interpretations. It first appears in the work of Bishop Ennodius of Pavia around 502, in the context of the controversies surrounding Pope Symmachus and the statement *prima sedes a nemine iudicatur.* Ennodius took Symmachus's side and declared that the pope could not be judged because he had received Peter's holiness along with his office.[9] This conclusion, incomprehensible to us today, can only be understood in light of ancient Christian penitential practice. We have no trouble in understanding that the pope confesses like the rest of us because he can sin just as any Christian can. This occurs within the internal forum and therefore does not detract from the claim that the office itself is not subject to others' judgment. But at that time serious sinners were subject only to the public penitential ordinances of the Church, and for those in ecclesiastical office such a judgment inevitably meant deposition from office. However, if the bishop of Rome was exempted from every kind of ecclesiastical judgment it was at least possible to conclude that he could not sin, or at least not seriously, and that he had received, along with his office, the promise that he would remain holy.

In the meantime, and especially during the *saeculum obscurum,* there had been some very "unholy popes," and Gregory VII was certainly aware of that fact. How, then, could he seriously maintain such a thesis? Probably he was not thinking of an automatic sanctity independent of human freedom, but of a kind of "sacramental" bestowal of grace through the office: Peter is present in the pope, acts in him and bestows on him his personal charism, at least when the pope opens himself to this gracious gift and makes himself an instrument in the hand of Peter.[10]

This in turn brings us to a "mysticism of Peter" as the true kernel of Gregory's notion of primacy. He believes that he stands in a mystical union with Peter, who acts, thinks, and speaks through him. The pope is Peter present on earth. His own authority is thus also and immediately that of Peter. Obedience to Peter now becomes the epitome of ecclesiality. In the name of Peter there followed, as a primary consequence, the strict imposition of the Roman liturgy especially in Spain and Milan, but also in southern Italy, which at that time still spoke Greek to a great extent.

"Accept the liturgical order of the Roman church, not that of Toledo or any other, but that of the church founded by Peter and Paul on the mighty rock through Christ and consecrated by their blood!"[11] So wrote the pope to Alphonsus VI of Leòn and Sancho IV of Navarre. This kind of demand was founded on the peculiar view of history that was dominant in Rome from the time of Innocent I: All the churches of the West originate in Peter, and therefore they have also received his tradition. Gregory traced the Spanish (Mozarabic) liturgy that deviated from that of Rome to heretical (Priscillian and Arian) influences. The Spaniards should receive their liturgy from the same source that gave them their origin, namely Rome!

2. Bernard of Clairvaux

In Bernard's work *De consideratione*, prepared around 1145 for one of his fellow monks of the Cistercian order who had become Pope Eugenius III, we have a genuine "mirror for popes" or "code of papal conduct." Bernard wrote in a period when the struggles of the Gregorian period were past and papal leadership was firmly established within the Church. The spirit of innovation and reform seemed to be waning even at Rome. The papacy of spiritual leadership threatened to become a papacy of legal ordinances.

To begin with, Bernard extends a pair of concepts that already had a long history indicative of the shift in the status of primacy relative to other Church officials. The pope is called *in plenitudinem potestatis* (to the fullness of power), others only *in partem sollicitudinis* (to a share in responsibility). This pair of concepts is first encountered in the writings of Leo the Great, but there it refers not to the relationship between the pope and the bishops, but specifically to the bishop of Thessalonica as the apostolic vicar of the pope for Illyricum and Greece.[12] The next step then followed with Pseudo-Isidore, who said that the Roman church has called other churches to act as its representatives in such a way that they are called to a share in pastoral care, but not to a fullness of power.[13] In context, this concerns the right of bishops to appeal to Rome at any time. The "other churches" here are therefore the metropolitan sees; their authority, especially in cases involving bishops, is "representative" of the Roman church and a sharing in its power.

With Bernard there now appears for the first time—not directly, but *en passant*—the application of these terms to the relationship between the pope and the bishops. What he is saying to the pope, of course, is: your (the pope's) power extends throughout the whole world, while that of the others applies only to their individual churches.

Bernard expands this in a typical medieval allegorical exegesis: when, according to John 21:7, Peter recognizes the Lord and throws himself into the sea while the other apostles follow in their ships, this means that the sea is the world and the ships the individual churches; Peter does not have a ship of his own to conduct, as the others do, but instead the whole world is under his leadership. The same is true of Matthew 14: The apostles remain in their ship, their individual church, while Peter walks on the water as Christ does; according to Revelation 17:15 the many waters are many nations; therefore Peter is the sole representative of Christ who is to preside not over a single nation, but over all the peoples of the world.[14]

However, the primary accent in this papal code is a critical one. Bernard is opposed to spiritual leadership being swamped by administrative and legal matters. He advocates a primarily spiritual and charismatic understanding of the papal office, not a jurisdictional and administrative conception. The pope's prime responsibility is to inspire, not to give orders. In Rome the "laws of Justinian" must not supplant the law of Christ; the pope must be the successor of Peter, not the "successor of Constantine."

In this context Bernard emphasizes that the "fullness of power" that is given to the pope is not to be a license for arbitrary centralization and interference with the rights of the bishops. The pope holds his office as service, not as lordship. He is to preserve the normal order of the Church, not to destroy it. In particular the document opposes the multiplication of exemptions:

> The dissatisfaction and sorrow of the individual churches speak through me. They cry out and complain that their branches and members are being cut away. . . . Abbots are removed from [the jurisdiction of] bishops, bishops from archbishops, and other bishops from the patriarchs and primates. . . . You are put in place to protect the grades of honor and dignity and the place of each. . . . Do you really believe that you are permitted to lop off the members of the Church, to destroy order and confuse boundaries as your predecessors have done?[15]

These words express a justified and shrewd critique of a development that, while it surely arose more from the needs and desires of the periphery than from the center, in the long run inevitably had to result in the destruction of Church order rather than its preservation. Of course the historical limitations of this critique cannot be overlooked. Bernard's judgment ultimately rests on a conservative understanding of hierarchy. He emphasizes in this passage that the order of the Church corresponds to that of the angels in heaven, and that therefore if a bishop does not want to be subject to an archbishop or an abbot to a bishop, but desires to be directly subject to Rome, it is as if an angel in heaven were to say, "I do not want to be subject to the archangels, but directly to God." Behind this lies an entire perspective on life: the idea of order peculiar to the high Middle Ages, which does not even permit this rigid *ordo* to be disrupted from above.

The events of the thirteenth century, when the mendicant orders were made directly subject to Rome and this specific idea of hierarchy was ruptured, no longer fit within this scheme of thought. In the mid-thirteenth century William of St. Amour could argue much in the same vein as Bernard when he took a stand at the University of Paris against the mendicant orders and their position in the theological faculty: he drew his points from the argument of Pseudo-Dionysius that every hierarchical order may always act only and immediately on the level beneath it. The pope can thus act upon the bishops, but cannot go over the bishops' heads and give assignments to monks; moreover, the duty of monks, as monks, is to do penance because they belong to the *perficiendi*, not the *perfectores* (and therefore cannot exercise any official Church office). Here the pope is the hierarchical pinnacle of the Church structure, but he is not the authority from which everything derives; the other hierarchical levels are also part of the divine ordinance, and the pope cannot arbitrarily go around them. This, however, was an argument that was not accepted by a new ecclesiastical reality. This rigid view of hierarchy could not deal with the mendicant orders or, on the whole, with the demands of the new world of the cities. It had to be shattered "from above" by the papacy.

3. Innocent III (1198–1216)

The next stage in the idea of primacy, corresponding in general to the function exercised by the papacy through the new mendicant orders, was embodied in Innocent III. It has been of the utmost consequence even to the present time. The notion we take for granted, that the pope is Christ's representative (or vicar) pure and simple, can be traced to Innocent. Now for the first time "vicar of Christ" became the pope's proper title. Until the eleventh century the king was also considered the *vicarius Christi*, and the same title was applied to the bishops.

Bernard of Clairvaux still thought that Peter, and in turn the pope, was "the only vicar of Christ who presides not over a single nation, but over all peoples."[16] For him the other apostles and the bishops were still regarded as vicars of Christ. Innocent in turn quoted this passage from Bernard with its allegory of Peter who does not remain in the ship with the other apostles but throws himself into the sea in a letter to Patriarch Johannes Kamateros of Constantinople in 1199—but without the restriction. According to Innocent, the pope is simply "the sole vicar of Christ."[17] This title thus replaces the earlier appellation, "vicar of Peter," that from Leo I onward had been the pope's proper self-designation and held a central place in Gregory VII's mysticism of Peter. Innocent expressly rejected the title "vicar of Peter" as inadequate, because he was "the successor of Peter," but "the vicar of Christ."[18]

As Christ's representative, moreover, the pope is *caput ecclesiae* (head of the Church). The image of head and members, appearing in the words of popes of the fourth and fifth centuries to describe the relationship between the Roman church and the other churches, is now adopted with the aid of the Pauline imagery of the body of Christ as a consistent depiction of the whole, making the Roman church the source of the entire life of the other churches. As Christ is the head of the body of the Church so that all members live only through him and receive their functions from him, so all power and authority in the Church come from the pope who represents Christ the head; as a result it can be said of the pope as of Christ that "from his fullness we have all received" (John 1:16).[19]

The relationship of head and members corresponds to that between the *plenitudo potestatis* (in the pope) and the *pars sollicitudinis* (in all other Church offices). Just as, according to the ideas of the time, life ("the plenitude of the senses," *plenitudo sensuum*) was concentrated in the head and flowed downward to the members, so all Church power, as *plenitudo potestatis*, exists originally in the pope, comes from him, and flows to the lesser authorities, the patriarchs, archbishops, and bishops. This in turn is derived from a strange etymology (not a new one, for it is found in the work of Optatus of Mileve at the beginning of the fifth century): According to John 1:42, Peter was called "Cephas," which in Hebrew means "rock," but in Greek corresponds to *kephalē*, "head."[20] Two further consequences for the relationship between pope and bishops follow from this:

- The pope can at any time reserve to himself, as needed, the duties that otherwise belong to other authorities. Again and again we read that in this way the pope distributes to others a share in pastoral care, but the "fullness of power" remains with him, and he can always intervene in the affairs of individual churches if he so desires. Thus Innocent with this formula laid a positive foundation for the reservations and ruptures of normal Church order that had increased in frequency since the twelfth century. It is true that in Innocent's practice this represented no essentially new stage in Church centralization. His interpretation of office and his attitude toward other ecclesiastical authorities were thoroughly governed by the principle of subsidiarity. What was new, however, and contrary to the previous tradition, was the application of this principle to the Greek church, which had been tricked into submitting to Rome during the "Latin crusade" of 1204. From that time on Innocent repeatedly reminded the Greeks that if he respected their traditional rights he did so out of pure generosity, because the apostolic see had called the other churches *in partem sollicitudinis,* but the *plenitudo potestatis* remained with him.

- Finally, this pair of concepts meant that all Church power, at least the supra-diocesan power of patriarchs and metropolitans, but ultimately that of bishops as well, came from the pope. This went so far that a whole series of passages even say that because the pope cannot do everything himself and he has not been given the gift of bilocation, there are other authorities in the Church whose presence replaces his own.[21]

Thus even more clearly than in Gregory's time the pope is regarded as the source of all power in the Church. The title "vicar of Christ" points in the same direction. Its exclusive nature leads to a very dangerous elevation that threatens to place the papal office above the Church rather than in the Church. If the title "vicar of Peter" still meant that the papal office was located within the apostolic college and the Church, even though certainly wielding a special authority given it by Christ, this new title had the deceptive consequence of placing the pope above the Church.

4. Innocent IV (1243–1254) and the Theorists of Absolute Papal Monarchy

A further step was taken by Innocent IV on the basis of a more sharply defined division between divine and human, or Church, law.[22] The keenness of the distinction was new. The older conception, still to be found with Gregory VII, had regarded traditional Church law as a whole that was to be faithfully preserved, or at most interpreted anew as the times required. Here the pope, despite his authority to issue laws, was not placed simply above the law; he remained subject to it.

This was now replaced by the idea that the pope is subject to divine law but is above all Church law. He can abrogate Church laws or dispense from them in individual cases. In fact he can even validly dispense arbitrarily, although he is morally obligated not to do so without good reason.

Innocent IV combined the idea that the pope is above positive Church law with the concept in Roman law that the prince is the one who stands above the law *(princeps legibus solutus)*. However, this concept introduced the principle of arbitrariness into the notion of primacy in a very dangerous way, even if *legibus solutus* was to be understood only legally and not morally. In practice it had dangerous consequences in the supposed right of the pope to abolish orders recognized by the Church; this was generally acknowledged as a right in the modern era and was put into practice in 1773 with the suppression of the Jesuit order. In principle the consequence of such a right is that the orders are no longer the ancestral inheritance of the rich spiritual diversity in the Church effected by the Holy Spirit, to be protected and preserved by the pope, but are special personal troops that the pope can establish and dissolve as any monarch would. The pope, who originally was supposed to be bound more than anyone else by the Church and its traditional order, now stands even farther above the Church, not within it. This dangerous idea of the papal office as arbitrary power was still exercising its influence in the *nota praevia* to the Second Vatican Council's Dogmatic Constitution on the Church, which says that the pope can make use of his supreme authority even without the college of bishops *ad placitum* (as it pleases him).

The system of absolute papal monarchy was perfected by authors of the early fourteenth century like Aegidius Romanus (d. 1306) and Augustinus Triumphus (d. 1328) to the point that the pope is the Church *(papa, qui potest dici ecclesia)* and the Church becomes "the pope's body." For Augustinus Triumphus the relationship between pope and Church is strictly one-sided. The head receives nothing from the members; they receive everything from it: "Thus the pope is the head of the whole mystical body of the Church in such a way that he receives nothing of power and authority from the members, but only exercises influence on them, for he is purely and simply the head."[23]

And yet this system of papal monarchy still had some crucial cracks by means of which the whole system was overturned in the late Middle Ages. In the first place, the practically unlimited *plenitudo potestatis* with regard to jurisdiction still corresponded to no sort of infallibility in the realm of teaching. Although papal authority also had something to do with decisions in controversies over matters of faith, the development was by no means so advanced in this realm as in the primacy of jurisdiction. Many canonists of the high Middle Ages recognized that in matters of faith a council is more than the pope alone. In addition, almost everyone was convinced that an individual pope can very probably fall into heresy.

The "heresy clause" was the decisive crack in the entire system. In case of heresy the pope can be judged by the Church, as we have seen. By way of Humbert of Silva Candida the heresy clause entered the collection of Church law called *Decretum Gratiani* (ca. 1140): the general principle *prima sedes a nemine iudicatur* (the first see cannot be judged by anyone) here permitted the exception *nisi devius a fide deprehendatur* (except when he is convicted of deviation from the faith).[24] Some historical examples were already known, although the case of Honorius had been forgotten by the Middle Ages. Most frequently cited were the (unhistorical) case of Pope Anastasius II (496–498), who was said to have communicated with an adherent of Acacius during the time of the Acacian schism,[25] and that of Marcellinus (296–304), who was supposed to have apostasized during the persecution of Diocletian and handed over the sacred books.

Taking this together with the doctrine that a council, as representative of the entire Church, was more than the pope alone, canonists drew the logical conclusion that in cases of heresy, and in fact in case of any serious offense, the pope could be judged by the Church, that is, by a council. In crisis situations therefore, even in the high Middle Ages a cry was repeatedly raised for the summoning of a council to bring the pope to account; however, it was only in the late Middle Ages that this principle acquired a special significance.

III. Primacy in Relation to Councils and Bishops

We have seen that Gregory VII did not yet interpret his primacy as centralized power from which all rights were derived. Correspondingly, the reform movement he initiated had as its first intention the restoration of the communal structures of the early Church, reflected in the traditional law of the Church but submerged by the involvement of the Church in the governmental system of the early Middle Ages. That movement desired to restore synods and councils and reinstitute the election of bishops. Nevertheless, by the late Middle Ages these synodal and episcopal structures had lost their independence, falling victim to an absolutist papacy on the one hand and to the established church systems of the early modern states on the other. It would certainly be an oversimplification to attribute this solely to the papal will to power. In large measure the failure lay at lower levels in the Church as well because they did not succeed in creating collegial structures inspired primarily by a unified ecclesial spirit, since episcopates and cathedral chapters almost without exception conceived themselves as the representatives of the interests of particular noble families.

1. The Resumption of Councils

The ancient institution of the ecumenical council was associated with the imperial Church from the beginning. At least in its organizational structure it was dependent on the emperor. It began with Constantine and declined to the degree that the imperial Church ceased to unite East and West.

The restoration of the institution of the ecumenical council came about in the West first of all not in continuity with the ancient councils but as a derivation from papal synods. Even during the first millennium the popes had been accustomed to make important decisions, especially in matters of doctrine, but also regarding the deposition of bishops not alone, but in synods at which the primary participants were the bishops of the ecclesial province of Rome. From the time of Gregory the entire Western Church had increasingly taken part in these synods. Important reforming decisions for the entire Church were proclaimed at the Roman "fasting synods": the enforcement of celibacy, the prohibition of lay investiture, but also, for example, the excommunication and deposition of Henry IV. Another important stage was reached when these synods began perforce to take place outside of Rome, in France and elsewhere, because Rome was occupied by the emperor and an antipope. Thus step by step an "internationalization" of the participants was achieved. It was no longer only the bishops in the neighborhood of Rome and other Italian bishops who were invited, but more and more frequently bishops from other countries. Abbots and representatives of the nobility also attended. These synods became the most important instruments of Church reform; the increasing number of participants shows that the papacy had succeeded in making the Gregorian reform a concern of the entire Church and expanding its basis.

The next stage was represented by the "general councils" of the twelfth century (the "first," "second," and "third" Lateran Councils in 1123, 1139, and 1179). In Bellarmine's later enumeration all three were regarded as ecumenical councils, but that did not clearly reflect the understanding of the time, even though the distinctions are somewhat fluid. In the view of the twelfth century these three councils did not necessarily rank higher than other Church assemblies also led by the pope that took place mainly in France (eleven in the period from 1119 to 1179 alone). What was decisive for the superior status of a council was the presence of the pope.[26] The sources do not indicate exactly who was invited to these councils. The first council in the Middle Ages that consciously understood itself to be ecumenical and in continuity with the ancient councils was the Fourth Lateran, called by Innocent III in 1215.

This brought the development to its conclusion: We now have an ecumenical council called and led by the pope, a feature that reveals the traces of its origin in the papal synods. At such councils the pope was dominant from the outset, even if they were not in every case the pope's obedient tools and could even on occasion express opposition to the point of accusing him of heresy. Nevertheless, these councils no longer had the independence of papal authority that characterized those of the first millennium. The transfer of synodal authority represented by the requirement of papal confirmation as expressed in the work of Pseudo-Isidore no longer encountered any difficulties.

2. From Election to Appointment of Bishops[27]

That within two centuries (from 1200 to the end of the fourteenth century) the bishops came to be appointed from Rome was not only a remarkable step toward papal centralism, it appeared to be a complete reversal of the Gregorian reform. That reform took as a principle that the freedom of canonical elections (which had been replaced almost everywhere by royal appointment) should be restored. *Libertas ecclesiae* for the Gregorians meant primarily the free election of bishops, which was regarded as having a deep spiritual significance and as being an ecclesiological necessity. The relationship of the bishop to his church was seen as a spiritual marriage; like the assent of the partners in a marriage, the church's "yes" to its bishop must be freely given. The imposition of a bishop, for example by a king, was spiritual rape, the pollution of the bride; simony made the bride of Christ a whore. For Gregory VII the church's election was the only "gate of the sheepfold" (John 10:1-10) through which the true bishop could come to his flock.

The restoration of canonical elections in the eleventh and twelfth centuries meant that by 1200 at the latest the cathedral chapter as a limited elective body became responsible for the election of the bishop. The laity were now totally excluded from the election itself, as were most of the clergy. Still the reforming papacy by no means saw it as its duty to take over the appointment of bishops; instead, its intent was to renew the elective system and to take care that free elections were restored and maintained. The confirmation of the bishop's election was restored to the metropolitan. It is true that Innocent III insisted on a principle that could appeal at least in part to *Dictatus papae:* that the resignations of bishops as well as transfers (translations) to other sees as the result of elections were only permitted with papal authorization. But this papal reservation was founded on the theory of spiritual marriage: the saying "what God has joined together let no one separate" applied to these unions as well. Only the pope, as vicar of Christ and therefore of God, can dissolve such a marriage; it cannot be dissolved by human authority.

Here, then, in principle the pope is in the first instance the advocate of the Church's freedom who guarantees that her husband cannot simply walk away from her! It is worth noting in any case that Innocent III did not simply derive his authority over the translation of bishops from the papal *plenitudo potestatis* over the whole Church, but rather from his special power as vicar of Christ. The relationship of the bishop to his church is still an immediate relationship to God.

But what was to happen if no clear election took place? That was very often the case, if only because the cathedral chapter, usually made up of members of the nobility, was frequently so divided by political rivalries that elections turned into bitter partisan struggles. Moreover, there was no clear majority required for an election. In general, unanimity was regarded as the sign of a genuine election, but when it was lacking the result was a divided choice. Appeals to Rome multiplied, especially when minorities more and more frequently saw their opportunity to win through such an appeal. Thus, for example, Mainz after 1284 had almost nothing but divided elections that were then decided in most cases by the pope, who quite often passed over the two rivals and chose an entirely different candidate.[28]

It is true that beginning with Innocent III Rome claimed the "right of devolution," that is, the right to name a bishop if the cathedral chapter proved incapable of carrying out a canonical election within the time allotted. In this way the controlling power of the metropolitan was gradually transferred to Rome. Nevertheless, most popes before the end of the thirteenth century still resisted the pressure to reserve the filling of episcopal sees to themselves. Thus in 1274 at the Second Council of Lyons Pope Gregory X introduced the two-thirds majority, previously required only for papal elections, as a rule for episcopal elections as well. In spite of this the appeals did not diminish, and when a two-thirds majority was not achieved, as was very often the case, any minority could still regard itself as the *sanior pars* (the better part) and appeal to Rome.

Add to this that from the middle of the thirteenth century onward, on the basis of the new understanding of the Church as a "papal monarchy" in which all ecclesiastical authority flowed from the pope, the bestowal of a bishopric by the pope was no longer regarded as an abnormal situation but as corresponding to the proper order of things in the Church. The groundwork was laid by the extraordinary emergency measures required during ecclesio-political conflicts when the free right of election by the cathedral chapter was suspended for a time over a large territory and the bishops were appointed from Rome. This happened with greater frequency after 1246 when Innocent IV in his struggle with the Hohenstaufen emperor Frederick II imposed such measures on the whole empire (Germany, Italy, and Sicily). Innocent IV appointed these bishops *de plenitudine potestatis* (out of the fullness of his power). The background for this, of course, was the idea of the pope as *princeps legibus solutus* who could intervene in the normal legal arrangements of the Church at any time. This went so far that Aegidius Romanus wrote in 1301 that, just as God normally acts in the world through "secondary causes" but in special cases can intervene immediately through a miracle, bypassing natural causes, so the pope normally acts in episcopal elections through the "secondary cause" represented by the cathedral chapter, but because he possesses the "fullness of authority" he can also intervene directly and name the bishop himself.[29] One might conclude from this that a Church in which bishops are chosen by Rome in principle and often in practice would have to be as absurd as a world in which nothing happened by natural causes and everything was a miracle. Still it is a fact that in this way the idea that papal appointment of bishops was something quite normal became fully accepted. When the cathedral chapter continued to choose the bishop, it did so no longer on the basis of local church autonomy, but because it was assigned this task by the pope as a matter of papal privilege. It is true that there was criticism in ecclesiastical circles of the steadily increasing number of matters reserved to the pope, but these criticisms referred usually to the manner in which this was done, especially when money played a role, and never, or scarcely ever, to the principle as such.

The ultimate step toward a systematic reservation of the appointment of bishops was taken by the Avignon papacy in the fourteenth century, primarily for financial reasons. In the meantime the appointment of bishops had become a lucrative source of income for the papal curia. Institutions and customs had been developed that were nothing but simony under a papal cloak. Notorious among these were the "annates" (the first year's income from a benefice whose occupant had been named by the curia had to be paid to Rome) and the "expectancies" (a candidature for a benefice for which annual payments were made). As it gradually came about that in more and more cases the appointment was reserved to the curia, Pope Urban V drew the line in 1363 by reserving all archbishoprics, bishoprics, and abbacies with incomes above a certain sum (!) to the curia. The "free election of bishops," fought for in the Gregorian period, founded on and protected by the highest spiritual and theological arguments, was thus abolished almost silently by the papacy itself, not for pastoral reasons, but purely on financial grounds. From then on in the Latin Church the principle was that bishops were canonically appointed by the pope. When after the fifteenth century it was sometimes the case that the papacy had to share the appointment of bishops with the royal houses, the official ecclesiastical appointment of the bishop chosen by the king still came from Rome. The same was true in those instances in which (as in Germany) an ecclesiastical election by the cathedral chapter was reinstituted.

This development also had a necessary reciprocal effect on theory because now for the first time in the Church's history it was really true that all authority came from the pope. The doctrine proposed by Augustinus Triumphus at the beginning of the fourteenth century according to which the episcopal power of ordination is the only power directly conveyed by Christ in the consecration of a bishop while the episcopal jurisdictional authority is given by the pope remained the dominant Roman position until Vatican Council II. It was, in fact, supported by the real situation in the Church. Thus theory and practice lent one another mutual support to the point that many authors of the period of Vatican Council I and later were fully convinced that it could not be otherwise: the pope appoints bishops, and if in the past other ecclesiastical authorities such as patriarchs or metropolitans had exercised that right, it was only because the power had been delegated to them by the pope. Of course such an interpretation bore no relation to the real events of history.

IV. The Crisis of Primacy in the Late Middle Ages

The papacy experienced the most dangerous crisis in its history, and its most significant loss of authority to date, in the great schism of the late Middle Ages (1378–1417) when for almost forty years no one knew who was the legitimate pope; this was followed by a series of struggles between council and pope.

1. The Papal Schism

When the long period of the Avignon—practically speaking, French—papacy (1309–1377) came to an end in 1378 with the election of a new pope in Rome, an Italian this time and not another Frenchman, it seemed that the Church had returned to normal. In fact the new pope, Urban VI (1378–1389) was reform-minded and zealous, but he was not equal to the problem of overcoming the national jealousies that separated him from the college of cardinals, still largely French. He lorded it over them in brusque fashion, with the result that after only three and a half months the French cardinals attacked his election as invalid. The election had undoubtedly occurred under massive pressure from the streets and in circumstances that scarcely permit it to be called a free choice. Another question, as difficult to answer then as now, is of course whether and to what extent an election that may have been invalid at the outset had been "rehabilitated" in the months immediately afterward by the actual acknowledgment of the new pope, so that the cardinals had relinquished the right to question the validity of the election. In any case they met at Fondi, near the border of the kingdom of Naples and elected another pope who called himself Clement VII (1378–1394).

Thus came about the greatest and longest papal schism in history, lasting almost forty years (1378–1417) and splitting Christianity in two. Germany, Italy, northern and eastern Europe, and England stood by Urban VI and his successors who resided in Rome, while France, the Iberian peninsula (except Portugal) and Scotland adhered to Clement VII and his successor, Benedict XIII (1394–1417), who again took up residence at Avignon. Because both popes had successors and the political power blocs and opposing forces cemented the schism, it put down deep roots. The difference between this and previous schisms was that in this case it soon became evident that neither of the two popes would succeed in being acknowledged by all Christianity.

How was the Church to escape from this blind alley? During the next three decades most hopes rested on a solution within the system itself in cooperation with the popes, without reference to a foreign authority. Historically speaking, this was understandable. In earlier periods people had experienced three schisms lasting up to two decades (1080–1100, 1130–1138, 1159–1177), all of them resolved without conciliar arbitration because ultimately one of the two popes achieved general recognition. Hence whenever in this period one of the popes died an attempt was made to apply pressure on the cardinals not to choose a successor; if one was elected, attempts were made to get him to resign or at least to declare his willingness to do so if his rival would also resign.

The ultimate means thus envisioned for resolving the schism was the so-called *via conventionis* or *compromissi:* mutual resignation through bilateral agreement. The advantage of this solution was that neither of the two popes was required to surrender his claim to legitimacy in favor of the other, and the cardinals could then proceed to elect a new pope without being encumbered by the past. In fact it seemed that such an agreement had been reached in 1408, thirty years after the beginning of the schism. Both popes agreed to a meeting at Savona on the Riviera, where they would mutually announce their resignations. The Avignon pope, Benedict XIII, went to Savona, but his Roman rival, Pope Gregory XII (1406–1415), did not. Finally Benedict went part way to meet Gregory; at the end the two popes were only about fifty kilometers apart. Nevertheless, the "papal summit" never took place. That ended the last chance for the divided papacy to restore the unity of the Church through its own efforts.

The behavior of the two popes, which in retrospect seems so grotesque, can only be understood if we take account of factors beyond the personal. Each of the two popes was convinced of his own claims and identified them with the claims of the papal office itself; he thus believed he could not resign without surrendering the claim of the office not to be subject to judgment by any higher authority. The popes of the schism were ultimately the prisoners of their own system, namely an exaggerated papal theory that they, of course, carried to the limits of absurdity because they could not cope with the situation. In truth it was that absolutizing of the papacy that had led the Church down the blind alley of the schism in the first place and was incapable of bringing it out again. This system led, for example in the case of the Roman Pope Boniface IX (1389–1404), to the absurd conclusion that even in the situation of an evil and insoluble schism one must simply trust in divine providence, and that any human intervention (for example, by a council) would be a "presumptuous interference with God's ordering of things." The answer could only come from a completely new ecclesiology.

2. Conciliarism

"Conciliarism" (or better, the conciliar idea) is understood to mean the doctrine according to which a council stands above the pope, at least from a certain point of view, as a controlling authority and barrier against papal misuse of power, either in specific exceptional situations (schism, *papa haereticus,* or other types of total failure of the papacy: this is the "moderate" conciliar theory) or in general and at all times (this is the more radical type of conciliarism). For the whole Church and the ecumenical council as its fullest "representative" are the fundamental bearers of all types of authority including those that belong to the papacy when it is functioning normally. In its most moderate form (as represented, for example, by Pierre d'Ailly), conciliar theory therefore would say that the pope in himself has the "fullness of authority" and the council cannot detract from it. But it remains the controlling authority in emergency situations, deciding whether the pope has surpassed the limits of his authority or acted contrary to the meaning of his office. To put it in modern terms, the council represents a kind of highest constitutional court in the Church.

The conciliar idea is thus clearly separate from a bold papal theory like that of Aegidius Romanus or Augustinus Triumphus according to whom the pope, as head of the body of the Church and source of all authority within it, represents the Church *eo ipso* and is answerable to no human being, but only to God; further, the council receives its authority from the pope and therefore can never act on him, even in exceptional situations.

What was the source of the conciliar theory? It certainly developed in this form only in the fourteenth century and achieved its influence because of the schism. Still, the roots of conciliarism are much older. It was created in the first place by expanding traditional "conciliar" elements of canonical theory from the high Middle Ages, or rather by making the "cracks" in the papal theory mentioned above the central point for a new way of thinking about the problem. Primary among these weak points was the *papa haereticus* as an exception to the principle *prima sedes a nemine iudicatur*. Ultimately, in addition, there was the conviction of many authors that a council possessed greater authority especially in questions of faith. These elements, some of them also found in the works of papal authors—although not in combination with any otherwise consistent system of papalist thought, but more as unassimilated relics of older tradition—were now systematically thought through and made central to an understanding of the Church.

The concrete occasion, of course, was the historical experience of a papacy that slid into schism. As early as 1380, at the very beginning of the schism, two German masters in Paris, Konrad of Gelnhausen and Heinrich of Langenstein, appealing to the traditional doctrine of the Church's law of necessity, proposed the *via concilii* as the only way out of the schism. At that time, however, their theory seemed too novel even at the University of Paris; it was not accepted and they had to leave Paris. An entire generation's experience was needed to show that there really was no way out of the schism except a council superior to the popes. From the beginning of the fifteenth century the University of Paris, under the leadership of masters Jean Gerson and Pierre d'Ailly, became the center of conciliarism it would long remain. For even if the papal office derives its authority from Christ it did not follow that the individual pope was set apart from all human judgment. He could be deposed, not solely for reasons of personal guilt, but also if he objectively stood in the way of the unity or the common good of the Church.

The other impression was that "reform of the Church in head and members" was only possible by means of a council and as things stood this could not be achieved through agreement with the papacy; it would have to be extracted by compulsion. From the time of the Council of Vienne (1311–1312) there had been no end of voices asserting that the papacy had become the greatest obstacle to reform. With its reservations, annates, and expectancies, in which finance had become the dominant force guiding the whole government of the Church, it was corrupting the Church and conducting simony under a papal cloak. Closely associated with this was the misuse of ecclesiastical punishments: thus in 1328 John XXII excommunicated thirty-six bishops and forty-six abbots because they had not paid the fees they owed. The complaints about these matters had swelled since 1300 into an irrepressible torrent. But characteristic of the dilemma of these reformers who left the principle of papal omnipotence unchallenged is the figure of Guillaume la Maire at the Council of Vienne. After complaining eloquently about the Roman practice of reservation (then only in its infancy) he observed resignedly that if the pope nevertheless insists upon the "fullness of his authority" we must submit to it, "for no one can say to him: why are you doing this?"[30]

The later conciliar movement would no longer be content with that answer. At Constance, Jean Gerson thundered against the "terrible and dreadful obstacle" blocking the way to Church reform, namely the idea that no one could say to the pope, "why are you acting in this way?" because he was not bound by the laws and stood above the law; this would have meant twisting the papacy into a "tyranny that would destroy the Church."[31] It is true that a contemporary historical and sociopolitical model played no small role here. This was the "corporative" or *universitas* model. The fourteenth century was a period when models of stratified participation and communal association were being developed in the political and social realms. Among these were the parliaments or assemblies of estates in the kingdoms, representing the "people" in the late medieval sense (as a nation divided into estates or "orders") and placing restrictions on royal power. However, the example of communal self-government in the medieval cities, the universities, and then in the new religious orders in which the chapter as representative of the whole exercised the highest authority was still more influential.

This *universitas* model lent the Middle Ages, which until the twelfth century knew only personal governance in stratified hierarchies (king, duke, count), a new model of community. In these corporations the *universitas*, represented in an elected body, exercised the highest authority (sovereignty), especially the making of laws. The "rector" was above the individual members, but not above the *universitas* because he was its agent. Conciliarism interpreted the relationship between pope and council in similar fashion: the pope is above all the members of the Church, but not above the Church as a whole, or: the council has the authority to make laws, the pope to carry them out, or: the principle *prima sedes a nemine iudicatur* means that no individual can judge the pope, but it does not hold for the whole Church and its representatives in a general council, which in fact can depose the pope not merely for heresy but also for other serious reasons (for example, if he causes notorious scandal in the Church, or if the Church cannot otherwise be cleansed from schism), or: the papal office does indeed derive from Christ, but the individual pope does not receive his office directly from Christ. He receives it through human beings, or rather the Church, and therefore, if necessary, he can be removed by the Church as well.

In turn it was true that later in the fifteenth century the champions of the papal theory also oriented their thinking by secular models, especially the principle of *princeps legibus solutus* in Roman law. The fifteenth century was a time when central monarchical power was again on the rise and was suppressing late medieval constitutionalism. Here we can see a striking parallel between ecclesiastical constitutional development and contemporary political developments:

- First there were a number of independent levels of authority in a graded hierarchy, with the lower orders subordinated to the upper, but not deriving their authority from the highest order as its source. Sovereignty was divided. Politically, this corresponds to feudalism, ecclesiastically to the old (pre-Gregorian) relationship between pope and bishops.

- Then comes the *universitas* model, in which the *universitas* is the bearer of a single, undivided sovereignty. The political counterpart were the corporations (cities, universities, the new orders); the ecclesiastical counterpart was conciliarism.

- Finally came the absolutist model, where the *princeps* (the prince, king, etc.) incorporates a single, undivided sovereignty and is the source of all authority. This corresponds to the beginnings of royal absolutism, and in the Church to papalism.[32]

Thus, on the one hand, conciliarism had very strong roots in its contemporary world. Still, we should not forget that on the other side it rested on the ancient synodal tradition of the Church and the awareness that the divine promise is given to the Church as a whole.[33] The old *communio* ecclesiology was revived in it, after having been suppressed since the early Middle Ages not primarily by the papacy but because the Church was enmeshed in the political order of governance.

3. The Councils of Pisa (1409), Constance (1414–1418), and Basel (1431–1449)

When the last opportunity for the divided papacy to restore unity to the Church by the *via conventionis* had been rejected, the hour of the *via concilii* had arrived. The initiative for calling a council belonged, according to the interpretation current at the time, to the college of cardinals, which represented the Roman church against a heretical pope. Thus the cardinals of both obediences separated from their popes and called a general council at Pisa. It met in 1409, put both popes on trial, and finally deposed them as "heretics" and "schismatics." They were declared heretics (important because only a heretical pope could be deposed) because, by refusing to resign in order to facilitate union, they had violated the article of faith that calls the Church one and holy. The council elected Alexander V (1409–1410) as the new pope; he was followed by John XXIII (1410–1415).

What happened in Pisa was in principle anything but "revolutionary." It stood within the framework of the traditional doctrine of the emergency law of the Church and councils in cases involving heretical popes. But it did not succeed in restoring unity. Since the two popes did not resign, the end result was that there were three popes instead of two—no longer a "disreputable duo," but a "cursed trinity" *(trinitas non benedicta, sed maledicta)*. It is true that the greater part of Christianity supported the conciliar pope, but the other two still had their adherents, even though reduced in numbers: Benedict XIII was supported by Spain and Scotland, Gregory XII by some regions of Germany and for a time by the kingdom of Naples.

A second attempt was made to resolve the schism by means of a council, namely Constance (1414–1418). That the tragedy of Pisa was not repeated was due on the one hand to the fact that there now existed, in the person of the German king Sigismund, a dominant figure and central authority who took control of the council with superior diplomatic skill and guided the infinitely tedious negotiations. Working together with Pope John XXIII, Sigismund succeeded at first in calling a council only of those who were obedient to John; it is true, however, that this represented the majority of Christianity. The proceedings against the other two popes were also conducted more "diplomatically" than at Pisa. Instead of putting them on trial immediately the council attempted to build "golden bridges" for them: negotiations were undertaken in order to persuade them to resign voluntarily and thus no longer to pose obstacles to unity. They could even formally call the council anew and then declare their resignations. Thus the greatest concern was shown for the different popes' views of legitimacy in order to enable them and their supporters to maintain their formal claims. The chief goal was to achieve unity by whatever reconstructive means necessary.

In this connection, however, there remained the problem of what to do with John XXIII. In the first place, the Council of Constance was a council of his obedience. For him and for a majority of the council fathers the first task was to obtain general acknowledgment of his papacy and to cause the "schismatics," Angelo Correr (Gregory XII) and Pedro de Luna (Benedict XIII) to resign. These resignations should be obtained by gentle means if possible, but if that failed they should be deposed. This is readily understood also from the fact that John XXIII owed his authority to the very principle to which the fathers of the Council of Constance appealed, namely the emergency power of a council over the pope. If the decision at Pisa were overturned the council ran the risk of having not three, but four popes; above all it seemed that the one legal basis on which they were able to proceed might be destroyed. Nevertheless, Sigismund's position finally prevailed. As he saw it, the solution to the question of unity demanded the resignation of the Pisan pope as well, especially since it appeared scarcely imaginable that the other "popes" would resign at the behest of a council called by John XXIII.

John at first agreed to resign, but then an event occurred that threatened to destroy the whole carefully constructed structure of unity at a single blow. John XXIII fled Constance during the night disguised as a stableboy and reached Schaffhausen, where he declared that he had not felt himself secure and free in Constance. This was the greatest crisis of the council. The council fathers were seized with panic. King Sigismund was immediately master of the situation, rescuing the council and thus the road to union by issuing a decree closing the city of Constance so that no one could leave. All was not yet lost. Messengers went back and forth between Constance and Schaffhausen. Then came another stroke of bad news: the pope had fled from Schaffhausen to Breisach; he had revoked his promise to resign, saying that it was forced and therefore invalid, and he had called on the cardinals to leave the council and come to him. It was the council's fatal hour.

Now it was purely a question of survival: Should they admit that the pope could dissolve the council and thus abandon all hope of escaping the dead end of schism for the foreseeable future, or should they stand firm on the basis of their own rights? Under the leadership of the chancellor of the University of Paris, Jean Gerson, they chose the latter course.

The fruit of this decision was the decree *Haec sancta* of April 6, 1415.[34] Its most important statements are the following: The synod solemnly declares that it possesses its own authority stemming immediately from Christ. It is "legitimately assembled in the holy Spirit," represents the Church, and receives its power immediately from Christ. The practical consequence that follows is that everyone of whatever condition or status, including the papal, is bound to obey it in "those matters which pertain to the faith, the eradication of the said schism and the general reform of the said church of God in head and members." Although this first statement applies only to the current council at Constance the second part, threatening punishment of everyone of whatever dignity, "even papal," who refuses obedience, is more general in scope: it applies not only to the current council, but also to the decrees of "any other legitimately assembled general council" called on the same principles, that is, for matters of faith, the eradication of schism, or Church reform.

We will discuss the problem of interpretation below. In any case this decree was the basis on which the council continued to meet even without the pope and ultimately put an end to the schism. John XXIII was put on trial; he was arrested, taken to Radolfzell as a prisoner, and finally deposed. Of the three popes only Gregory XII, the pope of the "Roman" line, acceded to gentle persuasion. He finally announced his resignation, but not without first formally calling the council. This mode did not succeed with the pope of the "Avignon" line, Benedict XIII, who had the greatest personal integrity of the three popes but was possessed of a rigid notion of legitimacy. He was still backed by the Spanish kingdoms and Scotland. King Sigismund negotiated with him in Perpignan on behalf of the council. When Sigismund presented the point of view that since the outbreak of the schism in 1378 there had been no legitimate pope at all, Benedict gave an answer that was as logical as it was estranged from reality. He said that in that case no cardinals had been legitimately appointed either. And since he himself was the only living cardinal who had received the purple before 1378, he consequently had the sole right to elect a pope; he would elect a pope, promising at the same time to elect someone other than himself. It was thus impossible to deal with him, but Sigismund did succeed in separating his Spanish adherents from him. A game was played similar to the previous one with Gregory: Benedict's supporters and the "assembly at Constance" mutually invited one another to a newly-constituted ecumenical council in Constance. They were thus permitted to construe the law to mean that the council only became ecumenical when they joined it. Benedict himself (Pedro de Luna) was deposed in 1417. Residing in his castle of Peñiscola on the Aragon coast, his "Noah's ark," he continued to regard himself, until his death in 1423, as the only legitimate pope, and excommunicated all the rest of Christendom. He was tolerated and protected by the king of Aragon who kept him as a bargaining chip in order to promote his own demands on the new pope.

The further question at Constance was whether the council should first undertake the tedious "reform of the Church in head and members," running the risk that it might take years and that thus the election of a new pope could be delayed indefinitely, or whether the first step should be a new papal election, in which case there was danger that the urgently necessary reform, particularly of the head, would again be put off *ad infinitum,* as bitter experiences of the very recent past had adequately demonstrated. But was not a council without a pope only an emergency measure? Was not the council's first duty to see to it that there should again be a legitimate head of the Church? But in that case, could the newly-elected pope be bound by the council?

The result was a compromise that dealt with the concerns of both parties. On the one hand, a decision was made to give the papal election priority over reform; on the other hand the council issued the decree *Frequens* even before the election of the new pope. It obligated future popes to hold councils at regular intervals (the first to be held five years after the conclusion of the Council of Constance, the next seven years later, and ultimately every ten years). The popes could shorten but not lengthen the intervals. This meant in the first place that the papal election was not further delayed, but also that Church reform was no longer to be subject to the arbitrary decision of the pope; a certain institutional guarantee had been created that was to carry reform and the conciliar idea (inseparable by nature) beyond Constance. Then the new pope, Martin V (1417–1431) was elected; after nearly forty years, the Church again had an undisputed head.

However, the expectation that *Frequens* would create an institutional guarantee for the continuance of the conciliar structure was disappointed. It is true that the decree was respected at first. The next council met five years later in Pavia and Siena (1423–1424) but it was poorly attended and was dissolved in short order. Seven years later followed the Council of Basel (1431–1449) which very quickly fell into an ongoing conflict with Pope Eugene IV (1431–1447). From the outset it was a question of fundamental structure: is the pope above the council, or the council above the pope? Did the pope have the right to dissolve the council or to transfer it to another place (namely Italy)? The majority of the council fathers at Basel resisted this attempt, resting their case on *Haec sancta,* which established once and for all the superiority of the council over the pope. In the first phase of the conflict the council was the stronger: the majority of Christians were on their side, and Pope Eugene IV had to give in. But a new ecclesio-political constellation restored his freedom of action: the people involved in the negotiations for union with the Greek Churches preferred, simply because of the difficulties of travel, to have the meetings take place in an Italian city rather than in the northern Alps. Moreover, they were primarily concerned with reaching agreement with the pope; the cause of unity was not served by a council that was in ongoing conflict with the pope. Now Eugene IV felt strong enough to transfer the council, first to Ferrara, and then in 1439 to Florence. Then came the final break between pope and council. The moderate minority in Basel followed the papal call; these included Nicholas of Cusa, heretofore one of the pillars of conciliarism. The majority remained in Basel and decided to issue a dogmatic definition of strict conciliarism as a general and unconditional superiority of a council over the pope. This was the decree *Sacrosancta*, which defined the following as true:

1. A general council is above the pope.

2. The pope cannot dissolve or interrupt a council, nor can he transfer it to another place.

3. Anyone who denies these truths is a heretic.

Since Eugene IV denied these "truths" he was deposed as a "heretic." In the same year in which a deceptive union with the East was created, the final papal schism broke out in the West: the fathers in Basel elected Count Amadeus of Savoy as Felix V (1439–1449). Things had gone awry again, but this time there were not only two popes, there were two councils in conflict with one another. In addition, this time the question was not one of formal claims of legitimacy as in the great schism, but of fundamental differences regarding the matter of Church structure. Everything pointed to another schism.

The struggle lasted ten years. Superficially the restored papacy was again victorious over conciliarism. Felix V resigned in 1449. The council, meanwhile transferred from Basel to Lausanne, now elected as pope a "Thomas Parentucelli from Sarzana," who was none other than the reigning pope Nicholas V. Then the council dissolved itself.

This was, however, by no means the death of conciliarism. It remained a major undercurrent from the sixteenth to the eighteenth centuries especially in France but in some parts of Germany as well. It had been suppressed, but this Pyrrhic victory had been achieved at a price far greater than the good it accomplished. In the first place, the true winner was the established religion of the emerging modern princely states. The states collected a great price for their support of Pope Eugene IV. This included not only the beginnings of state supervision and control of the Church (the *placet* or *exsequatur* as permission for the publication of Church edicts, *recursus ab abusu* as recourse to the state authorities against Church punishments, etc.). In addition, and of special importance, it included the right to nominate bishops, which remained in effect in almost all the major European nations well into the nineteenth century, either officially guaranteed through a concordat with Rome or simply exercised in practice. In the Holy Roman Empire, where the bishops were independent princes, the corresponding move was the restoration of election by the cathedral chapter. But the forces that had been awakened by the conciliar idea sought new—i.e., centrifugal—outlets that destroyed or at least disrupted unity; these forces were propelled into the arms of the state-church movement.

Of course there were more profound reasons for the collapse of conciliarism than Pope Eugene IV's drive for power. One was that regular councils as required by *Frequens* proved to be an excessive demand given the travel conditions of the time. Basel suffered from a notoriously small number of bishops present. The council's ambitious claim "to represent the Church as a whole" was in striking contrast to the deplorable actual representation. In fact those who gathered there were a group of professional conciliar experts (primarily professors and members of religious orders) chosen on the principle of availability: men whose "benefices" allowed them to be absent for years at a time. Some form of representative selection from the episcopates of the individual states might not have been impossible, but that would have required a genuine spirit of cooperation within the national episcopates. That such a true ecclesial spirit was not present in the great majority of bishops was the real and deeper reason for the failure of a moderate conciliarism that would have corresponded thoroughly to the ancient tradition of the Church.

Nevertheless, as soon as the battle standards were raised and the pointed question of superiority (who is over whom?) governed the whole fray, it was perfectly natural that the greater efficiency and political abilities of a monarchical papacy would gain the victory.

4. The Problems with the Decree Haec sancta

For a conception of the Church oriented to Vatican Council I the events of those times, and especially the Council of Constance's decree *Haec sancta*, remain a hard nut to crack. Even to the present time they have not been thoroughly examined by theologians. A number of questions arise: How is this decree to be interpreted? Does not the superiority of a council over the pope that it claims contradict the later teaching of the Church, and especially of Vatican I? Can it be that *Haec sancta* is also a dogmatic definition contrary to Vatican I, so that one of the two must necessarily be wrong?[35]

To begin with, *Haec sancta* must be seen within its contemporary situation. It was an extreme action in defense of the Church in a hopelessly muddled situation when the papacy had failed to bring about unity. *Haec sancta* intends only to legitimate the council in this situation so that it can continue its work toward unity. From that point of view one may surely say that the historical circumstances themselves do not point to a desire for a dogmatic definition. In terms of the situation itself, it was a pragmatic maxim for Church action at a moment of extreme emergency when the times called for immediate action and not for the quiet reflection required for a definition. Add to this that in its attitude to the supporters of Gregory XII (and also those of Benedict XIII) the Council of Constance clearly did not insist upon *Haec sancta* so long as unity could be achieved, for even after *Haec sancta* the council fathers permitted Gregory XII to call the council before he resigned. They permitted him and his followers to interpret the law to mean that only their participation caused the council to begin (and that therefore all its earlier meetings, including the one at which *Haec sancta* was proclaimed, were not valid conciliar sessions). They patiently listened to the bull calling the council as if they had not previously declared in explicit terms that the council was legitimately gathered in the Holy Spirit, that it received its authority from Christ, and that all, no matter what their dignity or status, were required to obey it. Thus in a certain sense Constance relativized the conciliar principle for the sake of unity. When unity could be achieved without *Haec sancta*, as in the case of Gregory's supporters, the council fathers did not insist on it.

The interpretation of *Haec sancta* is a different matter. Does it refer only to cases of schism or does it apply to other extreme and exceptional situations? Should it then be interpreted in the sense of the traditional doctrine of "emergency law"? Such an interpretation would not require *Haec sancta* to be read as formally contrary to Vatican I since the latter presumes the normal situation of the Church when a valid and undisputed pope exists. It takes no account of exceptional situations. One could assume from this that in situations when Christians of good will cannot know who is the legitimate pope there really is no pope at all, but only pseudo-popes. *Haec sancta* would then in reality not have declared the superiority of a council to the pope, but only to supposed popes.

The strongest support for such an interpretation is that the argumentation at the council itself was conducted purely in light of the current problem. Those who spoke did not look beyond their own situation. They always had in mind the schism, the current emergency, and the failure of John XXIII. They did not argue in universal terms nor with a view to the orderly, normal condition of the Church.

On the other hand, the version proclaimed on April 6 (but not the version of March 30!) contains passages that go beyond the traditional doctrine of emergency law and are more difficult to restrict to exceptional situations or specifically that of schism. This is true especially of the statement that not only in questions of eradication of schism, but also in those of faith *and* the general reform of the Church in head and members everyone of whatever degree, including the pope, must obey the council; further, that this is true not only of the present council but of all councils in the future. These statements, too, may possibly be interpreted in the sense of emergency law. There are indications that "reform of the Church in head and members" was not understood as the task of every council, but as a special historical emergency. When the decree then speaks of "any other legitimately assembled general council" with regard to "the eradication of the said schism and the general reform of the said church of God in head and members" one could understand this to mean an extreme situation, even though possibly subject to repetition, so that the Church might also face such conditions in the future. However, such an interpretation seems very artificial.

In fact at the first reading on March 30 this passage was omitted. In the intervening week the council received the news of John XXIII's second flight. In this extremely tense and embittered atmosphere, the decree was passed on April 6 in its sharpest form. Most of the council fathers scarcely appreciated the consequences of the passage. It was a time for action, not for placid theological reflection. When there is a fire to be put out there is no time to debate the responsibilities of the fire department. This was in some sense a life or death operation, the consequences of which could not be foreseen, but of which one could say that if it were not done there would be (at least in human estimation) no other chance to save the patient!

Nevertheless, even in such a situation the Church cannot go beyond the order established by Jesus Christ. Therefore one should probably say that even if *Haec sancta* is not a dogmatic definition it retains its function as a model for the Church in later times (and even as a corrective to Vatican I). It is an important fundamental decision regarding the always possible circumstance of an extreme failure of the papal office, something that should be much more carefully considered than it normally is, and an eventuality to which we should not blind ourselves by ignoring all history and simply trusting in the guidance of the Holy Spirit who "would not permit such a thing."

The events of that time, moreover, have an unmistakable significance for the Church in all times: any ecclesiology that simply binds the Church to the pope, and not the reverse as well, is refuted by the historical experience of the great schism and the events connected with it.

The example of Constance itself shows that truth lies not only in Ambrose's famous saying, *ubi Petrus, ibi ecclesia* (where Peter is, there is the Church), but in its reverse, *ubi ecclesia, ibi Petrus* (where the Church is, there is Peter). It is not always the case that Peter is the more definite entity who sets norms for the less defined reality of the Church. It can also be the other way around, and it must therefore be the case in normal Church situations as well that the Church, through its witness and its reception, sustains and supports the pope and his decisions.

Excursus 1: *Primacy and the Separation from the Eastern Church: The Council of Florence*

What role did the question of primacy play in the separation between the Eastern and Western Churches? Ordinarily the mutual excommunications exchanged by the papal legate Humbert of Silva Candida and Patriarch Michael Cerularius in 1054 are said to mark the date of the separation. In reality that event was only one prominent incident within a process that lasted approximately from 1000 to 1200. Since the time of Gregory VII the popes had regarded the Greeks as "disobedient" because they did not recognize the form of papal primacy that had developed in the West; on the other hand, they did not think of them as *eo ipso* excommunicated.

For the Greeks the unilateral introduction of the *filioque* into the Credo (which actually took place in Rome for the first time in 1014 and was the work of the German King Henry II) was a major accusation against the West; quite apart from the dogmatic question, this was seen as an offense against the principle of ecclesial charity and communion because the West made the insertion unilaterally and without consulting the East. There was thus a breach of communion on both sides and the transition to a genuine schism between the Churches was gradual. Later attempts at union undertaken for political reasons at the urging of the Byzantine emperor collapsed for various reasons. The popes repeatedly made the mistake of dealing directly with the emperor, presuming in Byzantium a caesaropapism that no longer existed there. Moreover, it was no longer possible to create a "union from above" because the people, and especially the conservative monasteries as guardians of orthodoxy raised a consistent opposition to all such attempts.

Ultimately, however, it was the question of primacy that was the decisive reason why union was never again achieved. The West repeatedly attempted to impose on the East a monarchical ecclesiology that saw the pope as the only visible head of the Church, and for which a reunion only seemed imaginable in terms of a return to obedience to the apostolic see. It was impossible to achieve insight into the Greek way of thinking because the West was ignorant of history and thus lacked an awareness of the historical conditioning and relativity of its own standpoint. The papacy was inclined to consider any forms of autonomy that might be recognized in the Eastern Church (for example, the rights of the patriarchs) merely as papal concessions and privileges, and not as the acknowledgment of independent rights. "In [the holy Roman church] such a plenitude of power rests that she receives the other churches to a share of her solicitude," and that included the patriarchal churches.

From Innocent III to the second Council of Lyons in 1274 attempts were made to describe the relationship in terms like these, as foreign to Greek thought as they were to historical reality.[36] The suggestion that the divisive questions should be discussed at a general council was rejected by the papacy for a long time because Rome was thought to hold its position not through the decisions of councils but by the Lord's institution, so that the primacy of Rome was not at the disposition of a council. The Greek objections to the western idea of primacy were most powerfully formulated as early as the twelfth century by Nicetas, the Greek partner in a dialogue with Anselm of Havelberg:

> But the Roman church, whose primacy among these sisters (the patriarchal churches) we do not deny, and whose foremost rank in honor as presider at a general council we acknowledge, has separated from us because of its pride, seized an autocratic rule that does not belong to its office, and divided the bishops of West and East as the empire itself is divided. . . . Although we are not divided in our faith from the Roman church, how can we, since at present we celebrate no councils with it, accept its decrees, which are written without our knowledge or participation? If the pope thunders against us on the exalted throne of his glory and from the heights of his majesty tries to hurl commands at us, not according to our advice, but according to his own good pleasure, as he claims—what kind of fraternity, indeed, what kind of fatherliness can there be in this? Who could quietly endure such a thing? For then we could no longer be called sons of the Church; we would no longer be sons, but truly slaves. . . . Freedom would then be enjoyed by the Roman church alone, which would make the laws for all others while remaining lawless itself. It would no longer be a gentle mother to its children, but the severe and tyrannical mistress of slaves. To what end then the biblical scholarship, the spiritual erudition, the theological studies and the noble wisdom of the Greeks? The Roman bishop alone, with his superior authority, makes all that empty and void. He alone would then be bishop, teacher, and preceptor. He alone should give an accounting for all that is entrusted solely to him before God, the one and only good shepherd![37]

To these reproaches Anselm could at first only reply that he had had much more positive experiences of the Roman church and that those who knew it better found it to be a model of gentleness, care, and justice. That was, of course, the very reason why appeals to Rome were increasing in the twelfth century: people expected to find more objectivity there than in a local church that was often thickly encrusted with political interests and family feuds.

The first genuine discussion of these questions came at the Council of Florence in 1439.[38] Still, here again there was no genuine negotiation, but instead a kind of comparative statement (as in the decree of union, *Laetentur coeli,* of 1439).[39] On the one hand, the pope's universal power of teaching and leadership was emphasized in the western understanding and using classic western terminology: the pope holds primacy over the whole world; he is the successor of Peter, the vicar of Christ, the head of the whole Church, and in Christ he has been given the "full power" of tending, ruling, and governing the whole Church. But the Greeks were only prepared to concede the position of Rome as the first see of the pentarchy. They demanded that the papacy be limited by the rights of the other patriarchs; if such a passage were not included, "the matter should be broken off." They achieved a statement of the order of the pentarchy and an affirmation that its privileges and rights should remain intact but there was no explanation of how the two bodies were related to each other. It is true that the decree avoided deriving the power of the patriarchs from Rome's *plenitudo potestatis,* as was still the case in the formula of union at Lyons II. But for western representatives only the statement about the pope was dogmatic, as even the text suggests, while the second passage simply paid heed to a venerable custom. For most Greeks, Rome was recognized as the head only in the sense of being head of the pentarchy, so that the second passage was a genuine restriction on the first; in particular, they regarded the clause "as it is contained also in the acts of ecumenical councils and in the sacred canons" as a limitation on papal power, not a confirmation of it. The union achieved at Florence collapsed just as its predecessors had.

Nevertheless, the definition of primacy at Florence had a turbulent history in the West, because the council was by no means universally recognized in the West since it was in opposition to Basel. Even at the Council of Trent (1545–1563) the ecumenicity of Florence was disputed; the French rejected that council and its definition of primacy. In all the subsequent centuries, the ecumenical character of Florence was the object of dispute between the group including many, though not all Gallicans (who recognized *Haec sancta* and the Council of Basel) and the "Roman" faction, which relied on Florence.[40] Only from the beginning of the nineteenth century onward, with the defeat of Gallicanism, did Florence and its definition of primacy gradually win the upper hand. How much the lines of contention had shifted was evident at Vatican I (1869–1870). At that council it was the minority who appealed to the Council of Florence, arguing that a definition of the pope's infallibility was not required since everything necessary regarding his primacy and rights had already been clearly defined at Florence.[41] When the Munich church historian Ignaz Döllinger disputed the ecumenicity of Florence, at that time some of the minority German bishops savagely denounced him for stabbing them in the back.[42]

Excursus 2: *Origins of the Doctrine of Papal Infallibility*

In 1972 Brian Tierney entered the discussion surrounding Hans Küng, attempting to prove that the doctrine of papal infallibility was not merely a relatively late phenomenon, but even had heterodox origins, beginning as a criticism of the pope.[43] "Infallibility" on the one hand, "sovereignty" or *plenitudo potestatis* on the other—inseparably linked to one another in the nineteenth century since Cappellari and Joseph de Maistre were originally opposites at enmity with one another. For "infallibility," as both its defenders and opponents clearly recognized at the beginning, meant a restriction on the freedom of action and independence of the papacy because it implied an irrevocable commitment for all time to come. The origins of the doctrine of papal infallibility were said to lie in the controversy over Franciscan poverty in the thirteenth and fourteenth centuries, concretely in the work of the spiritual Franciscan Peter Olivi, who taught around 1280 that papal decisions in questions of faith or morals were irrevocable and remained valid for all time. In saying this he intended to nail the papacy fast, once and for all, to the rigorist position on the poverty question, which Pope Nicolas III had supported in the spring of 1279 in the bull *Exiit qui seminat.*

The question at issue was whether Christ and the apostles had owned anything, individually or in common. In the conception of the time, this was certainly a question of faith. It was an issue of the ultimate interpretation of discipleship which, the spiritual Franciscans believed, Francis of Assisi had restored in its full purity. Tierney further emphasizes that it was precisely the defenders of an unrestricted papal *plenitudo potestatis* who opposed this new teaching because they accurately saw in it a limitation of the field of papal actions. The question became acute in 1323 when Pope John XXII declared the teaching that Christ and the apostles owned nothing either individually or in common to be heretical. When the spiritual Franciscans, in turn, declared John XXII a heretic—appealing to the principle that what had once been defined by the popes through the "key of knowledge" (*per claves scientiae*, i.e., magisterially) was a truth of faith and could no longer be called into question by a successor—the pope condemned that principle as "false."

In the two years following the publication of Tierney's book his positions provoked a lively discussion.[44] The most thorough reworking of the question, and most persuasive in its overall historical perspective, was provided by Ulrich Horst.[45] It appears that Olivi by no means played the key role in the development of the doctrine of infallibility that Tierney ascribes to him. On the one hand, the earlier period of the Decretists and still more that of high scholasticism, with Thomas Aquinas and Bonaventure, came closer to the doctrine than Tierney acknowledges. On the other hand, the crucial next step was not taken by Olivi and the authors who followed him, but only occurred as a result of the conciliarist debates beginning in the fifteenth century.

What, then, were the origins of the doctrine of "papal infallibility"? Here, as with almost all the rights, laws, or convictions associated with papal primacy, it is impossible to fix a single author or era as the starting point. First we must recall that, as far back in history as we can see, the special esteem given to the Roman church community was always associated with fidelity in the faith and preservation of the *paradosis* (the faith as handed down). The "faith . . . proclaimed throughout the world" of the Roman believers (Rom 1:8) became a fixed saying found again and again from the third century onwards. The conviction of the purity of faith of the Roman church, which has never erred, is more easily traced from the fifth century, first with Theodoret of Cyrus, who wrote in 449 after the Latrocinium, "This most sacred throne takes precedence over all the Churches of the world for many reasons, but primarily because it has been preserved from every stain of heresy and no one who thought to the contrary has sat there, but instead it has preserved the grace of the apostles intact."[46]

The conviction that established itself especially but not exclusively in Rome beginning with the Hormisdas formula in 519, that "the Roman church has never erred (and will never err)" of course differed from the later "infallibility of the papal magisterium" especially in that it did not refer specifically to individual dogmatic definitions but to the whole of the faith as handed down and the tradition of Peter preserved intact by the Roman church. In addition, it did not exclude the possibility that individual popes could become heretics because its reference was primarily to the Roman tradition as such, and not exclusively to the person of the pope.

But who embodied the Roman church against a possibly erring pope? The Decretists (commentators on the *Decretum Gratiani*) in the twelfth and thirteenth centuries discussed this problem. Most obvious was the interpretation in the sense of the local church at Rome, especially identified with the college of cardinals, to whom, in cases of heresy or other serious defection by the pope, the protection of the unfailing "Roman Church" is entrusted. But there was also another interpretation. For some of them, as for Huguccio of Pisa, the teacher of Innocent III, around 1188, the *Romana ecclesia* is identified with the *universitas fidelium*, i.e., the universal Church in communion with Rome, which as a whole cannot lose the true faith.

The special contribution of the canonists and theologians from the twelfth to the fourteenth centuries was then the increasingly strong emphasis laid not only on the passive preservation of the faith but on the active role of the pope as leader in the Church's definition of that faith. Nevertheless, there was not yet any disciplined reflection on the question why, ultimately, such decisions are absolutely certain: because of the pope alone, or because they are accepted by the whole Church? The argument was not framed in terms of conflict situations; instead, the pope and the Church, the pope and the council were more likely to be seen as existing in a natural and obvious harmony.

To begin with, the canonists of the twelfth century and afterward, taking up the statement of the *Decretum Gratiani* that in all questions of faith one must refer to the pope, said that "it is the office of the pope to decide questions of faith."[47]

Thomas Aquinas then took an important further step, writing that the pope could issue new formulas of faith (*ad papam spectat editio symboli*).[48] But in giving reasons for this statement he regards the pope primarily as the head and apex of the council, since it is agreed that a council can issue definitions of faith. However, the council is assembled by papal authority and confirmed by papal decree. Therefore the pope has the final decision and final responsibility in conciliar definitions; it belongs to him *finaliter determinare ea quae sunt fidei* (to settle authoritatively what is of faith). Thomas does not reflect further on the relationship between pope and council. He sees the two as obviously in harmony, but at the same time he quite clearly acknowledges that the pope has the last word and exercises the ultimate authority. The background for Thomas's ideas was furnished by the papal general councils of the high Middle Ages, especially the Fourth Lateran Council of 1215. That was the model from which he derived his description of the functioning of the Church's magisterium.

Another important piece of background was the situation of the new mendicant orders, especially the Franciscans, who were well aware that their way of life was a rediscovery of the true evangelical following of Christ. For them the question arose: How reliably does the

Church stand behind this new way of life, which may be felt to be revolutionary? As a consequence, they laid claim to the infallibility of the
Roman church in support of the conformity of their way of life to the
gospels. This did not originate with Olivi, but with Bonaventure. He
argued that if the pope had erred in this case (that is, in establishing
the Franciscans) the universal Church had erred, and that is impossible.[49] Here the pope and the Church merge with one another and are
practically interchangeable. But even with Bonaventure the train of
thought is still unusually fluid. On the one hand it appears that the
pope, "whose decision it is by no means permitted to oppose," represents the Church *eo ipso,* so that his word is in itself the Church's
word.[50] But in another place it appears that the real reason is that the
universal Church has obeyed the pope's word and accepted the
Franciscan order, "for it is certain that the universal Church throughout the whole world accepts this way of life and its statutes."[51]

This tendency to insure the security of one's own way of life, felt to
be something new, is then found also in the work of Peter Olivi, now
against the background of the Franciscans' internal struggle over
poverty. With him we find the first explicit use of the term "freedom
from error" with regard to papal dogmatic definitions. Of course, in
the crucial question he does not go beyond Bonaventure. The pope is
free from error to the extent that he expresses the faith of the universal
Church, which as a whole is without error. But if he ceases to do so and
becomes a heretic, he ceases to be the head of the Church.[52]

The consistent position of the authors of this period remains that the
pope's freedom from error (the expression "infallibility," Latin *infalli-
bilitas,* was then ordinarily reserved to God alone) is founded on that
of the Church, and by no means the reverse. The pope is free from
error as long as and to the extent that he relies on the faith and teaching of the Church. Thus Hermann of Schildesche wrote about 1330:

> The pope's decision is founded on the Catholic Church, which cannot
> err or fall away from the infallible truth, just as the judgment of the head
> is rooted in the body. . . . Thus the pope will never make a false judg-
> ment in such things or err *if he is well integrated into the body of the Church*
> (*si bene corpori Ecclesiae coaptetur*).[53]

It is noteworthy here that the head/body symbolism is used differently from the way it is applied to the *plenitudo potestatis* in the realm
of jurisdictional authority. In that case, since the time of Innocent III,
the image is almost always used to demonstrate the one-sided dependence of the body on the head alone. But in matters of faith and doctrine it is apparently of equal importance that the head is not separated
from the body, but remains in living relationship with it.

On the other hand, there is a much greater shift of infallibility to the pope as head in the anti-conciliarist authors of the fifteenth century. They refer primarily to Thomas Aquinas, but no longer against the background of the experience of the fourth Lateran Council; now the background is Constance and Basel. At this point the emphasis lies on the fact that a council alone does not offer complete security. As experience has shown, especially with the decree *Sacrosancta* of Basel that was issued with a claim to dogmatic validity, councils by themselves can err. Ultimate security can therefore only be given by the pope, and it is only through his approval that the decree of a council becomes absolutely binding and infallible. It must be recalled that this took place in the context of the dispute over the doctrine of the "infallibility of a council," which was first passionately advocated by the conciliarists, especially the theologians of the Council of Basel.[54] The doctrine of "conciliar infallibility" in the strict sense has no priority over that of "papal infallibility;" both developed together and in competition with one another. Of course the councils recognized by the Church, especially the first four, have long been regarded as free from error. No one could dispute their definitions without being a heretic. But if it was asked how one knew that what they defined was true, it was sufficient to say that it was because they were recognized by the Church, which as a whole cannot err. To that point, we cannot pinpoint with the same degree of clarity any doctrine that the truth was guaranteed by an ecumenical council as such, under specific formal conditions and independently of its reception by the Church. However, this claim to infallibility was made explicitly by the conciliarists, precisely because they found themselves locked in a struggle and the recognition and reception by the Church of the councils in question (Pisa, Constance, and especially Basel) was still lacking or unclear. And because a council laying claim to infallibility had deposed a pope who rejected this "infallible" definition (Basel, with its decree *Sacrosancta* against Eugene IV) it was now emphasized on the papal side that a conciliar decision offers no absolute security unless it is confirmed by the pope.

Certainly infallibility as such was not immediately transferred to the pope alone. At first it was only the ultimate guarantee of the council's actions that was made dependent on the pope's affirmation. But for the authors of this period, especially the Dominicans, it is usual for the pope still to be strongly bound to the universal Church, so much so that at Vatican I their texts were most often cited by the minority, and less frequently by the infallibilist majority. There still remained the borderline case of the *papa haereticus,* and in such instances the superiority of the council to the pope remained intact. In other terms it was said (for example by Torquemada) that in matters of faith the pope cannot set himself against an ecumenical council that makes its decisions with an overwhelming majority, not so much because the council is above the pope as because of its more perfect ability to judge.

Antoninus of Florence (d. 1459) employed an important distinction first found in the work of the Dominican master general Herveus Natalis (d. 1323):[55] The pope can err *ut persona singularis, ex proprio motu agens* (as a private individual when acting on his own accord), but not *utens consilio et requirens adiutorium universalis ecclesiae* (when making use of the counsel of the whole Church and seeking its aid).[56] This formula was later cited repeatedly by the minority bishops at Vatican I.

In addition according to most authors, the pope must not only inquire of the Church before making a definition; the counsel of the Holy Spirit is not available to him as something coming directly from God, but only by way of the medium of an inquiry addressed to the Church as a whole; in so inquiring he is relying on the Church, which is infallible primarily as the Church universal. Of course, if one asks these authors how this questioning of the Church should be done, different individuals give different answers. It may be said that, depending on the importance of the matter and especially on the degree to which it is clarified by the tradition or not, a general council may be needed; otherwise an inquiry of the cardinals may suffice. What is here expressed is on the one hand the awareness that the ultimate decision in matters of faith belongs to the pope and without him an infallible decision is impossible; but on the other hand it is also true that the pope is not autonomous, but is dependent on the Church and its faith. He has no "personal" infallibility of his own that could function alongside that of the Church and be founded on some kind of special "enlightenment." In other words, the mutual dependence of pope and Church are always emphasized.

For these authors, of course, the era of the schism was still a vivid memory. They knew that the papacy had failed in their own time and, even though they were by no means conciliarists, they could not abstract from this experience even in their theology. But the farther that period receded into the past, the more were its experiences forgotten or repressed. This is true, for example, of Cardinal Cajetan and the other Dominican theologians at the beginning of the sixteenth century.[57] Cajetan made use on the one hand of the same distinction as Antoninus of Florence: the pope as an individual can err, but not when he definitively binds the entire Church. As with Antoninus, this is then demonstrated on the basis of the infallibility of the whole Church, which cannot fall into error. Nevertheless, the reversal of the traditional argument is striking: if Antoninus proved this by the fact that the pope, *when depending on the Church,* cannot err, now it is said that *because the pope binds the Church,* and the Church cannot err (although an error of the pope in a faith definition would necessarily lead the Church into error) an error on the part of the pope is also impossible.[58] For Antoninus, then, it is primarily the Church as a whole that is infallible; the pope, as its voice and representative, participates in its infallibility. For Cajetan it is primarily the pope who is infallible; the Church's infallibility is prior to that of the pope only as a final cause, but not as an efficient cause. "The former idea of the Church as the primary reality that then in a certain sense transfers its own truth to its presiding head is now interpreted in such a way that the causality takes its beginning from the top and then penetrates the whole."[59]

The authors tend more and more to recommend nothing but prayer and reliance on God (who will cause such a pope to die quickly) as means of combating papal misuse of power (heresy or the like). It is even said that the fact of a *papa haereticus* must be directly attested by God, perhaps through a miracle. Still further we read that one must obey even a heretical pope, just as one must submit to an irreligious prince. Faced with this kind of naive, simplistic reliance on divine providence, one could get the impression that there had never been a great schism; but the problems of reform that beset the lifetime of these authors and the scandal of the Renaissance papacy are just as thoroughly repressed.

It is true that another factor plays a role here, namely the greater acceptability, in that time and place, of absolute monarchy as a form of government. It was argued that a monarch was necessary to create unity out of multiplicity and to preserve order. The arguments of the Dominican Torquemada are significant in this regard: Just as the prince must be above the laws of the state in order to be able to "move it in all things" *(movere rempublicam ad omnia)*, so the pope must "move and lead [the Church] through his teaching office" *(magisterio movere et dirigere)*.[60] The crucial concept here is *movere*. It is no longer simply a question of "preserving" the Church (or the state) in the traditional order of what is right and true, but now it is a matter of "moving" them. That requires new decisions for which, by nature, a monarchical power free of all kinds of restrictions and limiting laws is more efficient. The static notion of government by a supreme judge has been replaced, in both Church and state, by a dynamic concept. The development toward the absolute monarchical state, no matter how centrifugal its effects in Church politics (as in French Gallicanism), promoted a mentality that readily accepted papal absolutism: Thus the Church, in its very opposition to the states and in the assertion of its own independence, again became an image of the world and political domination.

NOTES

[1]Cf. D. Gerhard, *Das Abendland. Ursprung und Gegenbild unserer Zeit* (Freiburg, 1985) 74–75.

[2]Joseph Ratzinger, "Der Einfluß des Bettelordensstreites auf die Entwicklung der Lehre vom päpstlichen Universalprimat, unter besonderer Berücksichtigung des heiligen Bonaventura," *Theologie in Geschichte und Gegenwart*, Festschrift for Michael Schmaus (Munich, 1957) 697–724, at 705.

[3]W. Ullmann, *The Growth of Papal Government in the Middle Ages. A study in the ideological relation of clerical to lay power* (London, 1955); F. Kempf, "Die päpstliche Gewalt in der mittelalterlichen Welt. Eine Auseinandersetzung mit W. Ullmann," *Miscellanea Historiae Pontificiae* 21 (1959) 117–69; H. Barion, review of Kempf's article, *Zeitschrift für Rechtsgeschichte, kanonische Abteilung* 46 (1960) 484–501; F. Kempf, "Zur politischen Lehre der früh- und hochmittelalterlichen Kirche," *Zeitschrift für Rechtsgeschichte, kanonische Abteilung* 47 (1961) 305–19; idem., "Kanonistik und kuriale Politik im 12. Jahrhundert," *AHP* 1 (1963) 11–52; W. Kölmel, *Regimen Christianum. Weg und Ergebnisse des Gewaltverhältnisses und des Gewaltenverständnisses (8.–14. Jh.)* (Berlin, 1970); see F. Kempf's review of Kölmel's book in *AHP* 9 (1971) 430–39.

[4]"*Oportet autem gladium esse sub gladio, et temporalem auctoritatem spirituali subici potestatis.*"

[5]See number 3 in "Texts," p. 185.

[6]On this, see especially L.F.J. Meulenberg, *Der Primat der römischen Kirche im Denken und Handeln Gregors VII* (s'Gravenhage, 1965).

[7]*PL* 20.473A.

[8]On this, see Meulenberg, *Primat*, 92ff.

[9]*CSEL* 6.295, 316.

[10]Similarly Meulenberg, *Primat*, 30–33.

[11]*Reg.* 1.64: E. Caspar, ed., *Das Register Gregors VII* (Berlin, 1920) 93.

[12]*PL* 54.671.

[13]P. Hinschius, ed., *Decretales Pseudo-Isidorianae et capitula Angilramni* (Leipzig, 1863) 712.

[14]*De consideratione* 2.8 (*PL* 182.752B/C).

[15]*De consideratione* 3.4 (*PL* 182.766–69).

[16]*De consideratione* 2.8 (*PL* 182.752).

[17]*Reg.* 2.209 (*PL* 214.760A).

[18]"*Nam quamvis sumus apostolorum principis successores, non tamen eius aut alicuius apostoli vel hominis, sed ipsius sumus vicarii Jesu Christi.*" *Reg.* 1.326: O. Hageneder and A. Haidacher, *Die Register Innocenz III* (Graz and Cologne, 1964) 1:473.

[19]*Reg.* 1.320 (in ibid., 1:465) and 6.188 (*PL* 215.205).

[20]*PL* 11.947.

[21]*Reg.* 1.345, 445, 495, 499 (Hageneder and Haidacher, *Register,* 1:515–16, 668, 724, 727); 2.123, 202, 213 (*PL* 214.676, 750, 772); 7.209 (*PL* 215.523).

[22]See the citations in L. Buisson, *Potestas und Caritas. Die päpstliche Gewalt im Spätmittelalter* (Cologne and Graz, 1958) 82–86.

[23]*Summa de potestate ecclesiastica* (1326) 6.5 (printed at Rome in 1584) 61D.

[24]*DG* 1, dist. 40, p. iii, c. xi.

[25]*DG* I, dist. 19, c. ix.

[26]Cf. F. J. Schmale, "Systematisches zu den Konzilien des Reformpapsttums im 12. Jahrhundert," *AHC* 6 (1974) 21–39.

[27]On this, see especially K. Ganzer, *Papsttum und Bistumsbesetzungen in der Zeit von Gregor IX bis Bonifaz VIII. Ein Beitrag zur Geschichte der päpstlichen Reservationen* (Cologne, 1968).

[28]F. Jürgensmeier, *Das Bistum Mainz. Von der Römerzeit bis zum II. Vatikanischen Konzil* (Frankfurt, 1988) 113, 115, 121, 126, 132–36, 138, 140, 142, 148.

[29]*De ecclesiastica potestate* 2, ch. 9; cf. Ganzer, *Papsttum und Bistumsbesetzungen* 59, 67–68.

[30]J. Lecler, *Vienne* (Mainz, 1965) 152.

[31]Sermon of July 21, 1415, reproduced in J. Gill, *Konstanz und Basel-Florenz* (Mainz, 1967) 375–88, at 379.

[32]On this, see especially J. A. Black, "Politische Grundgedanken des Konziliarismus und Papalismus zwischen 1430 und 1450," in R. Bäumer, ed., *Die Entwicklung des Konziliarismus*, WdF 279 (Darmstadt, 1976) 295–328.

[33]On this, especially the Council of Basel, see W. Krämer, *Konsens und Rezeption. Verfassungsprinzipien der Kirche im Basler Konziliarismus* (Münster, 1980). In addition, see H. J. Sieben, "Der Konzilstraktat des Nikolaus von Kues 'De concordantia catholica,'" *AHC* 14 (1982) 171–226.

[34]See number 4 in "Texts," p. 186.

[35]On this, see H. Riedlinger, "Hermeneutische Überlegungen zu den Konstanzer Dekreten," in A. Franzen and W. Müller, eds., *Das Konzil von Konstanz* (Freiburg, 1964) 214–38; A. Franzen, "Das Konstanzer Konzil. Probleme, Aufgaben und Stand der Konzilsforschung," *Concilium* 1 (1965) 555–74; H. Jedin, *Bischöfliches Konzil oder Kirchenparlament? Ein Beitrag zur Ekklesiologie der Konzilien von Konstanz und Basel* (Basel, 1966); W. Brandmüller, "Besitzt das Konstanzer Dekret Haec sancta dogmatische Verbindlichkeit?" *Römische Quartalschrift* 62 (1967) 1-17; R. Bäumer, "Die Interpretation und Verbindlichkeit der Konstanzer Dekrete," *Theologisch-Praktische Quartalschrift* 116 (1968) 44-52. The essays by Brandmüller and Bäumer can also be found in R. Bäumer, ed., *Die Entwicklung des Konziliarismus* (Darmstadt, 1976).

[36]W. De Vries, "Innocenz III. und der christliche Osten," *AHP* 3 (1965) 87-126; the formula of 1274 is in *DS* 466.

[37]*Dialogues* 3.8 (*PL* 188.1219).

[38]On this, see A. Leidl, "Die Primatsverhandlungen auf dem Konzil von Florenz," *AHC* 7 (1975) 272-89.

[39]Cf. number 5 in "Texts," p. 188.

[40]Cf. H. J. Sieben, "Vom Florentinum zum Ersten Vatikanum. Zur Ökumenizität des Konzils von Florenz und zur Rezeption seiner Primatslehre," *ThPh* 65 (1990) 513–48.

[41]Mansi 51.678B/C, 680C/D, 683A/B, 685B.

[42]Klaus Schatz, *Kirchenbild und päpstliche Unfehlbarkeit bei den deutschsprachigen Minoritätsbischöfen auf dem 1. Vatikanum* (Rome, 1975) 161–69.

[43]Brian Tierney, *Origins of papal infallibility 1150-1350. A study of the concepts of infallibility, sovereignty and tradition in the Middle Ages* (Leiden, 1972).

[44]The most important contributions were by Alfons M. Stickler, "Papal Infallibility—A Thirteenth-Century Invention? Reflections on a Recent Book," *CHR* 60 (1974) 427-41; Brian Tierney, "Infallibility and the Medieval Canonists: A Discussion with Alfons Stickler," *CHR* 61 (1975) 265-73; Alfons M. Stickler, "A Rejoinder to Professor Tierney," *CHR* 61 (1975) 274-79; Yves Congar's review of Tierney's book in *Revue d'Histoire Ecclésiastique* 68 (1973) 162-67; the review by Remigius Bäumer in *Theologische Revue* 69 (1973) 441-50 and the subsequent exchange: Brian Tierney, *Theologische Revue* 70 (1974) 186-94; R. Bäumer, *Theologische Revue* 70 (1974) 194-95.

[45]"Infallibilität und Geschichte. Ein Rückblick," in U. Horst, *Unfehlbarkeit und Geschichte. Studien zur Unfehlbarkeitsdiskussion von Melchior Cano bis zum 1. Vatikanischen Konzil* (Mainz, 1982) 214-56.

[46]*Letters* 116, SC 111, 70.

[47]*"Quoties fidei ratio ventilatur,"* DG II, ch. xxiv, q. 11, c. 12.

[48]*Summa theol.* 2.2ae q. 1 art. 10.

[49]*Apologia pauperum,* 11.10, 16; *De perfectione evangelica* q. II art. 2 t. 5.

[50]Thus in *Apologia pauperum,* 11.

[51]*De perfectione evangelica* q. II, art. 2 t. 5.

[52]On this, see Horst, *Unfehlbarkeit und Geschichte,* 227-28.

[53]Hermann of Schildesche, *Tractatus contra haereticos negantes immunitatem et iuris-dictionem sanctae Ecclesiae,* ed. A. Zumkeller (Würzburg, 1970) part II ch. 9, pp. 77-78.

[54]On this, see especially H. J. Sieben, *Traktate und Theorien zum Konzil* (Frankfurt, 1983).

[55]Horst, *Unfehlbarkeit und Geschichte,* 234.

[56]*Summa theol.* III, tit. 22, ch. 3.

[57]On this, see U. Horst, *Zwischen Konziliarismus und Reformation. Studien zur Ekklesiologie im Dominikanerorden* (Rome, 1985).

[58]*De comparatione auctoritatis papae et concilii,* ch. IX, nos. 131-32.

[59]Horst, *Zwischen Konziliarismus und Reformation,* 29.

[60] Quoted by Black (see n. 32) 324.

SELECTED BIBLIOGRAPHY

Bäumer, Remigius, ed. *Die Entwicklung des Konziliarismus.* Wege der Forschung 279 (Darmstadt: Wissenschaftliche Buchgesellschaft, 1976).

_____, ed. *Das Konstanzer Konzil* (Darmstadt: Wissenschaftliche Buchgesellschaft, 1977).

Congar, Yves. "Der Platz des Papsttums in der Kirchenfrömmigkeit der Reformer des 11. Jahrhunderts," in Jean Daniélou and Herbert Vorgrimler, eds., *Sentire ecclesiam.* Festschrift for Hugo Rahner (Freiburg: Herder, 1961) 196–217.

Franzen, August, and Wolfgang Müller, eds. *Das Konzil von Konstanz* (Freiburg: Herder, 1964).

Horst, Ulrich. *Zwischen Konziliarismus und Reformation. Studien zur Ekklesiologie im Dominikanerorden* (Rome, 1985).

Imkamp, Walter. *Das Kirchenbild Innocenz III., 1198–1216* (Stuttgart: Hiersemann, 1983).

Kempf, Friedrich. "Die Eingliederung der überdiözesanen Hierarchie in das Papalsystem des kanonischen Rechts von der gregorianischen Reform bis zu Innocenz III," *AHP* 18 (1980) 57–96.

Maccarrone, Michele. *Vicarius Christi. Storia del titolo papale* (Rome, 1952).

Meulenberg, L.F.J. *Der Primat der römischen Kirche im Denken und Handeln Gregors VII* (s'Gravenhage: Staatsdrukkerijen Uitgeverijbedrijf, 1965).

Pennington, K. *Pope and Bishops: The Papal Monarchy in the 12th and 13th Centuries* (Philadelphia: University of Pennsylvania Press, 1984).

Schatz, Klaus. "Papsttum und partikularkirchliche Gewalt bei Innocenz III. (1198–1216)," *AHP* 8 (1970) 61–111.

Sieben, Hermann Josef. *Die Konzilsidee des lateinischen Mittelalters 847–1378* (Paderborn: Schoningh, 1984).

_____. *Traktate und Theorien zum Konzil. Vom Beginn des Großen Schismas bis zum Vorabend der Reformation 1378–1521*. Frankfurter Theologische Studien 30 (Frankfurt: Knecht, 1983).

Tierney, Brian. *Foundations of the Conciliar Theory. The Contribution of the Medieval Canonists from Gratian to the Great Schism* (Cambridge: Cambridge University Press, 1955).

_____. *Origins of papal infallibility 1150–1350. A study of the concepts of infallibility, sovereignty and tradition in the Middle Ages* (Leiden and New York: E. J. Brill, 1972).

PART FOUR:
PRIMACY AS A MARK OF CONFESSIONAL IDENTITY IN THE MODERN ERA

I. From the Reformation to the Enlightenment

At first sight it must seem peculiar that there was no definition of primacy at the Council of Trent (1545–1563) although this council issued dogmatic definitions on all the other points of Catholic doctrine that had been attacked by the Reformers. In view of the Protestant polemics about the "Antichrist," a dogmatic defense of the divine right of the papacy would have seemed quite opportune, but it did not take place. This was neither because some of the council fathers did not acknowledge a divine law of primacy nor because there was no discussion of the question. There was, in fact, scarcely any set of problems that was so controversial at Trent or that brought the council so close to collapse as the question of primacy and the relationship between the primate and the episcopate.[1] This is true especially of the final year, 1563, when the French were also present. It was then obvious that there was no consensus possible about the concrete meaning of primacy and the rights of the primate. The attempt to enact the definition of primacy from the Council of Florence was defeated by the resistance of the French council fathers who did not recognize Florence and were not prepared to accept a "complete authority" of the pope to pastor and rule the Church as defined there.

Another bitter conflict broke out over the origins of episcopal jurisdictional authority in connection with the decree on the sacrament of orders. The Roman group upheld a thesis in line with papalist theology since Augustinus Triumphus that episcopal jurisdictional authority was given by the pope, while both the French and Spanish council fathers saw it as given immediately by Christ. Here again the debate came to no conclusion, as in the still more hotly discussed question of the *ius divinum* (divine law) regarding the bishop's obligation to reside in his diocese. The debate on this point was so hot and bitter because here once again the problems of reform were irrevocably tangled with ecclesiological issues. The question was whether the bishop's duty to reside in his own diocese (as well as the associated prohibition on holding a plurality of bishoprics) was so inseparably bound up with the nature of the episcopal office that even the pope could not dispense from it.

Ultimately this was another confrontation between two concepts of the Church, one primarily focused on the universal Church, the other on the local church. For the upholders of *ius divinum* (the Spanish and French) the episcopal office was essentially and inseparably ordered to the local church; because it was instituted by Christ and not by the pope, the pope could not change its essential character. Therefore even the pope could not bestow bishoprics on persons who were not expected to reside in their dioceses. Sham bishops who really lived at the Curia or in princely courts and appointed representatives for their dioceses were in that case an illegitimate phenomenon in principle and there could be no valid and legal dispensation for such a practice, not even from the pope. The contrary view, represented mainly by Italians, held that the episcopal office was primarily ordered to the Church universal. According to this the bishops received their jurisdictional authority from the pope; they were in some sense a mobile set of functionaries who could be employed in a variety of ways. Here again, no consensus could be reached.

The unresolved questions of papacy and episcopate were thus left for future decision. At the end of the council the papal legates wrote to Rome that in their opinion the Church would find no peace and be unable to avoid divisions if these questions were not somehow decided. The dilemma was simply that on the one hand the decision could only be made by a council, since only the decree of a council had a chance of being accepted by everyone, "but in that case it is to be feared that a council, being a council of bishops whose interests are at stake, would decide in their favor."[2] What is astonishing is that just over three hundred years later it was a council of bishops who defined papal privilege in a way that was unthinkable at Trent.

1. The Strengthening of Papal Authority in the Post-Tridentine Period

In spite of all this the Council of Trent strengthened the role of the papacy in the Church in the long run precisely because in spite of all the tensions that again and again brought it to the brink of collapse, its concrete course in fact showed that it was possible to carry out a reform of the Church in cooperation with the papacy and without constitutional restriction of papal authority. It was important in the sequel that the papacy again accepted its leadership role in the Church with more vigor and placed itself at the head of the Tridentine reform. Roman directives continued the reforming work of Trent in its centralist tendency and intervened in many areas of Church life to establish order and set norms.

One aspect of this, as early as 1542, was the establishment of the central Roman Office of the Inquisition, later called the Holy Office. Of course the Spanish and Portuguese inquisitions already existed independently of Rome; they by no means always acted in conformity with Rome in disputed matters. Conflicts arose over relationships between king and pope or when the Spanish inquisition acted against bishops, which was contrary to the principle of the sole responsibility of Rome in *causae maiores*. Nevertheless, at Rome two schools of reforming thought continued to struggle back and forth for decades in this and other problem areas: one was more open and humanistic, the other more strict and rigorist, seeking to effect reform primarily through discipline imposed from above. Ultimately the latter school prevailed under Pius V (1566–1572).

Not least among the accomplishments of Pius V was the final prescription of the norms for the liturgy according to the Roman rite, especially through the Missal issued in 1570 and in use until after Vatican II. Begun in the Carolingian period and continued in the Gregorian era, the process of acceptance of the strict Roman liturgy throughout the western Church was now essentially complete apart from some minor exceptions. But what was completely new was that from now on the regulation of the liturgy in the Latin Church was strictly reserved to Rome. In spite of all the tendencies to accommodation to the Roman form, promoted especially by the Franciscans, until that time it was still possible for a variety of alterations and new elements in individual rites, Mass formularies, prayers and solemnities to originate elsewhere. From now on that could no longer happen: the liturgy of the Mass, the sacraments, and the breviary was fixed, and Rome alone was responsible for any future changes.

Of the greatest importance for the future was the establishment of the permanent nunciatures, especially under Pope Gregory XIII (1572–1585). From the eleventh century onwards there had been papal legates with special assignments. The establishment of the permanent nunciatures (the first in Venice in 1500; the highly important nunciature for Germany was founded at Cologne in 1584) was connected with the custom that had grown up since the beginning of the modern era of having permanent embassies at the various courts. From the beginning the nuncios were important figures in the Church for the accomplishment of the Tridentine reforms (especially because in this matter, particularly in Germany and France, the bishops were very dilatory) and the battle against the Reformation.

With regard to the Church's missions, we should mention the founding in 1622 of the Congregation for the Propagation of the Faith, which was responsible until 1908 for most of the countries under Protestant rule. Through this congregation Rome sought to bring missionary work under its own control, although until the nineteenth century it had little success.

It was also crucial that the papacy and acceptance of it became a sign of Catholic confessional identity over against Protestantism. Even though Trent had deliberately refrained from defining the primacy, and even though episcopal counter-tendencies continued to represent separate centers of power, their advocates now found it repeatedly necessary to acknowledge that as Catholics they quite obviously recognized the papal primacy and its divine right. In any case, from this time until Vatican I the papalist point of view always had the advantage of appearing "undoubtedly Catholic." Wherever the primary interest was establishing confessional boundaries and a clear profile of what was confessionally Catholic, this position presented itself as the most consistent. It is true that on the other hand where overtures were made toward community and building bridges to Protestantism, conciliarism and Gallicanism presented themselves as potential ecumenical approaches; this was especially evident during the Enlightenment period. But because over time maintaining clear confessional identity came to be seen as the desirable goal the more ecumenical school was left behind. It introduced a hint of insecurity into the Catholic principle of unity and clarity. In the end this was most clearly expressed by Archbishop Manning at Vatican I. Manning himself was a convert: as an Anglican in search of truth he had had the feeling that insecurity about the infallibility of the pope obscured the otherwise secure Catholic teaching about the infallibility of the Church; English Protestants themselves regarded papal infallibility as a necessary consequence of Catholic teaching. They regarded Gallicanism as not genuinely Catholic and were happy to bring it forward as an argument against the genuineness of supposed Catholic unity.[3] However, three centuries would elapse before this was fully resolved.

Finally, another very crucial factor was the Jesuit order, established in 1540. It was not only more centralized than the other orders; it was also distinguished from the mendicant orders of the thirteenth century by the fact that its connection to the pope was not merely an authorization to work in all parts of the Church. Instead, work for the greater glory of

God in the service of the most important tasks of the whole Church at any given time and submission to the pope constituted the original purposes of the order. For Ignatius Loyola and his original companions the first goal was to have been to live in the Holy Land. Only when that plan collapsed because there was no ship available at Venice did it become urgently necessary for the community to accept the best solution available: submission to the pope so that he might send them wherever their service to the Church would be most vital, whether among the Turks, the pagans, or any kind of heretics. This tie to the pope is most clearly expressed in the fourth vow (willingness to be sent by the pope to any place at all). The spirit behind this is that of "indifference" to all human ties, including local ones; positively it is a dedication to the "greater glory of God." Ecclesiologically, in turn, this means that there is no ultimate inner tie to any individual church, but instead service to the whole Church and willingness to allow oneself to be sent where one is most needed. Any intention of supporting an endangered papal authority by this means was completely foreign to Ignatius's thinking. He turned to the pope in order not to go astray, and in order to work where God wanted him and where the Church needed him. The pope here represented simply the common good of the Church, of course not as a purely human instrument but as the "vicar of Christ."

It was of course quite natural that the Jesuits became the strongest support of papal authority as they found it being attacked by Protestant "antichrist" polemics. For Peter Canisius as for Polanco and Nadal, the Jesuits were the "true knights of St. Peter," called "to serve the Holy See in this, its hour of greatest need," and dedicated to the service of all humanity "but with special devotion to the pope and the Apostolic See." This attitude was already clearly apparent in the last phase of the Council of Trent (1562-1563) when the Jesuit theologians Lainez and Salermon were the most determined in their support of papal rights, resisting all attempts to use the Council to set limits on the pope's power.[4]

All these factors now played a part in the development of the Roman theology of primacy in the sixteenth and seventeenth centuries and especially in the idea of papal infallibility, which was understood in a stricter and more absolute sense.[5] The reservations advanced by the Dominican theologians until the fifteenth century were gradually demolished. Even in the Dominican school of Salamanca, in the work of such men as Francisco de Vitoria (d. 1546) and Melchior Cano (d. 1560), while on the one hand it was affirmed that the pope must make use of "human means" for seeking truth and thus listen to the Church before making a definition, on the other hand God would guarantee that he would always do this. It is characteristic that the latter is specifically emphasized as something that must be maintained in order to provide no basis for "heretical excuses." These tendencies were still stronger among the Jesuit theologians, most important among whom was Robert Bellarmine (d. 1621). There was still discussion of the "extreme case" of a heretical pope, but this was increasingly of purely academic interest. It is true that it was still emphasized that the pope before making a definition had to make use of human means for discovering the truth, study Scripture and tradition, and inquire of the Church. But this was seen more and more as purely an individual moral obligation of the pope, not an ecclesiological necessity; it was a subject belonging essentially to papal morals, not to ecclesiology. No one any longer said that the assistance of the Holy Spirit was mediated to the pope through these same *media humana* (and therefore that the pope is infallible because he listens to the Spirit who lives in the entire Church) as the Dominican theologians had emphasized. Increasingly the emphasis was solely on the dependence of the Church on its head, and not the reverse.

If we inquire about the background of this development, we discover three factors at work:

- The era of the schism was now far in the past; papal leadership in the Church was experienced in a more favorable light; particular reservations that formerly were not merely abstract and academic, but founded on bitter historical experience, were therefore set aside more and more often.

- Also of the highest importance was the spirit of the Counter-Reformation. Ecclesiology was practiced primarily as controversy. Its dominant interest was to answer Protestant questioning about the true Church, and the papacy served this interest in offering the greatest possible security about where the true Church and the true faith are to be found. Anything that introduced a factor of insecurity, anything that relativized the principle *ubi Petrus, ibi ecclesia* as the ultimate, Archimedean point from which the true Church could be discerned was excluded and suppressed.

- Finally, the relationship of the Jesuit order to the pope also had an influence because it regarded the papacy as the authority through which the will of God for the order (but not only for it) was most clearly discerned.

2. Centrifugal Counterforces

Despite all this, up to the time of the French Revolution the papacy was still confronted with some strong counterforces within the Church. Ultimately it was the French Revolution and consequent phenomena that overcame those counterforces because the centrifugal forces within the Church were closely aligned with the political order of the Ancien Regime.

First we should mention the dominant system of state control over the Churches associated with the great monarchies since the fourteenth and fifteenth centuries. Even in places where in theory full papal authority over the Church was not disputed, this system maintained gigantic barriers against its full realization before the nineteenth century. In many regions until the eighteenth century Rome could practically do no more than conduct rearguard actions in maintenance of principle. This was especially true because the princes were extremely important for carrying out the Counter-Reformation and the Tridentine reform decrees could often be enforced more efficiently through determined rulers than by bishops, even if the latter were willing to carry them through. In addition, Roman politics moved toward a strategy of "domesticating" the existing state Churches by means of concordats and formally granting as papal "privileges" the rights that could not be recovered from the states. In this way principle was preserved even if the reality could scarcely be altered. This was the case especially for the right of regional rulers to nominate bishops, which was current in all the major monarchies. What was crucial (apart from papal confirmation of the chosen bishop) was simply that this be recognized as a free papal privilege, and not as the ancient right of majesty or something belonging to state sovereignty. There was especially extensive royal control over the Church in the Spanish and Portuguese patronage of missions, which through numerous papal privileges guaranteed the Iberian kings an almost unrestricted right of control over the missions; for Portugal this extended to the Asian missions outside the narrow sphere of Portuguese jurisdiction. The founding of the Roman congregation *De propaganda fide* in 1622 came too late because the ground was already occupied. Against the further secular claims to control and supervision (including *placet, recursus ab abusu*, etc.) that were not acknowledged by Rome there remained only a maintenance of principle, usually toothless. One example of this was the "Lord's Supper bull," still read every Holy Thursday until 1770 that among other things imposed excommunication as punishment for these state Church practices; ultimately its reading was suppressed in most countries by the use of the *placet* that, according to the bull itself, should in fact have been followed by excommunication. In general, Rome tolerated a very extensive system of state control over religion as long as the prince was a good Catholic.

There were much sharper conflicts beginning in the last third of the eighteenth century as the traditional state religions underwent a transformation influenced by the Enlightenment. The system of state control over Churches became much more doctrinaire and principled, claiming for the state a comprehensive responsibility in the entire "external" sphere, that is, for everything that had any politico-social aspect, or in other words for anything in the Church order that was changeable and subject to alteration. The maxim in this sphere was to be: "The Church is in the state, not the state in the Church." This combined with Enlightenment trends within the Churches that, in turn, had joined with theological and ecclesiastical movements of the recent past that had been rejected by Rome, especially Jansenism.

In addition to the system of state-regulated Churches there were also traditional episcopalist schools of thought that continued to develop in combination with the still influential conciliarist school especially in France, but later in Germany as well. In those countries since the fifteenth century these schools of thought had been firmly embedded in the national and imperial consciousness. The episcopalist schools, which preferred to appeal to the systems of the ancient Church, in fact continued tendencies and movements that had been present from the beginning of the Church alongside and against the centripetal movement toward Rome. Their historical uniqueness at this period was due to their association with the modern nation-states.

The most important and strongest force of this type was French Gallicanism. To begin with it was the form in which conciliarism lived on in combination with the politico-ecclesial self-definition of the French monarchy. Its first programmatic manifestation was the Pragmatic Sanction of Bourges (1438) by which the French Church adopted the reforming decrees of the Council of Basel, especially those that were directed against Roman reservations. When a strong royal house stood behind the state Church, Rome was unable to wrest the rights claimed by such a Church out of its hands. All Rome could do was conclude a concordat acknowledging the situation, formally bestowing the rights claimed *via facti,* especially the royal nomination of bishops, as "papal privilege" in order to save the principle. This was done in the concordat with France in 1516. The background was again an acute manifestation of conciliarism that immediately threatened the unity of the Church, combined with French national consciousness. Because Pope Julius II (1503–1513) had practiced an anti-French policy in his military campaigns aimed at enlarging the papal states, a group of cardinals opposed to him received the support of the French king when they called a council at Pisa in 1511. They gave good conciliarist reasons for their action, citing the permanent neglect of the decree *Frequens* and the popes' systematic delaying of all types of reform. It is true that this Council of Pisa never numbered more than thirty prelates and remained entirely French in its makeup; nevertheless it was a serious challenge.

The battle over conciliarism had thus entered another critical phase. Pope Julius II tried to take the wind out of the conciliarists' sails by calling his own council at Rome (the "fifth Lateran Council," 1512–1517). That council did enact a number of important reforming decrees but remained ineffective in practice because the pope never had any intention of using it except as an alibi. Now there were, as there had been seventy years earlier, two councils, one papal and the other conciliarist. The danger posed by Pisa was only removed by the succeeding pope, Leo X (1513–1521), who broke with his predecessor's anti-French politics and concluded the Concordat of Bologna with the French King Francis I in 1516. The Pragmatic Sanction of Bourges was revoked, although the corresponding rights were bestowed on the king as a "papal privilege." Rome thus hoped that it had conquered Gallicanism. But all that had been eliminated was the immediate danger of schism; Gallicanism remained the dominant doctrine for another three hundred years in France and finally, in the eighteenth century, it spread throughout Catholic Europe.

"Gallicanism" is a collective term for a variety of very different movements shading from radical to very moderate. One line was "conciliar" in the sense of the fundamental superiority of a council or a prior consensus of the whole Church over the pope. This school of thought was sometimes radicalized to the point of advocating an ecclesiastical parliamentarianism; according to it, the legislative authority in the Church belongs to the councils, the executive authority to the pope and bishops. The ultimate sovereignty in the Church is sometimes ascribed to all priests (this was the idea of Edmond Richer in the early seventeenth century) or even to the whole body of the faithful. But since a council was impossible under the conditions obtaining in absolutist Europe, it was more and more frequently replaced in this line of thought by a recourse to the *ecclesia dispersa,* the Church distributed throughout the world: in particular, papal doctrinal decisions are said to be binding only if they are accepted by the *ecclesia dispersa.* This, of course, meant *de facto* a recourse to state authority, since there were no collegial structures that could have manifested the consensus of the *ecclesia dispersa.*

As early as 1641 in the work of Pierre de Marca[6] and for a whole series of authors from the end of the seventeenth century onward the people of the Church or the community of all believers is represented by the sovereign. As this consistency clearly demonstrates, the national-church line was thus more effective than the conciliar-universal Church line. Here the ecclesiastical and political aspects are indissolubly joined. The issue was the securing of ecclesiastical-political national unity against Roman assaults, especially when they were combined with requests for money. It required, on the one hand, a principled rejection of papal hierocratic claims over the kingdom in the sense of the bull *Unam sanctam,* and on the other hand and primarily, from the internal Church point of view, a relative autonomy of the French Church with respect to Rome and the preservation of that Church's special traditions.

These different tendencies are reflected in the true Magna Carta of Gallicanism under Louis XIV, the "Four Gallican Articles" of the French clergy congress of 1682.[7] The theses adopted there embody a still relatively moderate Gallicanism. The following central statements are important: The first article, appealing to the words of Jesus ("My kingdom is not from this world . . . ," "Give to Caesar the things that are Caesar's . . .") and the early tradition of the Church, rejects every kind of papal claim to secular power and emphasizes the independence of secular authority in its own sphere. No one dealing with Gallicanism should fail to take this most important article into account. Without the whole entanglement of the universal authority of the papacy with hierocratic claims in the sense of *Unam sanctum* from the time of the struggle between Boniface VIII and King Philip the Fair in 1300, the conflicts and debates within the Church itself cannot be understood. Universal papal authority within the Church was, for the Gallicans, inseparably bound up with papal claims to superiority over secular authority.

The second article makes strict conciliarism its own. It expressly emphasizes the superiority of the council to the pope in the sense of the Constance decree *Haec sancta* and rejects any interpretation of that decree in the sense of a mere emergency law to be applied in cases of schism.

In the third article it is emphasized that the pope is not superior, but subject to the canons of Church law, for even if they were originally promulgated by the pope they receive their validity from the fact that they are received by the whole Church; therefore they cannot be independently abrogated by the pope or evaded in particular cases. However, the pope is bound not only by legal provisions of the universal Church but also by those of the different parts of the Church, especially the traditional customs of the Church in France.

The fourth article, finally, restricts papal authority in teaching. Its formulation shows that it is a compromise: papal decisions regarding faith do indeed have a certain binding character for the entire Church, but they are finally irrevocable (and thus infallible) "only when they have received the consent of the Church." It was this article against

which the formula *non autem ex consensu ecclesiae* ("and not by the consent of the Church") in Vatican I's definition of infallibility would be
directed. Gallican authors who were more friendly to Rome, such as
Bossuet and Tournely, made use of a different distinction: individual
popes could err, but not the Roman church or the "see," which they interpreted as the sequence of popes or the continuing magisterium of
Rome beyond the lifetime of any given pope. This was an attempt to
interpret Roman magisterial authority in the sense of the ancient doctrine of the freedom of the Roman church from error not so much in
terms of individual definitions, but more as an ongoing historical continuity, and thereby also to separate it from the person of the current
pope—a distinction that was certainly better able to circumnavigate
particular historical shoals and, above all, to deal with the fact that
Rome had seldom triumphed in doctrinal questions in the short run,
but almost always in the long run.

These Gallican articles were not merely theological theory; they
were proclaimed as imperial law and thus binding for theological
teaching. No one in France could occupy a theological professorship
without swearing an oath to uphold them. Even Rome before the nineteenth century never dared to condemn the content of the Gallican articles *through the magisterium,* if only because of the danger of schism.
Pope Alexander VIII only declared in 1690 that the proclamation of the
Gallican articles was *"ipso iure* void, invalid, ineffective, without force,
without any legal effect from the beginning and forever; no one is obligated by them, even if bound by an oath."[8] But this only meant that
the *obligation* to teach the Gallican articles was without legal force; no
position was taken on their content. Still Rome did not even succeed
on that point, for only in the eighteenth century was the Gallican system unchallenged in France, whereas until the end of the seventeenth
century there had still been voices that deviated from them.

The other important force was German imperial church episcopalism. As French Gallicanism rested on the Pragmatic Sanction of
Bourges of 1438, German imperial church episcopalism was founded
on the fifteenth century "concordats of the German nation," especially
the Vienna Concordat of 1448. Supported by these concordats, the
German imperial church defended the "liberties of the German nation" against Rome, especially the election of bishops by the cathedral
chapters. This episcopalism was the expression of the "imperial consciousness" of the Holy Roman Empire, embodied until secularization
especially by the prince-bishops, particularly the three episcopal electors of Mainz, Cologne, and Trier. One should not forget the profound
extent to which noble class interests played a role, for in the cathedral
chapters that elected bishops sat the younger sons of the noble fami-

lies, and the bishoprics in turn were political pawns in the imperial church politics of the leading dynasties, the Wittelsbachs, Habsburgs, or Wettins, who all had representatives of their interests within the cathedral chapters. On the other hand, one should not see imperial church episcopalism merely as a veil for egoistic class interests. There were also instances of justified episcopal resistance against forms of Roman interference that were not guided by pastoral concern but were driven by financial interests and contributed instead to confusion in the normal Church order. The German prince-bishops sought only to achieve for the Church in the empire the same relative independence that was guaranteed in France and Spain by a strong royal power.

Part of this was the German bishops' struggle to maintain their power to dispense from universal Church law. In fact this was primarily a question of money, since concretely these were dispensations that were customarily given, but required the payment of fees. The German bishops practiced *via facti* the right of dispensation from a whole list of impediments laid down in canon law, especially marriage impediments. Rome accommodated itself to this by permitting as a privilege what in fact it could not stop: from the seventeenth century onward the bishops were granted a number of faculties of dispensation by papal privilege every five years; this was the origin of the "quinquennial faculties" that since Vatican II have been permanently granted to bishops.

The other struggle was directed against the judicial powers of nuncios. The nuncio for Germany resided in Cologne; another was dispatched to Munich in 1784. The tendency was to reduce these nuncios to the ecclesio-political position of representative of the Holy See to the particular government without acknowledging that he had any right of supervision over internal Church affairs. In particular, battle was waged against the nuncio's claim to concurrent jurisdiction (including the granting of dispensations, administration of the sacrament of confirmation, etc.), which would significantly undermine episcopal jurisdiction and provided the basis for continual conflicts. At the beginning because of the passivity of many bishops the nuncios had borne the major burden of carrying out the Tridentine reforms. But to the degree that the bishops took account of their ecclesiastical duties, conflicts with the nuncios ensued.

Until the end of the seventeenth century imperial church episcopalism was generally pragmatic in its aims. It had no particular ideology because German conciliarism had not survived the Reformation, and since the end of the sixteenth century the Jesuit theologians in German university chairs had effected a victory for Roman papalist doctrines. But from the end of the seventeenth century onward French Gallicanism also influenced Germany, where it combined with the trend to independence in the German imperial Church. Canonists like Bernhard

Van Espen in Leuven, Johann Kaspar Barthel in Würzburg, and Georg Christoph Neller in Trier propagated from 1700 until the middle of the eighteenth century the most far-reaching positions of the French Gallicans: the pope as merely a delegate of the college of bishops; the people of the Church as possessing the ultimate sovereignty (with the sovereign himself representing the people).

Added to this was the mentality of the emergent ecclesiastical Enlightenment, which lent a special coloring to these theories. Part of this was the "emancipatory" impulse of historical criticism, which recognized that the current position of the papacy had not existed from the beginning of the Church, and which distinguished the "essential" right of primacy from what was "accidental" and developed in the course of history. The reference back to the primitive Church, the *ecclesia primitiva* as enduring norm, was already characteristic of French Gallicanism, but it was now further strengthened: In general, the ecclesiastical Enlightenment, in opposition to a scholasticism divorced from the source, stressed a recurrence to the origins, to Scripture and the early tradition. Added to this was the "ecumenical" tendency, the hope that with de-emphasis on the right of primacy, decentralization, and emphasis instead on synodal elements, bridges could be built to connect with Protestantism.

All these elements were collected and put under a magnifying glass in a work that made a sensation in educated circles in Germany in 1763 and soon thereafter in all Europe. Its title was *De statu Ecclesiae et de potestate legitima Romani Pontificis liber singularis ad reuniendos dissidentes in religione christiana compositus* ("The constitution of the Church and the legitimate authority of the pope, for the reunion of separated Christians"). The authorial pseudonym "Febronius" concealed the identity of the auxiliary bishop of Trier, Nikolaus von Hontheim. Five months after its appearance Rome placed the book on the *Index*, but in doing so it only contributed to its publicity; moreover, it was symbolic of the ecclesio-political situation in Germany that the Roman condemnation of the book was not published by sixteen of the twenty-six German prince-bishops.

Febronius offered nothing new of his own; he compiled the ideas of others, especially Van Espen, Barthel, and Neller. The secret of his success was that he presented in summary form what many of his contemporaries desired. The pope was for him the *centrum unitatis* of the Church; that is, he had a full subsidiary power over individual bishops in the sense of a right of supervision when bishops failed. The concrete measure of the "essential right of primacy" without which the unity of the Church could not be preserved was the first eight centuries of the Church's history, that is, the time before the pseudo-Isidorean forgeries. Only the powers exercised by the popes in the centuries before that point were legally theirs; everything later was abuse and curial presumption. Concretely this meant that true authority in the Church, which is collegial and not monarchical, belongs to the council. The papacy is the executive authority responsible for keeping and carrying out the decrees of the council; its decisions, made provisorily between councils, are subject to the consensus of the Church as a whole.

This "Febronianism" was translated into ecclesio-political reality at the Congress of Ems in 1786, the last great uprising of German prince-bishops against Rome. Representatives of the three Rhenisch elector-bishops (of Mainz, Cologne, and Trier) participated, as did the representative of the fourth German archbishop, from Salzburg. The congress protested in Febronian terms against Roman centralism and demanded the restoration of conditions as they existed before Pseudo-Isidore:

> The Roman pope is and remains the principal overseer and primate of the whole Church and the center of its unity, and is furnished by God with the jurisdiction required thereby; to him all Catholics must always render canonical obedience and full deference. All the other privileges and reservations not associated with this primacy in the first centuries, but accruing to it from the later Isidorean decretals to the clear detriment of the bishops cannot be attributed to the scope of that jurisdiction now that the forgery and falsity of those [decretals] has been adequately demonstrated and is universally recognized. They belong rather to the class of interferences on the part of the Roman curia, and the bishops . . . are authorized to restore themselves to the exercise of the authority granted to them by God, under the supreme protection of His Imperial Majesty.[9]

The delegates demanded among other things the unrestricted authority of bishops to bind and loose, the removal of all exemptions, especially those granted to monasteries, the exercise of the quinquennial faculties as an original right of bishops, and finally the removal of the nuncios or at least their restriction to the role of diplomatic representatives to the courts without any competing ecclesiastical jurisdiction. Important further goals were the restoration of the rights of metropolitans as they had existed in the ancient Church and the calling of a national council. These goals were to be accomplished with the assistance of the emperor. Nevertheless these ambitions proved to be a tempest in a teacup: first of all because this imperial Church episcopalism existed within a political world that was dying. The Holy Roman Empire was but a shadow of what it had been. Emperor Joseph II had a fundamentally Austrian and territorial mindset; already sufficiently involved in conflicts with Rome, he showed little interest in burdening himself further with the concerns of the Rhenish electors. At the same time the prince-bishops were not overly anxious to support powerful metropolitans; they preferred the "pope at a distance" to the "archbishop close to home." Thus what had happened with Pseudo-Isidore in the ninth century was repeated in similar fashion. The fragile unified front of the archbishops quickly collapsed again, especially since the Mainz plan regarding primacy found little welcome among the others. Three years later the French Revolution broke out, and it quickly produced a whole new set of concerns for the Rhenish electors.

A correct assessment of the Gallican and episcopalist currents in the seventeenth and eighteenth centuries must not overlook the fact that we are confronted not by a unified system, but by a collection of different tendencies. They coincide only in that they are directed against the concentration of ecclesiastical authority in the pope alone, and they place a stronger emphasis on the autonomy of the individual Churches and the importance of communitarian and collegial realities such as consensus and reception, all this through an appeal to the ancient Church and its constitution. It would be correct from one point of view to emphasize that this view of history as represented for example by "Febronius" is archaic and rigid, and that it allows no room for legitimate historical development. But one should not forget that the opposing papal side—as represented for example by the Jesuit Father Zaccaria who wrote *Anti-Febronius* in 1767, or still more by Mauro Cappellari, the later Pope Gregory XVI, with his 1799 work *Trionfo della Santa Sede e della Chiesa contro gli assalti degli novatori* ("Triumph of the Holy See and the Church over the Attacks of the Innovators")—was equally incapable of historical thought or even less so, inasmuch as it did not even consider the possibility that there had been any historical deformation of the Church.

If the Febronians took the first centuries of the Church as their only yardstick, their opponents proceeded from the actual present situation as their norm and unhistorically transposed it to the past. The Febronians argued that "there can be no legitimate changes" (and therefore one must take the origins of the Church as norm); the papalists countered that "there can be no changes at all" and therefore, as Cappellari thought, one can spare oneself the effort of going back into the "confusion of antiquity;" instead, one may simply proceed on the basis of the Church as it now exists, because it is given *a priori* that its "essential form" is unchangeable, and therefore existed in the past as well.[10] The episcopalist authors would respond that only a consideration of the past and the entire history of the Church could show what in the present Church is its "essential form" and therefore unalterable. But for the papalists the present Church (that is, the Roman view of it) was sufficient. These two fronts would reappear in similar form at Vatican I.

One may not dismiss the episcopalist currents of the early modern period out of hand as "unchurchly" or even "heretical" from the historical standpoint of Vatican I. Nor is a blanket reproach of servility toward state power valid in simple terms even for French Gallicanism,[11] and certainly not for German imperial Church episcopalism, which desired to open a third way between the system of state-regulated Churches and Roman centralism. It is of course a different matter to ask objectively whether these movements were not destined by their internal dynamics to fall into the wake of the established Church system. This statement would probably be regarded as justified within the framework of a more comprehensive historical judgment and classification of the aims of episcopalism.

The uniqueness of episcopalism lay in the fact that it gave a stronger emphasis to the whole aspect of the Church as *communio* and thus attempted to give a higher value to consensus and reception. Undoubtedly this made binding authority and the ultimacy of decision in the Church less clearly defined, and even subject to dispute if the point were pressed. But the real problem was that there existed no tangible entity capable of action in the form of a collegial structure in the Church that could represent the *consensus ecclesiae* that in this view became the court of last resort. Since the *ecclesia dispersa* had replaced the council, recourse to consensus was always in danger of making it utterly impossible for the Church to make a binding decision or of provoking a situation in which the actual decision lay with the state because then the "people of the Church" were represented by their princes. The supporters of infallibility at Vatican I argued fundamentally on the basis of this experience, but so did Cappellari at the time. Among other things he objected that for the Gallicans "consensus" meant that the promulgation of a law would be followed by an extra-constitutional uncertainty that existed in no well-ordered state, and not even in republics.[12] By the force of its own inner logic episcopalism led the Church, whether the leaders of the movement intended it or not, into particularism and a kind of immobility, especially because, as the French Revolution would clearly show, it was closely bound up with the political structures of the Ancien Regime and thus was less well equipped than the papacy to survive catastrophe.

II. From the French Revolution to Vatican I

In 1800 it appeared that the papacy had reached the nadir of its modern existence. In the spring Pius VI died in Valence, a prisoner of Napoleon. It seemed certain that in future episcopalism would dominate the Church, and that there was no chance that the papacy would be strengthened. For most authors in Germany and France between 1800 and about 1820 the "papal system" and especially papal infallibility were regarded as passé and matters of only historical interest; it scarcely seemed worthwhile to engage in any further serious discussion of them. Even in Italy these ideas and some still more radical positions had been increasing in influence for decades, especially in the Austrian regions of the North and in Tuscany, where in 1786, the year of the Congress of Ems, the Synod of Pistoia under the intellectual leadership of Pietro Tamburini proposed a new image of the Church diametrically opposed to the Roman and papal view.

Nevertheless in the year 1799, when reality seemed to indicate anything but "triumph," Mauro Cappellari wrote his *Trionfo della Santa Sede,* mentioned above. From one point of view this work already anticipated nineteenth-century ultramontanism with its picture of a papal Church whose unchangeability enabled it to stand firm against the storms of changing times and turn back the attacks of all innovators, its derivation of infallibility from the idea of papal sovereignty, and finally its extreme notion that the pope is infallible "independently of the Church"[13] and that the Church is dependent only on the pope, not the pope on the Church.[14]

1. The Impact of the French Revolution

There can scarcely have been any event in history that was so important in laying the groundwork for the ultimate victory of the papacy at Vatican I as the French Revolution of 1789. In the first place, it removed the obstacles raised by the Ancien Regime in absolutist Europe, which had established insurmountable barriers to a complete victory for papalism. It brought about the destruction of the political and social order that had constituted the basis for episcopal and state Church independence from Rome. It is true that in the short run this handed the Church over to the secular power, but in the long run it strengthened Rome because the counterweights and power factors within the Church that had held Rome in check now ceased to exist.

In the first place, after the collapse of the old Church order the papacy was the sole authority that could bring about a rebuilding. This was accomplished in 1801 in Pius VII's concordat with Napoleon, and in the decade from 1817 to 1827 with the reorganization and redistribution of the German dioceses after the Congress of Vienna.

The events of 1801 made a particularly profound impression on contemporaries. After the revolution the French church was divided. The National Assembly had imposed the "civil constitution" on the church in 1790. This was an extraordinary radicalizing of episcopalist and state church ideas.[15] In fact its ultimate aim was a complete integration of the church into the revolutionary state. The first result was a division in French Gallicanism from which it never recovered. Those who saw the heritage of Gallicanism as the most seamless possible amalgamation of church and nation, or church and bourgeois society, or else in a universal impulse toward freedom, accepted the new arrangement. But those who thought that the heritage of Gallicanism lay in the episcopal and synodal constitution of the ancient church became opponents of the civil constitution. What remained unacceptable to Rome was the demand that a new order for the church in France be established without the participation of the pope. Because Rome opposed the civil constitution—too late, of course, and at a time when the great majority of the French clergy had already made up their minds—the result was a schism between the "constitutional" church and the church that refused to take the oath to the constitution, thus rejecting the civil constitution for the church and setting themselves up in opposition. Those who did so, however, even though their group consisted more of moderate Gallicans than of ultramontanists, were forced toward the papal position to a degree that by no means corresponded to their original attitude, for union with Rome was now the crucial confessional point for whose sake the non-jurors were persecuted and driven underground, sent into exile, or even put to death.

When Napoleon, as the man designated to carry out the will of the French Revolution, was prepared to come to an arrangement with Pius VII (1800–1823) it became clear that there could be no thought of recognizing only the non-juring church and simply forcing the constitutional church to submit. Instead, in order to end the schism in the French church Pius VII agreed with Napoleon to depose all the French bishops (to the extent that they were not prepared to resign "voluntarily" at the pope's urging) and to create a new episcopate and a new distribution of dioceses. This was a coup like none other in history before or since, but it was also a brilliant demonstration of papal power over the entire Church that necessarily had to have a significant impact on theology. How little this was understood at the time is evident from the fact that in 1790 the later Cardinal Maury, himself an opponent of the civil constitution, declared in the National Assembly that the pope himself did not have the right that the assembly was arrogating to itself through the civil constitution:

> We do not believe that the pope could by himself redraw the boundaries of all the dioceses in our kingdom without making a frontal assault on our [Gallican] liberties. These arbitrary changes would not be tolerated

even in the most ultramontanist countries, and the pope would be required by the entire Catholic world to negotiate with any Churches whose diocesan boundaries he wished to alter.[16]

However, under Napoleon none of the parties intended by this means to achieve a strengthening of the papacy. Certainly nothing of the sort could be said of Napoleon, for even after the concordat was signed he required, in the "Organic Articles" of 1802, that all French teachers of theology subscribe to the four Gallican Articles. But Rome was so little interested in seizing this opportunity to demonstrate its own plenary power that the papal secretary of state, Cardinal Consalvi, even pointed out to the French negotiators that the removal of the entire French episcopate as requested by Napoleon would surely have an effect the government could scarcely have in mind, namely giving a death blow to the Gallican system.[17] In fact Rome could scarcely have had any interest in the matter at that time because the disavowal of the "confessing bishops," who though they were Gallicans in the traditional sense had staked their very lives for the sake of fidelity to Rome and had refused to swear an oath to uphold the revolutionary principles of the civil constitution, in the short run could only weaken the authority of Rome, which here appeared to be a compliant instrument used to pacify Napoleon and to carry out a "massacre of the apostles." It was Napoleon who forced this violent measure, seen at the time as a manifestation of the ultimate weakness, not the strength of Rome; yet in the long run it worked to Rome's advantage.

Something similar can be said of the reorganization of the German church after the Congress of Vienna. After the secularization of 1803 Karl Theodor von Dalberg, the last elector-chancellor of the empire and elector-archbishop of Mainz, had attempted to continue the traditions of the German imperial church. But even at that time his plans no longer fit the political landscape, and he was compelled to depend heavily on Napoleon. At the Congress of Vienna one result of the weakness of Rome was that Cardinal Consalvi, the papal secretary of state, could not effect his plan for a general organization of church affairs in Germany at the level of the German federation and had to accept the fragmentation of the German church into isolated state churches that were powerless in face of the secular bureaucracies.

The result was the system that a high civil servant in Württemberg cynically described by saying: "All we need is someone to anoint; we can do the rest ourselves."[18] But here again the development worked in Rome's favor in the long run. This was already true from the very fact that the structures of the old imperial church had been destroyed and a completely new distribution of dioceses had to be created. No matter how much this new arrangement corresponded on the surface to the political desires of the new states, it obviously required a recourse to papal authority. As in France, the results were inevitable. For a new generation of lay people, priests, and bishops who were handed over to a system of state church authority and deprived of all the national church supports that had been destroyed by the secularization of 1803, there was no recourse except a close adherence to Rome. When the church considered how to maintain its freedom from the state, it became clear that the only independent church power lay with the papacy and Rome; the traditional episcopal power was finished.

The Protestant church historian Mirbt regards it as a "strange turn of events that the papacy itself became revolutionary in order to destroy the effects of the revolution."[19] The word "revolutionary" is accurate in the sense that the papacy set aside rights, historically developed traditions, and customs in an unprecedented manner. But in the same sense one could ask whether the Gallican church in France with its insistence on historically-developed traditions and rights that were to be preserved unaltered and the German imperial church with its adherence to the ancient Holy Roman Empire had not proved themselves incapable of surviving such a catastrophe, unlike a papacy that if necessary could rub out episcopates with a thousand years of history behind them by the stroke of a pen.

One could also ask how it happened that political crises and defeats worked at least in the long run to strengthen the spiritual authority of the papacy (which was drawn into them just as deeply) but this was not the case for episcopalism. Does this not indicate that the papacy, or at least the papal ideal, was stronger and better able to withstand crises, while episcopalism in its French and German forms could not survive the collapse of its supporting structures? It would then be possible to interpret these events in such a way that the revolution and resulting phenomena (such as the secularization of Germany in 1803), by destroying the order of the Ancien Regime, in the long run released the stronger spiritual forces that lay behind the papal ideal. In any case, Gallicanism was conquered not because it was theologically erroneous, but because it had become historically impossible.

2. The Victory of Ultramontanism

The decisive intellectual shift toward ultramontanism occurred for the most part within the thirty years from 1820 to 1850; it was intimately associated with the shift away from the Catholic Enlightenment and toward restoration. It is also noteworthy that the principal agents of this movement, including DeMaistre and Lamennais in France, Görres and Phillips in Germany, Donoso Cortès in Spain, Manning in England, and George Ward in Ireland, were almost all "converts" (not necessarily from Protestantism). Most of them were people who had passed through a phase of unbelief and had made a personal decision to adhere to the Catholic faith. For them the papacy, and to some degree papal infallibility itself, were not simply part of tradition, but a new personal discovery. These things appeared to them especially important as answers to the spiritual problems of the day and often the social problems as well.

Looking at the situation in detail we can again discern two types of movement although they were by no means sharply distinguished from one another and were very often intertwined. On the one hand there was the *restorative* movement with its slogan "authority against anarchy and autonomy." It is primarily connected with the name of the French restoration philosopher Joseph de Maistre, who was the French ambassador to the czarist court in St. Petersburg in 1819 when he wrote his book *Du pape* ("On the Pope"). De Maistre brought papal infallibility "out of the theologians' studies and into the homes of the laity."[20] Through his work the topic suddenly became enormously explosive even in the political and social order, because according to him the papacy and papal infallibility were the only guarantees of social order and stability in a world that had run off the track after the Congress of Vienna, a world in search of renewed security and something to hold on to after the shocks of the revolution and the Napoleonic wars:

> Christianity rests entirely on the pope, so that the principles of the political and social order over which he has been called by divine guidance to preside may be derived from the following chain of reasoning: there can be no public morality and no national character without religion; there can be no European religion without Christianity; there can be no Christianity without Catholicism; there can be no Catholicism without the pope; there can be no pope without the sovereignty that belongs to him.[21]

For de Maistre, infallibility meant that the principle of criticism and questioning that resulted in a destruction of human order must be eliminated once and for all:

> There can be no human society without a government, no government without sovereignty, no sovereignty without infallibility; and this last privilege is so absolutely necessary that one is compelled to postulate infallibility even in secular sovereignties (where it does not exist) if one is not to concede the ultimate dissolution of the social order.[22]

The influence of this author on the developments leading up to Vatican I cannot be overestimated. H. J. Pottmeyer has shown how powerfully de Maistre's concept of infallibility influenced a great many authors before Vatican I. That concept included especially the interpretation of infallibility as the final authority, with an overemphasis on decision making and the consequent decline of the concept of the magisterium as witness. The task of the magisterium was then no longer seen as primarily one of giving witness to what has been received, but as independent "decision," or "definition" for which in turn an individual and not a conciliar consensus is the more appropriate authority.

It is true that this is a typically modern shift of emphasis and can by no means be ascribed solely to de Maistre. The view of the magisterium as *determinatio fidei* (instead of *testificatio*) reveals an aspect of the modern awakening of the human subject, now more strongly aware of its active role in the shaping of history. To that very extent infallibility as understood by many nineteenth-century authors was a typical product of the modern era and its particular set of problems. If the underlying sense of the ancient Church councils was more affected by the idea that in the tradition and the faith as handed down Christ himself is transmitted through the Holy Spirit so that those who are clothed with the magisterium felt themselves sustained by this stream of divine truth, the new fundamental sense was that the magisterium "makes decisions" about the faith as transmitted. And since a "decision" or "definition" is required, the authority that makes such decisions must be unequivocally designated. Otherwise the foundation of the Church's faith is no longer clear. Such a concentration on formal authority is something typically modern and would have been foreign to the mentality of earlier times.

Let us consider one example of the influence of de Maistre's ideas at the time of Vatican I: In 1868 the Jesuit Matteo Liberatore, writing in the Jesuit paper *Civiltà Cattolica*, described the "restoration of the principle of authority" as the sole means for saving society; but this could only occur if the "principal authority, the rule and type of every other authority on earth," namely that of the pope, was restored to its full rights. Typical and characteristic is his view of history: the true original sin in western history and the beginning of the modern dissolution of order was the weakening of papal authority by the conciliarism of the fourteenth and fifteenth centuries. In turn, therefore, the process of healing could only be begun by a definition of papal infallibility: "And since the restoration of the idea of authority itself must come from the consolidation of this highest authority, and from the restoration of the idea of authority will come the salvation of the world, everyone must recognize how important this point is."[23]

Still it would be wrong to reduce the entire ecclesiastical movement culminating in 1870 to the formula "restoration, counterrevolution, and strengthening of the principle of authority." Genuine ultramontanism, beginning in the 1820s and 1830s, was essentially characterized by its critique of the state, its populism, and its tendency to dissolve the bonds between throne and altar. This feature was especially well expressed by Félicité de Lamennais, the founder of "liberal Catholicism" and the true head of the ultramontanist movement from 1830 to 1832. For him the future lay in a covenant between the papacy, the peoples of the world, and the cause of freedom, especially with the oppressed peoples struggling for their national and religious freedom, the Poles, Irish, and Belgians; indeed, it lay in the separation of Church and state, which would be the only means to afford the Church the liberty it vainly hoped to receive from the restored Ancien Regime of the Bourbons.

Lamennais articulated the experience that recurred throughout the nineteenth century: that a close association with Rome and freedom of the Church from the state go hand in hand; effectively that liberty could not be achieved in the long run by cooperating with the old political powers, but only through alliance with the democratic forces of the future. "Freedom for the Church as in Belgium," "freedom as in North America"—these were the dream and the battle cry of many who struggled for Church independence in the nineteenth century, and it was precisely those countries in which the pope truly ruled the Church more than anywhere else in the world outside the papal states. Even though Pope Gregory XVI condemned Lamennais' ideas in *Mirari vos* in 1832, that was not the end of "liberal Catholicism," which simultaneously sought a positive relationship with the ideas of freedom and democracy and (at least at the beginning) saw a strong papacy as the guarantor of the Church's freedom from the state. Beyond this, the "populist" line, which appealed to the ordinary people and was detached from state power, remained the enduring characteristic of the entire ultramontanist movement.

In Germany the "Cologne episode" of 1837 was especially significant: the arrest of Clemens August von Droste zu Vischering, archbishop of Cologne, by the Prussian government because of his stubborn maintenance of the Church's standpoint on the question of mixed marriages. This was followed by a public protest from Gregory XVI and by Joseph Görres's broadsheet "Athanasius." The result was the decisive rupture of the alliance between throne and altar that had been maintained at least superficially until that point. The Cologne episode was a crucial milestone for Germany however, not only in Church politics, but also in mentality and especially in the history of theology. One can indeed demonstrate that from that point onward the theological manuals, sometimes even those by the same authors, gave a much greater emphasis to the primacy of papal rights. In any case

German Catholicism was from that time forward much more "papal" in its orientation or, in other words, the "Cologne episode" accelerated the development that had certainly begun at some earlier time.

The transition to theses more friendly to the pope occurred in the French and German regions between 1820 and 1850, not abruptly, but gradually and in stages. One may observe in general, that strict conciliarism with its unconditional placement of the council above the pope was virtually without defenders. Febronius no longer found any support. Even if the infallibility of the pope alone was not yet acknowledged, the deciding word was attributed to him, for example, when there was a division between the fathers at a council; in any case no council could be ecumenical without him or against him. In the German regions, under the intellectual influence of romanticism, there was a theological trend most importantly represented by Johann Adam Möhler (d. 1838) that interpreted the relationship between the pope and the college of bishops, or the pope and a council, as that of a living organism in which every member is dependent on the others so that the question of who is "superior" to the others is inappropriate. Every kind of "division" was rejected, whether "Gallican" or "papalist." In its tendency, of course, this line of thought was more friendly to the papacy, especially since it had to contend more often against the extremes of state church particularism than against those of Roman centralism. In the course of the decades it moved more and more toward the papal side.

In 1856 the French historian Alexis de Tocqueville wrote in a letter: "The pope is driven more by the faithful to become absolute ruler of the Church than they are impelled by him to submit to his rule. Rome's attitude is more an effect than a cause."[24] This observation was completely accurate. One cannot understand the success of the ultramontanist movement in the nineteenth century unless one realizes that it began from the periphery. The decisive reorientation within the Church had already occurred by 1848, and even before Rome was in a position to give effective direction to the process. Only from that time onward was there a systematic and, in particular, an efficient Roman policy for combating the last vestiges of Gallicanism. This policy was conducted especially through the nuncios, the most important of whom was, of course, in Paris. A systematic policy for the nomination of bishops in the ultramontanist sense was possible in very few countries at that time because of the secular right to nominate or at least to participate in nominations. If the numbers of ultramontanist bishops gradually increased this was more attributable to the overall change of climate within the Church, emanating from below, than to Roman politics. Even after 1850 more deliberate Roman interventions were only possible because they were far more welcome to the majority of clergy and laity than they had been thirty years earlier.

There were a number of additional factors that accelerated the development after 1848. One was the increasingly antiliberal attitude of Pope Pius IX (1846–1878) and the curia, as well as the siege mentality that gradually seized both the papacy and the Church to the same degree that the cleft between the Church and developments in the modern world deepened. This was exacerbated in the 1860s because of the threat to the papal states posed by the unification of Italy. For the pope and for most committed Catholics in every country the pope, the Church, and the papal states were all on the same level. An article in *Civiltà Cattolica* of 1867 entitled "A Threefold Tribute to Saint Peter" shows how these motifs could be commingled:

> We have reached a point today when the war of the godless against the Catholic Church is totally concentrated in attacking the papacy, assaulting both its spiritual and its secular prerogatives. We may even rejoice in this rather than lamenting it, for in this way it is revealed that this is the unconquerable rock. . . . But because the supreme interest of every Catholic lies herein it is also our highest duty to bind ourselves as much as possible to this central point, and this contest involving all in the unity of faith, hope, and reverence for the protection of the see of Peter must be the salvation and the boast of all Catholic Christianity.

The author continues by saying that besides the tribute of money (Peter's pence) and that of blood (the volunteers from other countries who were rushing to the defense of the papal states) it was now time to offer the still more important and essential "tribute of reason." Then a formula was suggested for a vow by which one could pledge oneself always to defend the doctrine of papal infallibility even, if necessary, to the point of martyrdom![25]

It would certainly be wrong to suppose that the definition of papal infallibility was issued in 1870 to rescue the papal states, or that this motive played any essential role at the council. And yet it is clear from this text to what a degree solidarity with the pope in the cause of the papal states could exercise a psychological influence on one's willingness to accept papal infallibility.

This development can only be understood if we remember that ultramontanism responded in large measure to the expectations, desires, and hopes of the Church's "base," that is, active lay people and particularly the younger clergy. Especially from the midcentury onward ultramontanism succeeded in becoming a mass movement. The struggle for Church independence that began in very small circles in Germany and France in the 1830s and 1840s was carried on after the revolution of 1848 as a popular movement displaying the liberal and

France from early 1869 onward with the two sides working themselves up to higher and higher levels of intensity. In the first phase it was primarily the infallibilist circles (those favorable to the dogma) who deliberately promoted the idea of a definition of papal infallibility. Their leaders were the French journalist Veuillot with his paper, *Univers* (which advocated among other things the idea that a definition of infallibility could be produced without a long conciliar discussion; instead it could be passed by acclamation "effected by the Holy Spirit") and the Jesuit periodical *Civiltà Cattolica,* as well as Archbishop Manning of Westminster.

Alarmed by these initiatives, the opponents struck back, employing a massive mobilization of liberal public opinion against a definition they feared would bring an absolute end to any hope of reconciling the Church with notions of liberty as well as a post-facto confirmation of "medieval" papal claims to power over the states. These controversies were not merely about questions of internal Church structure or the traditional struggle between Gallicanism and ultramontanism. Both sides were essentially concerned with the relationship between the Church and liberal notions of freedom: Should the Church, at a time when the world was in turmoil, locate itself primarily beneath the standard of fixed and unchangeable authority, or present itself more as a historical reality also subject to history and even to change and accepting the modern development of liberty as something in accord with the Gospel?

The attitude of most of the council fathers was primarily shaped by this polarization. Most of them were convinced by the public controversy, at the latest by January 1870, that a decision was unavoidable; silence on the part of the council would be the equivalent of a negative.

It is true that alongside this special dynamic of polarization there was an undeniable element of deliberate direction. However, it did not come from the curia. It was Archbishop Manning of Westminster and Bishop Senestrey of Regensburg who, as early as June 28, 1867, on the eve of the 1800th anniversary of the martyrdom of Peter and Paul, under the direction of the Jesuit Matteo Liberatore, made a vow at the tomb of Peter in Rome to do everything in their power to bring about a definition of the doctrine of papal infallibility.[32] During the council it was primarily these two bishops who, at crucial moments, moved heaven and earth to cause papal infallibility to be dogmatically defined.[33]

The role of Pius IX himself was also of vital importance. It is certain that the pope, in February 1870 at the latest, came to the definite conclusion that silence on the part of the council about papal infallibility would be the same thing as a failure of the council itself. He then deliberately and consistently moved the council toward the goal. At decisive moments it was the pope who applied his authority in favor of the group led by Senestrey and Manning. In all this Pius IX had little sense of the pas-

democratic features of the age. In this struggle the papacy represented the refuge of Church independence against the still powerful institutions of bureaucratic state religion. Indicative of the way in which union with the pope could become the key to one's interpretation of the Church so that *sentire cum ecclesia* became effectively *sentire cum papa* is the reminiscence of the English Cardinal Wiseman, under whose leadership the English Catholic hierarchy was reestablished in 1850, of his student years at the Gregorian University. It represents at least to some extent the feeling of many priests from all nations who studied in Rome after 1820, adopting a "Roman" attitude as their measure of Church adherence, and who then became precursors of the Roman orientation of the Churches in their respective countries:

> From all corners of the earth aspirants to the priestly life streamed toward Rome; they came as boys, almost as children, speaking as many languages as were placed in the mouths of the apostles on Pentecost, and yet probably there was not a single one who did not enter into personal contact with the man to whom he had looked up from his childhood onward as the most illustrious person in the world. Soon after his arrival he received his early blessing on his future course, often accompanied by some kind words but always by a benevolent look. This brief moment was an epoch in his life, perhaps the starting point for his fortunate success. . . . The young man knew that every professor whose lectures he heard had been appointed directly and personally by the pope after a careful process of selection; that every schoolbook he read had received the highest blessing; he felt himself almost under the immediate supervision of the Holy See; no matter how pure and sparkling the brooks from which others drank, he placed his lips upon the very rock that had been struck by a magical divine blow, and he drew in the living words as they streamed forth.[26]

However much in this text we may attribute to romantic language, it certainly gives clear expression to the feeling that Rome was not merely a center of unity but the unique source of Catholic truth, while everything else was secondary and secondhand. This corresponded to the theological conviction, already evident in the work of Cappellari, that the pope is the ultimate basis for the church's infallibility.

The product of ultramontanism as a mass movement on the one hand and the increasing identification of Catholics with Pius IX as someone ridiculed by the world on the other hand, added to the unique personality of that pope, was the phenomenon of a specific papal devotion ranging from simple proclamations of faithful allegiance to a practical identification of the pope with Christ. Thus Auxiliary Bishop Mermillod of Geneva spoke in a sermon preached at the beginning of the council of a "threefold incarnation of the Son of

God" in the womb of the virgin, in the Eucharist, and "in the old man in the Vatican."[27] This is only comprehensible, of course, if we keep in mind that Pius IX was not the caricature of pathological autocracy that August Hasler sketched but rather a man whose charm, humor, and spontaneous heartiness made him a very pleasant person to deal with. In any case the phenomenon of "papal veneration" under Pius IX was something new, although it did have some precedents.[28] It represented something like a transposition of the papal ideal into the age of the masses. The simple fact that people now went to Rome "to see the pope" (and no longer, as previously, to visit and pray at the tombs of the princes of the apostles and to venerate the relics at Rome) signaled this shift from the ideal of Rome (which was more oriented to the institution and tradition than to the person) to one of papal devotion.

With regard to this papal devotion we should not overlook the degree to which the tendency to make supernatural reality as tangible, available, and localized as possible affected the idea of papal infallibility. When, for example, the Irish ultramontanist George Ward expressed the desire to have an infallible papal encyclical delivered every morning along with his breakfast and the *Times*,[29] he was only expressing what many others thought. Faith in the supernatural seemed often to be concentrated in faith in the infallible teaching of the pope, in whom people saw both the gate of heaven in this world below and the concrete appearance of the supernatural. This mentality can even be glimpsed among theologians and bishops. Bishop D'Avanzo of Calvi proclaimed in the conciliar hall on June 20, 1870, that ultimately papal infallibility meant an emphasis on the "supernatural order" against naturalism so that all peoples might see that "the pope is also an incarnation of the supernatural order . . . and therefore in the teaching pope the nations may behold the supernatural order and Christ within it, who therefore in all things and for all things is in the pope and with the pope and through the pope."[30]

It would be an oversimplification to see the whole movement toward a definition of the dogma of infallibility as nothing more than, or primarily, a fearful reaction. That aspect certainly cannot be denied. In particular, fear of the unpredictabilities and accidents of history led people to lock themselves up in a Church in which, thanks to papal infallibility, there could be no dangerous tensions and uncertainties and no risks of any kind. Still, we cannot regard ultramontanism as purely an anxious reaction and a defensive posture. It had an essentially dynamic, missionary and conquering character, a unique liberating function drawing people out of every kind of provincial self-satisfaction and state-Church narrowness.

Characteristic of this experience is the postulate of the Neapolitan bishops at Vatican I, written by Cardinal Riario Sforza, proposing that new bishops should be consecrated at Rome and there receive their mission and jurisdiction from the pope. In this way the bishops who were groaning under the heavy yoke of the state-Church structures would acquire an entirely new point of view at Rome and would breathe the universal breath of what it means to be Catholic:

> As soon as they emerge from the narrow confines of their country, their heart expands under the free skies of the Roman Church . . . and they truly experience what it means that the Church of Christ is catholic, that is, living throughout the world and spread from the Holy See to the ends of the earth; then they sense new powers and recognize what they are, namely princes in that community that breaks through all spatial boundaries and encompasses the whole earth; and they understand the meaning of their dignity and from then on courageously resist secular power; and now they are firmly convinced that the pope alone, who represents Christ on earth, has an episcopal dignity over that of all bishops.[31]

Apart from this dynamic proper to the ultramontanist movement its triumphal march and victory at Vatican I cannot be understood.

III. The First Vatican Council

1. Factors and Forces

The definition of the papal dogmas at the First Vatican Council (1869–1870) was on the one hand the result of a very long development, especially during the seventy years since the French Revolution. At the same time this does not mean that within that framework the definition of papal infallibility in particular was necessarily pre-programmed. There are a number of reasons why this was not the case. Of the cardinals and bishops polled before the council, only one-sixth (eight of forty-seven) mentioned this as one of the topics they hoped to see discussed at the council. On the one hand the great majority of the council fathers were certainly animated by a desire to counter liberalism by giving some special emphasis to the principle of authority. It is certain that within that overall framework most of them accepted papal infallibility and considered the time more or less ripe for its definition. But that does not mean that within this overall theme of "strengthening the principle of authority" infallibility necessarily had to become the dominant topic of the council to the point that everything else was made secondary. In the minds of most of the bishops it was one theme within a larger horizon, but by no means the central issue.

A highly crucial factor bringing the topic of infallibility to the fore was public polarization. This had manifested itself especially in Germany and

toral seriousness and important theological objections that underlay the reasoning of the minority. For him there was nothing behind the minority bishops' opposition but a timid "secular" attention to the spirit of the age, public opinion, or the desire to please certain rulers. He regarded it as a question of proper supernatural attitude whether one would offer unconditional support to the Holy See at a moment when the "gates of hell" were bringing all their forces against it, or whether at such a moment one would primarily give heed to one's own critical reservations. Thus his influence was altogether polarizing and contributed nothing to a reconciliation of the stiffening ranks on either side. We will return in a moment to a discussion of his behavior in the matter of Cardinal Guidi.

To explain the results of the council in terms of "manipulation" and compulsion, as Hasler has attempted to do, certainly ignores the facts. The definitions of papal infallibility and primacy of jurisdiction were more the natural result of a long process of historical development than the product of deliberate political manipulations by a few individuals. Even though there was some chicanery and restriction of freedom the council fathers as a whole certainly retained their independent power to decide, to obtain information, and to articulate their views. The minority, comprising twenty percent of the council fathers and presenting forty percent of the speeches on the primacy decree, had sufficient opportunity to make their views heard both orally and in writing. It is true that the principle of "moral unanimity" was violated because at the end the decree on primacy was not the result of consensus; it was a majority decision in face of a still considerable minority. During the council that principle was repeatedly advanced by the minority as the precondition for the validity of a conciliar definition in a matter of faith. Historically we should say that while this demand can certainly be found as a principle and an ideal throughout the whole of conciliar history, in practice it was by no means followed without exception by the councils acknowledged by the Church. In fact, as a strict condition for the validity of dogmatic conciliar decisions this principle is really quite recent. It was unknown to classical conciliarism and Gallicanism, both of which tended rather to support the majority principle. Its development begins among the Jansenists in the eighteenth century, after the bull "Unigenitus" (1713).[34] It is, of course, another question whether in this as in previous cases a good deal of later damage might have been avoided if the majority had made a serious effort to obtain consensus.

2. Tendencies and Positions

The minority opposed to a definition of infallibility comprised about twenty percent of the council fathers (some 140 out of 700); these came primarily from the more socially and intellectually developed countries. They included most of the German and Austro-Hungarian representatives, about forty percent of the French, a third of the North Americans, and a few English, Italians, and bishops from the East. On the whole one may speak of a tendency on the part of the majority and minority to hold different views of the relationship between the Church and the world and especially to have contrary ideas about the history of liberty in the modern world. The majority were inclined to see Church doctrine as "counter-dogma" against the principles of 1789 and, following de Maistre, to emphasize that the Church is called to bring salvation to the world by offering it a principle of authority that is lacking in the world, and without which it will end in chaos and destruction. Characteristic of this position are the words spoken in the council hall on July 16, 1870, two days before the solemn definition, by Vincent Gasser, the bishop of Brixen and speaker on behalf of the conciliar deputation for dogma:

> It cannot be denied that human society has come to the point at which the last bases for human social order have been shaken. There is no other means of healing this miserable situation in human society than the Church of God, in which there exists an infallible authority instituted by God, both in the whole body of the teaching Church and in its head. I believe it is in order that all eyes may be turned to this rock of Peter whom the gates of hell shall not be able to overcome that God has willed that in these days the doctrine of the infallibility of the pope should be presented to the Vatican Council.[35]

The minority was guided instead by a more nuanced judgment according to which at least some elements in the modern growth of liberty were regarded as legitimate. This view is expressed, for example, in the words of Bishop Ketteler of Mainz in his speech to the council on May 23:

> It is true that the whole world complains that in our day every authority, whether secular or spiritual, is being trodden under foot. All people of good will desire that we should defend and fully emphasize the role of authority. But the world is also overwhelmingly ruled by another conviction: namely the rejection of every form of absolutism from which has arisen so much evil for humanity, for absolutism corrupts and degrades the human being. Therefore, honorable fathers, proclaim to the whole world that the authority of the Church . . . is the foundation of all authority! But at the same time show that there is in the Church no arbitrary, lawless and absolutist authority, . . . that in [the Church] there is but *one* Lord and absolute monarch: Jesus Christ, who has purchased the Church with his own blood! Only the one who does both these things truly shows concern for the welfare of the Church and the authority of the Holy See.[36]

Most, although not all of the minority bishops came from countries that had concordats or similar agreements with Rome. They were concerned to prevent a total separation and divergent development of the Church and secular society. For the minority, the Church was deeply woven and embedded into secular society and its history. Consequently the theological aspect of infallibility could not be separated from its social and political aspects. For the majority, in contrast, the Church appeared from the outset as a contrast to the world and could in no way be dependent on it. In a world in turmoil the Church, especially through papal infallibility, was to represent something reliable and protective, the solid rock of authority. At the same time the definition of papal infallibility was regarded as the Church's self-definition in terms of its true and certain center at a time when the safety of the self-evident reality of a Christian society had ceased to exist.

The crucial objections to papal infallibility came from the arsenal of history.[37] In general the eighteenth-century positions were repeated, but with the difference that this time papal primacy of jurisdiction was disputed not at all in principle and by no means so strongly in its various modes as was infallibility. The infallibilists were more inclined to proceed on the basis of the current view of faith and doctrine and to interpret past history in that light. In the traditions of the first millennium they looked more to individual affirmations of doctrine that for them constituted an expression of the Church's normative mentality and from which conclusions were deduced concerning modern questions but corresponding to their own theory. For them the doctrines of papal infallibility and certainly of full papal primacy of jurisdiction were the secure possession of the Church until the conciliarist controversies of the late Middle Ages; only from that point on did they begin to be called into question.

The minority proved superior in their understanding of and feeling for history, except for the case of Honorius where their arguments were not the strongest. In particular they argued not only on the basis of individual documentary teachings but more from the whole sweep of Church praxis to show how questions of doctrine were decided in the first millennium. This, they said, had always taken place through a long and tedious process of consensus building; no one ever thought it possible to shorten that complicated process by means of the "short cut" of a papal pronouncement. The idea of the papal magisterium as a living oracle was regarded as contrary to the genuine historicity and humanity of the Church.

Theoretically, said Cardinal Rauscher of Vienna, God could have used the preaching of the apostles to anticipate all later false teachings by placing in it all later dogmatic formulations and precise definitions in a clear and unmistakable manner and in systematic order. In the same way, he could have said from the outset: Whenever disputed questions arise, simply ask the successor of Peter! Such a simple solution would seem most obvious to our human understanding. But God's ways are different: He preserves his Church in the truth through arduous struggles and seeking, as the history of the Church demonstrates.[38]

The contrary positions on the substantive theological question cannot be understood by simply setting up a contrast between proponents and opponents of infallibility. Most of the minority bishops at Vatican I were by no means the heirs of early episcopalism. Nevertheless they emphasized the reference of papal infallibility to the whole Church: when the pope speaks infallibly he is the voice, the speaker, and the representative for the entire Church; the assistance of the Holy Spirit is given to him not through a special "enlightenment," not simply as a direct gift of God, but inasmuch as he listens to the Church. Again and again the fifteenth-century formula of Antoninus of Florence was quoted: The pope is not infallible when he defines something of his own accord, but *utens consilio et requirens adiutorium universalis ecclesiae* ("when he makes use of the advice and assistance of the Church universal"). Thus at the end of the council the minority bishops called for formulae such as "relying on the tradition of the Church" or "relying on the witness of the Church" as a condition for their assent.

Consequently a highly regarded speech by the Dominican Cardinal Guidi on June 18 won broad acceptance by the moderates on both sides.[39] Guidi asserted that the pope depends on the bishops not on the level of authority, but on the level of *witness* "in order to learn from them what the faith of the entire Church is and what traditions exist in the various individual Churches regarding the truth in question."[40] The canons should not only reject the opinion that denies the infallibility of definitive teachings of the pope, but also the opinion that "the pope acts arbitrarily and of his own accord as independent of the Church, that is, separate from it, and not on the advice of the bishops who present the tradition of the Churches."[41]

Pius IX's disputed words against Guidi, "I am the tradition," do really seem to have been spoken after this.[42] In any case, to understand the reasons why a compromise formula of this kind was rejected we must look more closely at the dominant interests of the authoritative representatives of the majority. Among them there were certainly some "extreme infallibilists" for whom the pope was the source of the infallibility of the whole Church so that the Church possesses it only mediately through the pope. A characteristic example is that of Abbot Prosper Guéranger, who in one of his writings came to the extreme conclusion that "the pope receives nothing from the Church just as

Peter received nothing from the apostles. The pope stands in the place of Jesus Christ and the bishops in that of the apostles."[43]

Such voices also emerged in the conciliar debate, but they were not the rule.[44] For most of those who favored the definition it was a matter of course that the pope must listen to the Church and make use of "human means to discover the truth," and that his infallibility remains tied to the witness of the entire Church.[45] But they refused to define the way in which the pope is to take account of the faith of the Church. They emphasized especially that this reference to the Church could not be formulated as a condition since otherwise the infallibility of papal definitions *ex cathedra* could always be called into question. Hence they did not wish to speak about the necessity for the pope to rely on tradition or the witness of the Church in the formula of definition itself, but only in the introduction.

This was again connected with their primary interests. The majority wanted the definition of infallibility to be as efficient an instrument as possible for making swift decisions and preventing future conflicts like those that, from the period of Gallicanism onward, had used up such enormous quantities of energy in the Church. They took as their starting point the premise that in cases of conflict a decision must be made as quickly and effectively as possible and also with the greatest possible certitude (that is, without any risk of error, or in other words, infallibly)! But that meant that there should be nothing in the definition of infallibility that would blunt this weapon by introducing any uncertainty and offering an excuse for those who would seek to evade the authority of a papal dogmatic definition. The primary interest here was the avoidance of any danger to Church unity.

The most prominent characteristics of infallibility understood in this sense were speed and efficiency. Repeatedly the argument was advanced that it could take a very long time to call a council and years might elapse before the consensus of the Church and the episcopate was clear. In the meantime an error would have every opportunity to spread like a cancerous tumor. Therefore if the Holy Spirit were really to secure the Church against error there was need for an authority that could make instant decisions.[46] The other characteristic was the certain and unmistakable designation of this infallible authority, which would exclude any possible factor of insecurity. Therefore one must not make infallibility dependent on conditions that could be verified only with difficulty or after the lapse of a certain amount of time.

These interests were rooted in the historical options of the nineteenth century. The question at issue was how the Church was to present itself in a chaotic world. For the majority the primary requisites were clarity, stability, security, and the prevention of any kind of internal disruption.

3. The Outcome and Historical Importance of Vatican I

The papal constitution *Pastor aeternus* was originally intended to be the first part of a comprehensive constitution on the Church, but it was not completed because of the sudden interruption of the council following the capture of Rome by the Italian forces on September 20, 1870, and the fall of the papal states. On the other hand one should not be too quick to conclude from this that the constitution remained a torso contrary to the will of the council, and that it can only be understood in a larger context. In fact the chief initiators and Pius IX deliberately separated the chapter on the pope from the schema on the Church because they anticipated the possibility of an early end to the council and hence wanted to wrap up the most important and urgent matter as quickly as possible. In addition it was frequently argued in the council hall that the primacy was the "foundation" of the Church and must therefore be treated first, or that Christ had first said "You are Peter . . ." and only then ". . . on this rock I will build my Church."[47] We must therefore presume that this chapter was intended from the start to be comprehensible in itself.

Methodically speaking it is important for our interpretation that we distinguish what was intended in the historical context of the time from the way these statements can be explained in current theological thinking. In this chapter we will be concerned only with the first type of interpretation.

The constitution *Pastor aeternus*, solemnly adopted on July 18, 1870 (in the absence of the still protesting minority), contains four chapters: on the institution of the primacy by Christ in Peter, on its continuance, on its character as the highest jurisdictional authority, and finally on the infallibility of the papal magisterium. The first two chapters were in principle a matter of long-standing consensus; the genuinely new and disputed statements were found in the third and fourth chapters on jurisdictional primacy and primacy in teaching.[48]

On the whole, the third chapter on primacy of jurisdiction did not offer the same difficulties for the minority because it corresponded to a practice that had existed for centuries. But in fact this statement is more urgently significant for the Church's daily life than infallibility, which is employed only in exceptional situations. It is also more absolutely stated and contains fewer restrictions than the definition of infallibility. To begin with, the statement puts an end to centuries-old controversies. The dispute with conciliarism is decided in favor of the papacy as the final authority from which no appeal to another instance is permissible. Further, the pope has "supreme power" in the Church; that is, in principle there is nothing that is subject to Church authority and yet is withdrawn from the competence of the pope. The phrase *plenitudo potestatis,* regnant since the time of Innocent III, is explicitly sanctioned: It is emphatically stated against titular bishop Maret, dean of the theological faculty of the Sorbonne, the "last Gallican," that the pope has not only the principal part *(potiores partes),* but the absolute fullness of this supreme power *(totam plenitudinem huius supremae potestatis).* His authority is "ordinary" and "immediate" over all Churches and each individual believer.

One could conclude from this that papal jurisdictional authority is thus "absolutist" in the strictest terms of constitutional law to the extent that it is bound by no limitations of positive law and, within the legitimate sphere of Church decision-making, is in principle able to do anything at all. This conclusion follows from the positive description of the content, but it contrasts with another statement. If absolutism means that there is no other authority with rights of its own beside or under the central monarchical power, that very idea is rejected as far as the Church is concerned, because the same chapter had previously said in clear terms that the pope's supreme power does not detract from the power of the bishops, which is also ordinary and immediate, for according to Acts 20:28 the bishops were appointed by the Holy Spirit to be the successors of the apostles and "tend and govern individually the particular flocks which have been assigned to them."[49]

The defenders of Vatican I have always defended themselves against any interpretation of papal primacy of jurisdiction as "absolutism," most clearly in the collective statement of the German bishops against Bismarck in 1875, which was approved by Pius IX.[50] It is true that this by no means solves all the problems. It is difficult to deny that in fact the post-Vatican I position of the pope in relation to the bishops corresponds on the whole to the concept of "absolutism" in constitutional law, for although there are other independent authorities there is none that can legally set limits on papal authority in serious matters. One should probably say that the third chapter of *Pastor aeternus* has kept alive more problems than it has solved.

In the fourth chapter on the infallibility of the papal magisterium, infallibility is ascribed to the bishop of Rome when he speaks *ex cathedra.* But what does *ex cathedra* mean? The constitution says: "that is, when, in the exercise of his office as shepherd and teacher of all Christians, in virtue of his supreme apostolic authority, he defines a doctrine concerning faith or morals to be held by the whole Church." It should be said that the distinction of *ex cathedra* definitions not only from private papal utterances or purely pastoral initiatives but also from other magisterial decrees for the Church as a whole, which certainly have a relatively obligatory character but are not "definitive" and therefore not infallible, was not at all clear either in previous theological tradition or for the most part in the conciliar debates. Neither before nor afterward has there been any consensus about which of the papal magisterial decrees before 1870 were really *ex cathedra*. It is true that the official report by Vincent Gasser makes a clear distinction, something that was otherwise quite rare in the council hall: *Ex cathedra* definitions differ also from other, non-infallible magisterial definitions; "the intention to define a doctrine or to put an end to a state of doubt must be clearly expressed . . . a definitive final judgment must be given and the doctrine in question must be presented as something to be held by the entire Church."

This last, Gasser continues, is in some way proper to every doctrinal statement, but in this case it must be explicitly stated together with the character of the statement as a genuine definition.[51] Such a distinction was seldom found before this.[52] But it is important for what followed because since 1870 there has been only one clearly *ex cathedra* definition, namely that of the bodily assumption of the Mother of God into heaven (proclaimed in 1950). With this exception the entire papal magisterium has been conducted within the realm of non-definitive decisions.[53]

The statement that papal definitions are irreformable "of themselves, and not by the consent of the Church" *(ex sese, non autem ex consensu Ecclesiae)* condemns the fourth Gallican Article, which had asserted that papal magisterial decisions are only irrevocable "if supported by the consensus of the Church." This statement is often misunderstood. Formally it says only that *if* papal definitions occur, the very fact is sufficient to make the teaching final and irrevocable; it does not require an additional ratification by Church consensus. It certainly does not say that the pope is not dependent on the witness or faith of the Church. And it is absolutely not the case that the pope is said to be infallible "in and of himself," because *ex sese* means "of themselves" and refers to the definitions, not to the pope. On the contrary, the introduction states positively that this is not a question of inspiration, but of the assistance of the Holy Spirit. The papal magisterium is conservative and protective in character; it is by no means creative or innovative:

> For the holy Spirit was promised to the successors of Peter not so that they might, by his revelation, make known some new doctrine, but that, by his assistance, they might religiously guard and faithfully expound the revelation or deposit of faith transmitted by the apostles.[54]

It is true that the introduction only hints without saying as clearly as the minority demanded that this assistance includes the use of human means and therefore by its nature requires listening to and relying on the witness of the entire Church, since the popes are not privy to any special "enlightenment." The text just quoted is preceded by a statement that sounds more like a historical note:

> The Roman pontiffs, too, as the circumstances of the time or the state of affairs suggested, sometimes by summoning ecumenical councils or consulting the opinion of the Churches scattered throughout the world, sometimes by special synods, sometimes by taking advantage of other useful means afforded by divine providence, defined as doctrines to be held those things which, by God's help, they knew to be in keeping with sacred scripture and the apostolic traditions.[55]

After the council this text was a crucial sea anchor for a good many minority bishops and made it possible for them to accept the dogma. If it was regarded not merely as a historical statement, but as a reference to the essential way in which the papal magisterium functioned, it was possible to overcome any interpretation of papal infallibility as something purely "personal" and "independent of the Church." The fact that this was not stated more explicitly and clearly, of course, was due to the fear already mentioned that such a statement could easily be used as an excuse for rejecting the binding character of papal decisions. The shadows of the conflicts with Jansenism and Gallicanism in the seventeenth and eighteenth centuries and their continual hide-and-seek, together with the (certainly illusory) hope of being able to prevent dangerous internal rifts for all time to come played a major role in this.

In historical perspective certainly, the papal definitions of Vatican I must be seen essentially as an attempt by the Catholic Church to maintain its place within a world and a society that were becoming increasingly secularized. Once the secure and accepted world of Christian society had ceased to exist, it was tempting for the Church to concentrate around its own institutional center. This was true certainly for the primacy of jurisdiction. It is the expression of a Church that is emancipating itself from the state, especially in internal matters, by constituting within itself a clear and unmistakable center of unity. Church identity, to the extent that it had any point of reference in this world, lay not in one's own nation, but in a purely ecclesiastical center.

Something similar can be said of infallibility. The function of this dogma was probably not dependent in the first place on whether or how often it was actually put into practice by the issuance of *ex cathedra* definitions in specific matters. It was more a matter of the overall security it gave to the Church gathered around the pope as it pursued its way in the world. Here again the uncoupling of the Church from "Christian society" was important, and the issue was certainly seen by Vatican I in that context. In a Christian society papal infallibility was not "necessary" in the same sense. The Church in earlier epochs appeared able to live with the centrifugal tendencies of Gallicanism and episcopalism because they were not yet combined with an atmosphere of general insecurity and questioning; they did not shake the faith of ordinary Christians. That, at least, was the perspective of the ultramontanists.

It is true that when the Catholic Church set itself up independently of secular society and the state it made itself an image of the state, and to an increasing degree of the modern, centralized administrative state—something that was perhaps unavoidable to a certain degree, but in fact obscured the nature of the Church itself. The same is true to some extent of the magisterium, which unlike jurisdictional authority has no proper analogue in the public sphere. The overemphasis on decision making and formal authority, the interpretation of papal infallibility as "sovereignty," and the neglect of its witness character are all phenomena within this realm. We have seen, however, that the formulations of Vatican I still contain elements that allow these other dimensions to emerge, and that they reject an interpretation of infallibility that would ultimately make the will of the pope the standard of the Church's faith.

IV. After 1870: Is There a Future?

Does the history of papal primacy continue after 1870? Most of what is truly interesting in this period concerns the history of the papacy, but is scarcely part of the history of primacy. That history is not concerned with the exercise of the papal office in detail but with the development and expansion of its essential structures, or those that are considered essential. It seems scarcely possible that there could be any further expansion. Furthermore, a more than superficial demolition of the quasi-absolutist structures sanctioned by Vatican I appears, on the one hand a utopian notion in light of all the sociological and historical laws of probability, while on the other hand the dogma of 1870 seems an insuperable barrier to any such eventuality.

Nevertheless, between Vatican I and Vatican II there were some very significant developments. In general terms they tend to show that the expectations regarding the infallibility of the papal magisterium (whether positive or negative) have not been fulfilled as anticipated, and that the dogma of infallibility has not had the significance attributed to it in 1870 by its supporters or by its opponents. Instead, the papal primacy of jurisdiction has acquired a greater scope than it actually had in 1870.

1. Between Vatican I and Vatican II

The fact that since Vatican I formal magisterial infallibility has been unmistakably invoked only once, namely in 1950 with the dogma of the bodily assumption of Mary into heaven, was certainly not what was expected in 1870. Döllinger's prediction in "Janus" that in future "a question telegraphed to Rome will result within a few hours or days in a response immediately constituted as an article of faith and a dogmatic axiom"[56] was certainly a caricature that was disarmed and refuted by most of the infallibilists, at least the moderates among them. But even the latter believed that at least the more important papal statements on current controversies would be infallible. The fact that this did not happen is probably connected at least in part with the natural aversion of any institution to something that, purely from the point of view of its continued existence, has to appear dangerous: namely taking a position from which it cannot retreat. A pope making an "infallible" decision burns his bridges behind him and his successors; and if he has already reached a point at which he cannot obtain any support by other means it is doubtful whether, once he has crossed the Rubicon by uttering an infallible statement, he will really succeed. He may only provoke schism. As Brian Tierney has rightly observed, John XXII had seen that point clearly when in 1324 he condemned the thesis of the Sachsenhausen Appeal that something that had once been defined by the popes "through the key of knowledge" was irrevocable. That is one reason. The other is that the field of papal teaching activity below the level of infallibility has acquired a new status since Leo XIII (1878–1903) through the numerous papal encyclicals issued by Leo and his successors, and that papal teachings of this kind before *Humanae vitae* (1968) hardly ever encountered any significant opposition within the Church.

Let us recall that there was scarcely any mention in the controversies surrounding Vatican I of the possibility of definitive teachings issued by the pope as pope and valid for the whole Church, but not *ex cathedra*. There was at any rate no evidence of any awareness that this describes the overwhelming number of cases in which the pope teaches, and that infallible definitions are rare and extreme cases. Now, however, it would appear that the popes have attempted to answer the real questions of dogma, morals, and Christian social teaching in this way.

At the same time since Leo XIII an important new function of the papal magisterium has emerged. Before his time papal encyclicals were almost always condemnatory and limiting. They were more often stop signs than directional arrows. That now to a much greater degree, papal encyclicals seized positive occasions and tried to give

impetus and stimulation represented a new accent. Of course this was
in itself an expansion of the authority of the papal magisterium. At the
same time this normal papal magisterium has gradually acquired
something like a "nimbus of infallibility." From the papal point of
view, and in large part that of theologians as well, until Pius XII matters were treated as if an error was at least so improbable that in practice one need not even consider the possibility. Practically speaking,
from 1870 until 1962 the "merely" authentic papal magisterium fulfilled the function of the unused infallibility and largely answered the
expectations of the infallibilists of 1870.

A further important development was that by the eve of Vatican II
Rome ruled the Church in a much stronger fashion and intervened in
its life everywhere to a much greater degree than had been the case in
1870. This was partly due to the further expansion of the papal curia
and the centralization made possible by modern means of transporta-
tion and communication. But it was also owing to the fact that the state
church restrictions existing in many countries in 1870 had been eliminated by secularization, the separation of church and state, and the fall
of monarchies.

This was true especially of Rome's nomination of bishops. Only in
the twentieth century, for the most part since World War I in the new
concordats that followed the first codification of canon law in 1917, was
Rome's claim to appoint bishops, a claim that had been raised in principle since the fourteenth century, established in practice to such an extent that there were few remaining obstacles to its implementation. If
we think of the situation in 1870 we see that the right of the state government to nominate bishops was the rule in France, Bavaria, Austria-
Hungary, Spain, Portugal, Brazil, and many of the countries in formerly
Spanish America. At that time Rome named bishops completely without state cooperation or interference only in Holland, Belgium, Great
Britain, the United States, Canada, and Australia, as well as in missionary countries where there was still no regular Church hierarchy. This
changed in the twentieth century for the reasons given above. The 1917
Code of Canon Law stated that "the pope freely appoints them [the
bishops]."[57] Even where the collaborative rights of the cathedral chapter are retained, as in Germany, the concordats made under Pius XI restrict them to selection from a Roman *terna*. It seems, however, that a
systematic policy for the nomination of bishops in the sense of promoting specific trends and especially in the service of positions taken by the
magisterium has only manifested itself in our own time.

Another and very significant new form of papal self-presentation has
been the "traveling papacy" that emerged after Vatican II with Paul VI
and John Paul II. Controversial in detail and certainly with differing im-

pact in different countries and continents, it is at the same time the expression of a new papal self-concept in the context established by Vatican II. It is intended to symbolize a missionary approach to the world instead of a static presence as the center of unity. The papal mission is understood as primarily charismatic and spiritual in the sense of Christ's command to "strengthen your brothers" (Luke 22:32). It is true that it thus promotes as never before a concentration of all the Church's expectations in the person of the pope: he is supposed to be not only the Church's highest official, but also its supreme charismatic, and to represent in person the Church's credibility, openness, and contemporary utterance. This is, of course, a hugely excessive demand on anyone.

2. The New Accents of Vatican II and the Lack of Integration

Vatican Council II with its statements on episcopal collegiality, especially in paragraph 22 of *Lumen gentium*,[58] has certainly established a series of new accents that locate papal primacy in a different context. No longer are the universal authority of the pope on the one side and the special and limited authority of individual bishops on the other necessarily set in opposition or in contrast to one another. This earlier view almost inevitably led to the conclusion that episcopal jurisdictional authority was given by the pope. Instead of this pure ecclesiology of *jurisdictio*, the concept that now connects the two is "collegiality." Every bishop is not only an individual, but by receiving episcopal consecration becomes part of a "college," a *collegium*, so that the gifts of teaching and leadership given in episcopal consecration "by their very nature can only be exercised in hierarchical communion with the head of the college and its members."[59] This college, of course, has a structure: the bishop of Rome is its unifying center and it cannot act against him.

On the other hand Vatican II was unwilling to interpret the primacy consistently and exclusively as the center of the college. This was not only made clear by the *nota explicativa praevia* introduced by Paul VI, but before that by the changes made in the final text of *Lumen gentium* 22 as compared to the draft submitted in 1963.[60] The 1963 draft had already rejected any notion that the college could act without or against its head, and it was repeatedly emphasized that the college of bishops could only act and exercise its collegiality in union with the pope. What was new in the version of 1964 was an additional description of a "supra-collegial" position of the pope as vicar of Christ. While it appeared in the 1963 draft that the college of bishops, of course in union with the pope, was the proper agency of the highest authority in the Church, there now appears once more to be a twofold authority: on the one hand the college of bishops in union with its head, but on the other hand the head by itself. This was certainly strengthened still further by the *nota explicativa praevia*, which repeatedly emphasizes that the pope can exercise his office alone and "freely."

This, however, indicates that mediation was not completely successful. The ecclesiology of *jurisdictio*, or rather that of Vatican I, and the still older and now rediscovered ecclesiology of *communio* are placed side by side but remain unconnected, and this lack of connection is more serious in Church practice than in theology. The tension is exacerbated by the understandable Roman policy of permitting no weakening of Rome's own authority in face of crises in the postconciliar Church and making use of "collegiality" more or less as it seems opportune in service of more efficient direction of the Church but not permitting it to become a disturbing and critical element or a risk factor. Collegial decision is thus desirable whenever there is no possibility of unpleasant surprises, but not when there is a danger that it could trigger unanticipated developments.

Here a historical comparison can provoke reflection and concern. We have already experienced once before in the Church's history a situation in which mediation between two ecclesiologies was unsuccessful; at that time the monarchical ecclesiology, which proved itself stronger, more consistent, and more efficient in such cases was victorious. That was the period of the reforming councils in the late Middle Ages, particularly after Constance. At that time the alternative was that the council was superior to the pope, or the pope to the council. Mediation between the traditional papalist ecclesiology that saw the Church as a monarchy and a conciliarist ecclesiology that had rediscovered some forgotten aspects (including especially the Church as *communio*) but was also one-sided in its absolute perspective did not succeed. Then as now, the *communio* ecclesiology was strongly influenced not only by tradition but also by secular models (at that time the corporative and guild models, today that of democracy). Does this not suggest that if we do not succeed in achieving an integration the results will be similar? Will it not again happen that a purely monarchical ecclesiology will triumph in theory and practice, and the newly discovered collegial and conciliar aspects will once again be repressed, just as in the fifteenth century?

NOTES

[1] On this, see most recently Klaus Ganzer, "Gallikanische und römische Primatsauffassung im Widerstreit. Zu den ekklesiologischen Auseinandersetzungen auf dem Konzil von Trient," *Historisches Jahrbuch* 109 (1989) 109–63.

[2] Hubert Jedin, *Geschichte des Konzils von Trient* 4/2 (Freiburg, 1975) 57.

[3] Mansi 52.257–58.

[4]See H. J. Sieben, "Option für den Papst. Die Jesuiten auf dem Konzil von Trient," in M. Sievernich and G. Switek, eds., *Ignatianisch. Eigenart und Methode der Gesellschaft Jesu* (Freiburg, 1990) 235–53.

[5]On this, see especially the studies by Ulrich Horst in his *Unfehlbarkeit und Geschichte. Studien zur Unfehlbarkeitsdiskussion von Melchior Cano bis zum 1. Vatikanischen Konzil* (Mainz, 1982).

[6]*De concordia sacerdotii et imperii seu de libertatibus ecclesiae Gallicanae.*

[7]See number 6 in "Texts," p. 188.

[8]*DS* 2285.

[9]M. Höhler, ed., *A. Arnoldi, Tagbuch über die zu Ems gehaltene Zusammenkunft* (Mainz, 1915) 171–72.

[10]M. Cappellari, *Trionfo della Santa Sede,* "Discorso preliminare," §§ 14 and 15.

[11]Cf. Pierre Blet, *Le clergé de France et la monarchie, études sur les assemblées générales du clergé de 1615 à 1666* (Rome, 1959).

[12]M. Cappellari, *Trionfo della Santa Sede,* "Trattato sopra la infallibilità pontificia," ch. VI, 7.

[13]M. Cappellari, *Trionfo della Santa Sede,* "Trattato sopra la infallibilità pontificia," ch. II, 10.

[14]There is an accurate analysis of this book (which is seldom really read) in Horst, *Unfehlbarkeit und Geschichte,* 78–120.

[15]Cf. Klaus Schatz, "Ekklesiologie und politische Theologie in der Französischen Revolution," *Stimmen der Zeit* 207 (1989) 445–59.

[16]Quoted by Bernard Plongeron, *Conscience religieuse en Révolution* (Paris: A. et J. Picard, 1969) 201.

[17]Joseph Schmidlin, *Papstgeschichte der neuesten Zeit* (Munich, 1933) 1:53 n. 69.

[18]Quoted from Heinrich Brück, *Geschichte der katholischen Kirche in Deutschland im neunzehnten Jahrhundert* (Münster, 1903) 2:214 n. 2.

[19]*Geschichte der katholischen Kirche von der Mitte des 18. Jahrhunderts an bis zum Vatikanischen Konzil* (Berlin, 1913) 57.

[20]C. Latreille, *Joseph de Maistre et la papauté* (Paris, 1906) 95.

[21]Letter to Count von Blacas, May 22, 1814, in Joseph de Maistre, *Correspondance* 4:428.

[22]*Du pape* (2nd ed. Lyons: Rusand; Paris: Libraire Ecclesiastique, 1821) 123.

[23]*Civiltà Cattolica* 19 (1868) ser. 7, 3:528–30.

[24]In É. Ollivier, *L'Église et l'État au concile du Vatican I* (Paris, 1879) 314.

[25]*Civiltà Cattolica* 18 (1867) ser. 6, 10:641–52.

[26]*Erinnerungen an die 4 letzten Päpste und an Rom während ihrer Regierungszeit* (Schaffhausen, 1858) 18–19.

[27]Johann Friedrich, *Geschichte des vatikanischen Konzils* (Bonn: P. Neusser, 1887) 3:387; J. J. von Döllinger and J. E. Lord Acton, *Briefwechsel,* ed. Victor Conzemius (Munich: Beck, 1965) 77.

[28]For example, in the first "papal journey" of modern times, Pius VI's visit to Joseph II in 1782; on this, see E. Kovàcs, "Pius VI. Bei Joseph II. Zu Gast," *AHP* 17 (1979) 241–87.

[29]Roger Aubert, *Le pontificat de Pie IX* (Paris: Bloud & Gay, 1963) 302.

[30]Mansi 52.767.

[31]Mansi 53.401C/D.

[32]Edmund S. Purcell, *Life of Cardinal Manning* (London and New York: Macmillan, 1896) 2:420.

[33]On this, most recently see Ignatius von Senestrey, "Wie es zur Definition der päpstlichen Unfehlbarkeit kam," in Klaus Schatz, ed., *Tagebuch vom I. Vatikanischen Konzil* (Frankfurt: Knecht, 1977).

[34]H. J. Sieben, "Consensus, unanimitas und maior pars auf Konzilien, von der Alten Kirche bis zum Ersten Vatikanum," *ThPh* 67 (1992) 192-229.

[35]Mansi 52.1317.

[36]Mansi 52.210–11.

[37]I have attempted to give an overview of this discussion in my essay, "Päpstliche Unfehlbarkeit und Geschichte in den Diskussionen des Ersten Vatikanums," in Werner Löser, Karl Lehmann, and Matthias Lutz-Bachmann, eds., *Dogmengeschichte und katholische Theologie* (2nd ed. Würzburg: Echter Verlag, 1988) 187–250.

[38]Mansi 51.974.

[39]On Guidi's intervention, see Ulrich Horst, "Kardinalerzbischof Filippo Maria Guidi OP und das 1. Vatikanische Konzil," *Archivum Fratrum Praedicatorum* 49 (1979) 429–511; idem, *Unfehlbarkeit und Geschichte,* 164–213.

[40]Mansi 52.742C/D.

[41]Ibid., 747C.

[42]This appears from the personal notes of Archbishop Tizzani, a member of the curia who was close to the minority; he claims to have heard the report of it from Guidi himself: *AHP* 23 (1985) 275–76. Cf. the critical investigation of this testimony in K. Schatz, *Vaticanum I 1869–1870,* vol. 3 (Paderborn, 1994) 312–22.

[43]*De la monarchie pontificale* (Paris: V. Palme, 1870) 79.

[44]There was a clearly excessive view of primacy and infallibility along these lines in the speeches of Caixal y Estradé of Urgel (Mansi 52.911B/C) and Ferré of Casale (Mansi 52.948C/D) as well as in the speeches prepared but not given by Dreux-Brézé of Moulins (Mansi 52.1158–60) and Zunnui Casula of Ales-Terralba (Mansi 52.1172–74).

[45]Thus especially Pie of Poitiers (Mansi 52.36–37), Dechamps of Mecheln (Mansi 52.67–68), Regnault of Chartres (Mansi 52.406), Vitali of Ferentino (Mansi 52.903B), Freppel of Angers (Mansi 52.1041), and finally the *relatio* by Gasser (Mansi 52.1213–14).

[46]Thus, for example, D'Avanzo, the speaker for the dogmatic deputation, on June 20 (Mansi 52.765–66).

[47]This is found in the *relatios* of Bishop Pie of Poitiers (Mansi 52.29D), Cardinal Patrizi (Mansi 52.39B), Archbishop Garcia Gil of Saragossa (Mansi 52.86B), Cardinal Cullen of Dublin (Mansi 52.117), and Magnasco (Mansi 52.518–19).

[48]See number 7 in "Texts," p. 189.

[49]*DS* 3061.

[50]*DS* 3112–16.

[51]Mansi 52.1225C. As regards the historical significance of "Gasser's *relatio*" on July 11, it may be said that its effect on the minority and majority bishops at the time did not correspond to its subsequent importance. It is clear from the contemporary witnesses that its resonance was for the most part very small. Few of those who have later read the *relatio* in comfortable rooms have any idea of the conditions under which most of the council fathers, exhausted by heat, pressure, and general weariness, heard a speech lasting almost four hours, especially since almost all of them, both the minority and the majority, were convinced that every additional word was one too many, and most of them were only thinking of putting an end to the debate as quickly as possible.

[52]For example it is lacking in the written *relatio* of the dogmatic deputation presented at the beginning of May 1870 (Mansi 52.21–22).

[53]These statements were made in 1990 in the German edition. In the meantime a new situation has been created by papal rejection of the ordination of women in "Ordinatio sacerdotalis" (1994) and the condemnation of direct killing and abortion

in "Evangelium vitae" (1995). In all three cases John Paul II, in a particularly solemn manner and referring to his office of "strengthening his brothers," has issued a decision that, as he specifically emphasizes, is to be held definitively by all the faithful. According to the wording of the papal decisions, these would be "ex cathedra definitions" in the sense of Vatican I. The problem, however, is that even the Congregation for the Doctrine of the Faith does not give the character of the pronouncement as an "ex cathedra definition" as a reason for the "infallibility" of the specific decision on the question of the ordination of women, but argues instead on the basis of the clarity of the tradition (which in fact is precisely what has been under discussion, both as to the facts and their interpretation and hermeneutical significance). Thus we may say, for the moment, that this represents an unclear situation as regards the teaching office.

[54]*DS* 3070.

[55]*DS* 3069.

[56]*Der Papst und das Concil von Janus* (Leipzig, 1869) 51–52. English translation: *The Pope and the Council* by Janus (Boston: Roberts, 1870).

[57]Canon 329 §2. In the *CIC* for 1983 the corresponding statement is: "The Supreme Pontiff freely appoints bishops or confirms those who have been legitimately elected" (Canon 377 §1). The context of the earlier canon law was thus more open than actual Church practice.

[58]See number 8 in "Texts," p. 190.

[59]*Lumen gentium* 21.

[60]Cf. number 8 in "Texts," p. 190.

SELECTED BIBLIOGRAPHY

Aubert, Roger. "Die ekklesiologische Geographie im 19. Jahrhundert," in Jean Daniélou and Herbert Vorgrimler, eds., *Sentire Ecclesiam*, Festschrift for Hugo Rahner (Freiburg, 1961) 430–73.

_____. *Le pontificat de Pie IX* (Paris: Bloud & Gay, 1962).

_____. *Vatican I*. Histoire des conciles oecumeniques 12 (Paris: Editions de l'Orante, 1964).

Congar, Yves. "L'ecclesiologie de la Révolution française au concile du Vatican sous le signe de l'affirmation de l'autorité," in *L'ecclesiologie au XIX siècle* (Paris, 1960) 77–114.

Conzemius, Victor. "Das 1. Vatikanum im Bannkreis der päpstlichen Autorität," in Erika Weinzierl, ed., *Die päpstliche Autorität im katholischen Selbstverständnis des 19. und 20. Jahrhunderts* (Salzburg: A. Pustet, 1970) 53–83.

Hasler, August B. *Pius IX. (1846–1878), Päpstliche Unfehlbarkeit und 1. Vatikanisches Konzil. Dogmatisierung und Durchsetzung einer Ideologie* (Stuttgart: Hiersemann, 1977); see also the longer critical reviews by Klaus Schatz in *ThPh* 53 (1978) 248–76; Giacomo Martina in *AHP* 16 (1978) 341–69; and J. Hoffmann in *Revue des sciences philosophiques et théologiques* 62 (1978) 543–56; 63 (1979) 61–81.

Horst, Ulrich. *Papst—Konzil—Unfehlbarkeit. Die Ekklesiologie der Summenkommentare von Cajetan bis Billuart* (Mainz: Matthias-Grünewald-Verlag, 1978).

_____. *Unfehlbarkeit und Geschichte. Studien zur Unfehlbarkeitsdiskussion von Melchior Cano bis zum 1. Vatikanischen Konzil* (Mainz: Matthias-Grünewald-Verlag, 1982).

Klausnitzer, Wolfgang. *Das Papstamt im Disput zwischen Lutheranern und Katholiken. Schwerpunkte von der Reformation bis zur Gegenwart* (Innsbruck and Vienna: Tyrolia-Verlag, 1987).

Pottmeyer, Hermann Josef. *Unfehlbarkeit und Souveränität. Die päpstliche Unfehlbarkeit im System der ultramontanen Ekklesiologie des 19. Jahrhunderts* (Mainz: Matthias-Grünewald-Verlag, 1975).

Raab, Heribert. *Die Concordata Nationis Germanicae in der kanonistischen Diskussion des 17. bis 19. Jahrhunderts. Ein Beitrag zur Geschichte der episkopalistischen Theorie in Deutschland* (Wiesbaden: F. Steiner, 1956).

Schatz, Klaus. *Kirchenbild und päpstliche Unfehlbarkeit bei den deutschsprachigen Minoritätsbischöfen auf dem 1. Vatikanum* (Rome: Universita Gregoriana, 1975).

Sieben, Hermann Josef. *Die katholische Konzilsidee von der Reformation bis zur Aufklärung* (Paderborn: F. Schoningh, 1988).

Vigener, Fritz. *Bischofsamt und Papstgewalt. Zur Diskussion um Universalepiskopat und Unfehlbarkeit des Papstes im deutschen Katholizismus zwischen Tridentinum und Vatikanum I.* 2nd ed., edited and with a biographical introduction by G. Maron (Göttingen: Vandenhoeck & Ruprecht, 1964).

CONCLUDING REFLECTIONS

Let me begin these reflections with a story from the Talmud tradition:

> When the sages had reassembled in Yavneh after the destruction of Jerusalem they said: "The hour will come when someone will seek a word from Torah or tradition and will not find it." They decided to collect all the discussions and preserve them, together with the names of those who handed them down. Binding decisions should then be made by the majority. But why, they asked, are the minority voices preserved, even if it be the voice of a single sage? One thought that it was in order to deprive them of their influence by recalling and refuting them. But Rabbi Yehuda said: "they are preserved so that one may be able to rely on them when their hour has come."[1]

This story may not be unimportant for Christians and Catholics dealing with their own history and tradition.[2] Here, too, we are dependent on history and live essentially from it; we must constantly take care to remain aware of it. Forgetfulness of history threatens the Church in its very substance. But this history and these traditions contain very different and even contradictory evidence. There are tendencies that enjoyed official success and took control. In our case, such a tendency was the papalist and ultramontane line that triumphed at Vatican I.

But what about the minorities, the voices that disagreed; what value do they retain? The opinion that they are only worth remembering "in order to deprive them of their influence by recalling and refuting them" long dominated Catholic historical writing. In particular since Granderath[3] the minority at Vatican I was seen at best in its function as "devil's advocate" whose objections led to a more precise definition and a sounder demonstration of the victorious theses. Such an oversimplified view, of course, is inadequate to describe the complexity of real history. The defeated and "superseded" positions of yesterday can become the agents of the future tomorrow.[4] Their hour may come, and then it may be necessary to remember them. Of course Catholics are convinced that this cannot mean that the statements of Vatican I could some day be rejected as erroneous. But neither are the contrary positions "rejected" once and for all. The episcopalist and Gallican lines of thought also endure as a stimulus to the Church and as witnesses to a broad current of tradition that has to be taken seriously.

Nevertheless one must accept at the outset that a "majority vote" in the Catholic Church is something different, and one must seek to understand such a majority vote both historically and in its rightful theological position.

First of all, historically speaking the Roman primacy of jurisdiction and teaching as dogmatically sanctioned at Vatican I developed historically as a result of a great many factors. The recognition of the Roman church as the center of communion existed by the fourth or fifth century in the West, and in somewhat less clear fashion in the East as well. This recognition, of course, was historically still open to a more federal or episcopalist and conciliar Church structure, and there have been tendencies in that direction throughout the centuries. To that extent one must say, speaking historically, that Vatican I proposed and gave the stamp of approval to *one* particular line of tradition, one tendency that can be traced back to late antiquity. To identify that tendency specifically with Pseudo-Isidore, the Gregorian period, or some later point is to oversimplify the course of history. The origins of papal primacy of jurisdiction can no more be assigned to a specific and fixed point in time than can "papal infallibility." Every new appearance is anchored by a hundred rootlets to earlier motifs, ideas, formulas, and laws.

These multiple historical factors that led to primacy in the sense of Vatican I can, of course, be given a more precise description. In the first place it would be too simple to explain these developments in isolation or primarily in terms of deliberate Roman power politics because they repeatedly emerged to a decisive degree from the periphery. Similarly it was not the case that the leadership qualities or vision of individual popes or other personalities with curial influence were decisive factors in the long run. There were times when the growth of regard for the papacy on the periphery bore scarcely any relation to a corresponding achievement at the center.

In general we must be struck by the fact that the historical factors promoting papal primacy endured over time while the factors obstructing it, always present as well (for example the collapse of the Roman empire in the West, the case of Vigilius and dependence on Byzantium, the *saeculum obscurum*, the Avignon papacy and the great schism, the Reformation, the modern system of state-regulated Churches, and finally the French Revolution) only served as temporary hurdles, and sometimes contributed in the long run to strengthen the cause of primacy. Finally, we cannot ignore the fact that it was especially crises in the Church, but also other reorientations, that ultimately resulted in a strengthening of primacy; or, from another point of view, the overcoming of these crises was accomplished essentially by the application of the authority of papal primacy.

The single exception seems to be the great Western schism, brought about by the papacy itself, which the papacy was then unable to resolve. The collapse of Church order and previous orientations called for a previously abnormal recourse to the center of unity. This was true as early as the christological conflicts of late antiquity, then at times of the battle over iconoclasm in the East, the early medieval German mission in the West and the new order of the Carolingian period, the collapse of the early medieval union of the spiritual and the secular under the slogan *libertas ecclesiae*, the step from early medieval regionalism and local orientation into the world of the cities, Catholic confessional self-examination since Trent, and finally the disruption of the *societas christiana* after the French Revolution. These historical observations are essentially independent of one's Christian or theological evaluation of the events described.

In light of these historical experiences, it seems to me that the definitions of primacy at Vatican I were a historically justifiable response, providing that one shares certain theological presuppositions. The most important of these is that the Church must be understood as *one*, and that its unity is not purely spiritual, but also consists in genuine communion, that is, the mutual acknowledgment of this unity in faith as well as eucharistic community. This concept of unity is therefore not in the first place an idea of a centralist administrative combination under a single head, but rather the existence of community, not only imagined or purely objective, but historically realized in mutual recognition, an essential feature of which is eucharistic community. It must also be a unity that especially in questions of faith and in face of the challenges of new spiritual and intellectual movements is able to give clear answers that are universally recognized; it does not consist merely in the refusal to make clear decisions. The unity of faith must thus be able to maintain itself historically by producing answers to new questions as they arise. We are also acting on the assumption that this unity should not be uniformity, but *unity in diversity*; this means that variety in theology, spirituality, liturgy, discipline, and Christian life are also part of the nature of the Christian Church.

Once these presuppositions have been stated, the historian's experience also shows that the boundaries between them are never clearly definable and are usually quite vague. Between the demands of unity and diversity (or the "inculturation" of the Church and Christianity) there are not only tensions, with which the Church must always contend, but sometimes conflicts that have no solution. Theoretically it may be impossible for such unsolvable conflicts to exist, but in limited historical reality the two demands are continually clashing. This is true independently of whose guilt, shortsightedness, or mere historical limitation is at fault: it may be the shortsightedness of Rome or the blindness of an individual Church that does not realize it is in danger of throwing overboard essential Christian values or matters of faith, or it may be both.

The hard question of the priority of values in cases of conflict is thus unavoidable in the long run. If the insistence of a Church on going its own way (even though it may be justified) leads to a breach of communion with the other Churches and with the center of unity, which value has priority in extreme cases of conflict? This question is all the more unavoidable because turning away from it means *de facto* giving a clear answer. For if one seeks to avoid the issue by saying that such an answer can only be given in individual cases and in light of the existing problems, this means in fact that when there are really severe conflicts priority is given to the value of diversity over unity because in such conflicts all plausible arguments will initially favor one's own particular position. Add to this that in such difficult questions of priority in extreme cases of conflict one cannot orient oneself by some platonic ideal of Church unity (or a papal office always exercised solely "in the spirit of the Gospel"), but by the very unromantic, hard, and conflictual reality of Church communion as the mutual acceptance of sinful human beings. The dream of a *papa angelicus* leads away from reality now just as it did in the late Middle Ages. Even the Petrine office can only be accepted as something that is always sinful as well.

In this context we can see that the primacy definitions of Vatican I and especially that regarding jurisdictional primacy mean a clear choice in favor of unity. Under the presupposition, already undisputed within Catholicism, that the Roman bishop exercises the office of unity for the whole Church, these definitions mean that Church unity with him takes precedence over consideration for the special situation of particular Churches. No matter how justified and necessary the latter is, in cases of conflict (that is, when their demands collide for whatever reason) the value of Church unity has priority. This is true also when Rome is lacking in understanding for the legitimate needs of an individual Church or a particular trend within the Church. The latter, of course, is not a foregone conclusion. Blindness or prejudice may also lie on the other side. There are enough historical examples of each. The matter is still more complicated because Rome's effective service in the cause of unity cannot consist merely in putting on the brakes at the edge of the cliff. In that case it is probably already too late. If schisms are to be avoided this must usually happen far in advance; but that means acting in situations that do not allow us to perceive clearly afterward whether authoritative intervention was really necessary or not.

Obviously this principle applies thus unconditionally only when unity is really in question, that is, when the sole alternative is schism. It does not require capitulation at too early a stage and it does not exclude the possibility that first all means will be tried to prevent an extreme conflict that, in any event, will constitute a severe crisis of conscience for all concerned.

But if we desire unity not only "in spirit" but consisting in genuine community and mutual acknowledgment, historical experience seems me to suggest that it makes sense to give priority to the option for unity. Such a clear option looks the real historical burdens of unity in the face and is not simply guided by an idea of Christian unity. It also takes seriously the fact that such a unity is bought at a price. It has both advantages and disadvantages. The question of the greater weight of one or the other cannot be answered simply by putting them in the scales. Instead the first question will be what value, in terms of faith, is to be ascribed to concrete Church unity. From the perspective of Christian faith one can see the meaning of such an option in the sense that it is the ecclesiological form of faith in the unconditional fidelity of God to God's people in Jesus' self-surrender on the cross. It thus takes seriously the proposition that God never abandons the Church and thus, with all its burdens and trials, it always remains the place for faith and discipleship of Jesus. What is at issue here is faith and God's fidelity in face of all human sin.

But the "minority votes" that at some periods in history have constituted the majority retain their value as witnesses to the tradition. They show that genuine problems and historical experiences were not dealt with in the decrees of Vatican I; in part they may simply have been suppressed. The idea that with the definition of papal infallibility we once and for all have a Church to which "nothing can ever happen again" and in which there are no more dangerous rifts and controversies has proved to be a major illusion. The bishops in the minority recognized at the time that papal infallibility in the sense of an arbitrary "quick fix" that avoids the normally complicated historical process of clarification is contrary to the Church's historicity. "Some sensed that history has always known how to catch up with and punish those who minimize or despise its complexity and variety."[5] From that point of view we can certainly say that particular historical experiences involving the Church and primacy as those were described at Vatican I and only slightly modified at Vatican II have been neglected or forgotten:

- First of all, this applies to the embeddedness of the primate in the realities of *consensus* and *reception*. To eliminate those realities as completely irrelevant means ultimately to ignore real history. Roman dogmatic definitions are always one event, although a highly significant one, within a process of clarification that involves the whole Church. They have never been able to put a swift end to a disputed question unless the time for it was ripe for other reasons. Those papal teachings that have become binding documents of faith are the ones that have been received by the Church as such.[6] Of course this reception of both papal and conciliar decisions would be misunderstood if it were interpreted to mean that the Church is offered something and can then consider whether to accept it or not. That, in fact, has almost never described the historical process of reception, an essential part of which is the acknowledgment of an authority in which the word of the Holy Spirit is perceived. But in this acknowledgment the material element, that is, the acceptance of the faith attested, is inseparable from the formal element, that is, the acceptance of the attesting authority. The Church acknowledges that a definition reflects its traditional faith, and in doing so also acknowledges the authority that issues the definition.

- Church unity is a *layered* reality. From a historical point of view it was not achieved in the ancient Church by a movement directly from individual bishops' communities to the bishop of Rome. Instead it led by way of regional synods and Church provinces to the "principal churches" and finally to the patriarchates. The idea that the only theological entities are the individual bishop and the diocese on the one hand and the bishop of Rome and the universal Church on the other, while everything in between—especially the episcopal conferences—is purely a set of administrative units that are created by canon law is a construct that does violence to history. In the ancient Church, first of all, synods had authority beyond that of the individual bishops. It is especially important to note that even after the first ecumenical council at Nicea (325) it was a long time before it was universally acknowledged that such an ecumenical council possessed a qualitatively higher authority than particular synods. The real problem and task today, therefore, is not the strengthening of the episcopal office as exercised by the individual bishops. Instead it is the theological revaluation and practical strengthening of the functions of supra-diocesan structures whether those be national bishops' conferences or similar bodies on a continental scale.

Theologically these supra-diocesan structures must be seen as ecclesiastical authorities with their own rights and not as bodies that exercise papal power by delegation. They represent an independent expression of episcopal collegiality. Only those who think in categories of personal, monarchical, individual power can arrive at the conclusion, foreign to the ancient Church, that supra-diocesan authorities can have no power over individual bishops unless it is given them by the pope. In that case this single monarchical power would exist in the bishop for his diocese and in the pope for the universal Church. But since all bishops are equal it appears that none of them, and no synod or bishops' conference, could have authority over the others unless it was given them by the pope.

This overlooks the primary reality of episcopal collegiality. Theologically the supra-diocesan structures have a further basis in the fact that the universal church exists as a layered reality. To put it another way, there is not simply local church and Church universal, but a dynamic transition from one to the other. A particular council or an episcopal conference embodies the concrete Church in more than one locality and its voice in a particular historical situation. These groups embody the real, historical presence of the Church in some sense more than an ecumenical council, which is much more strongly controlled by the necessity of balancing all points of view because it must take account of very disparate situations and possible misunderstandings.[7]

• The problem of an internal Church corrective in case of the most severe types of failure or defection on the part of the personal occupant of the Petrine office cannot be suppressed in light of the historical experiences of the great schism, the Renaissance papacy, and other events. The mere possibility of a pope who became mentally deranged—something that is not excluded by any special grace of office—would provoke a serious structural crisis for the Church since it is not provided for in canon law. Medieval, and especially late medieval theologians and jurists were less content with pious evasions than the moderns have been; they soberly considered the most extreme possibilities. Pointing out that in the Church one can never create absolute security by means of legal regulations but must trust in the Lord in all human dangers and insecurities is an evasion whose alibi function is easy to see through, because when it is a question of the Church's being endangered by the failures of bishops and individual Churches no one is content with this kind of pious trust; here security has been guaranteed through the creation of very concrete rights of interference by Rome.

It is true that absolute security can never be achieved in the Church. But there is a need for certain limits so that in a serious case the Church is not handed over to unfettered personal instability. Certainly since Vatican I it has not been possible to establish a higher ecclesiastical authority over the pope. But there can probably be authorities (whether the College of Cardinals or an episcopal synod) that can declare with certainty that the see of Peter is vacant. Ultimate security can then exist of course only when an elected successor is acknowledged by the whole Church, or at least by an overwhelming majority.

At any rate the problem of a corrective against the misuse of power by no means arises only in this extreme case when a pope must be immediately deposed or declared to have forfeited his office. It will much more frequently happen that extreme tendencies of great consequence for the Church need to be curbed. For that, counterweights within the Church are needed and they must be capable of action. That these were gradually eliminated in favor of an absolutist papacy was due in part to the fact that they very frequently were placed in the service of particular political and national interests and that the spirit of ecclesial solidarity and responsibility for the whole Church was much too weakly developed. But it may well be necessary to reconstitute such counterweights and strengthen them.

A one-sided view of the relationship between primate and episcopate, blind to all conflicts and seeing the whole in terms of a model harmony, is certainly not justified by historical experience. Unity and communion in the Church have often been realities not existing in frictionless harmony, but having to be achieved laboriously and through the resolution of conflicts. Peter only received the assignment to strengthen his brothers "when once [he had] turned back" (Luke 22:32). It is not from the Peter whose self-confidence was unbroken, but from the Peter who has passed through the fire of humiliation and correction—from his brothers and sisters as well—that strengthening in faith can come.

NOTES

[1]E. Simon, *Entscheidung zum Judentum. Essays und Vorträge* (Frankfurt, 1979) 66–67.

[2]On this, see most recently Max Seckler, *Die schiefen Wände des Lehrhauses. Katholizität als Herausforderung* (Freiburg: Herder, 1988) 74–75, 206.

[3]Theodor Granderath, *Geschichte des Vatikanischen Konzils. Von seiner ersten Ankündigung bis zu seiner Vertagung.* 3 vols. (Freiburg: Herder, 1903–1906).

[4]Cf. Victor Conzemius, "Die Minorität auf dem Ersten Vatikanischen Konzil: Vorhut des Zweiten Vatikanums," *ThPh* 45 (1970) 409–34.

[5]Ulrich Horst, "Tradition—Lehramt—Dogma: Zur Debatte," *Themen der Katholischen Akademie in Bayern* (March/April 1989) 2.

[6]I have attempted to develop some more precise distinctions on this point in my essay, "Welche bisherigen päpstlichen Lehrentscheidungen sind 'ex cathedra'? Historische und theologische Überlegungen," in Werner Löser, Karl Lehmann, and Matthias Lutz-Bachmann, eds., *Dogmengeschichte und katholische Theologie* (2nd ed. Würzburg, 1988) 404–22.

[7]See the enlightening treatment of this subject in Hubert Müller and Hermann Josef Pottmeyer, eds., *Die Bischofskonferenz. Theologischer und juridischer Status* (Düsseldorf, 1989), especially the essays by Hermann Josef Pottmeyer and Gisbert Greshake.

TEXTS

1. Irenaeus of Lyons, Adversus haereses *3.3.1-2*[1]

1. It is within the power of all, therefore, in every church, who may wish to see the truth, to contemplate clearly the tradition of the apostles manifested throughout the whole world; and we are in a position to reckon up those who were by the apostles instituted bishops in the churches, and [to demonstrate] the successions of these men to our own times; those who neither taught nor knew of anything like what these [heretics] rave about. For if the apostles had known hidden mysteries, which they were in the habit of imparting to "the perfect" apart and privily from the rest, they would have delivered them especially to those to whom they were also committing the churches themselves. For they were desirous that these men should be very perfect and blameless in all things, whom also they were leaving behind as their successors, delivering up their own place of government to these men; which men, if they discharged their functions honestly, would be a great boon [to the church], but if they should fall away, the direst calamity.

2. Since, however, it would be very tedious, in such a volume as this, to reckon up the successions of all the churches, we do put to confusion all those who, in whatever manner, whether by an evil self-pleasing, by vainglory, or by blindness and perverse opinion, assemble in unauthorized meeting; [we do this, I say,] by indicating that tradition derived from the apostles, of the very great, the very ancient, and universally known church founded and organized at Rome by the two most glorious apostles, Peter and Paul; as also [by pointing out] the faith preached to men, which comes down to our time by means of the successions of the bishops. For it is a matter of necessity that every church should agree with this church, on account of its pre-eminent authority, that is, the faithful everywhere, inasmuch as the apostolical tradition has been preserved continuously by those [faithful men] who exist everywhere.

2. The Canons of Sardica 3, 4, 5 (343)[2]

CANON 3: "If a bishop is condemned (that is, deposed, as appears from the fourth canon), but thinks his case is a good one, so that a fresh sentence ought to be pronounced, then, out of respect to the memory of the Apostle Peter, a letter shall be addressed to Rome to Pope Julius, so that, if necessary, he may appoint a new court composed of the bishops near the province in question, and may himself appoint the judges. If it is not proved, however, that the affair requires a fresh inquiry, then the first sentence (of the Provincial Synod) shall not be annulled, but shall be confirmed by the Pope."

CANON 4: "Bishop Gaudentius said: 'If pleasing to you, it shall be added to this judgment, which you, Hosius, have brought forward, and which is full of pure love, that if a bishop has been deposed by sentence of those bishops who are in the neighbourhood, and he desires again to defend himself, no other shall be appointed to his See until the Bishop of Rome has judged and decided thereupon.'"

CANON 5: "If a bishop deposed by his comprovincials (the bishops of the same region) has appealed to Rome, and the Pope considers a fresh examination necessary, then he (the Pope) shall write to the bishops living nearest the province in question, that they may thoroughly investigate the matter, and give sentence in accordance with the truth. But if the appellant can induce the Bishop of Rome to send priests of his own to constitute, with the appointed bishops, the court of second instance, and thereby to enjoy the authority belonging to himself (the Pope),—*i.e.* to preside in the court, as even the Gallican Marca allows to be the meaning,—it shall be open to the Pope to do so. But should he think the bishops alone sufficient for this court of appeal, he shall do what seems to him good."

3. Gregory VII, Dictatus papae (1075)[3]

1. That the Roman church was founded by the Lord alone.
2. That only the Roman pontiff is by right called "universal."
3. That he alone can depose or reinstate bishops.
4. That his legate—even if of an inferior rank—takes precedence of all bishops in council; and he can give sentence of deposition against them.
5. That the pope can depose absentees.
6. That, among other things, we ought not to stay in the same house with persons excommunicated by him.
7. That it is permitted for him alone, according to the need of the time, to establish new laws, to form peoples into new congregations,

to make a canonry into an abbacy, and, on the other hand, to divide a rich episcopacy and unite needy ones.

8. That he alone can use imperial insignia.

9. That only the pope's feet are to be kissed by all princes.

10. That his name only is recited in churches.

11. That this is a unique name in the world.

12. That it is licit for him to depose emperors.

13. That it is licit for him to transfer bishops, under pressure of need, from see to see.

14. That he has the power to ordain a cleric from any church to whatever place he wishes.

15. That a man ordained by him can preside over another church, but not do military service; and that he ought not to receive a higher rank from another bishop.

16. That no synod ought to be called "general" without his command.

17. That no chapter or book can be held to be canonical without his authority.

18. That his sentence ought to be reconsidered by no one, and he alone can reconsider [the judgments] of all.

19. That he ought to be judged by no one.

20. That no one may dare condemn a person appealing to the Apostolic See.

21. That greater cases of any church ought to be referred to her [the Apostolic See].

22. That the Roman church has never erred, nor, by Scripture's testimony, will it ever err.

23. That the Roman pontiff, if he be canonically ordained, indubitably becomes holy through the merits of Blessed Peter, according to the witness of St. Ennodius, Bishop of Pavia, with many holy Fathers concurring, as is contained in decrees of Blessed Symmachus, the Pope.

24. That by his precept and license it is licit for subjects to bring charges.

25. That he can, without a synodal assembly, depose and reinstate bishops.

26. That no one is considered catholic who is not in harmony with the Roman church.

27. That he can absolve subjects of wicked men from fealty.

4. The Council of Constance, Decree Haec sancta *(April 6, 1415)*[4]

[Decrees of the council, concerning its authority and integrity, which had been abbreviated by cardinal Zabarella at the preceding session, against the wishes of the nations, and which are now restored, repeated and confirmed by a public decree]

In the name of the holy and undivided Trinity, Father and Son and holy Spirit. Amen. This holy synod of Constance, which is a general council, for the eradication of the present schism and for bringing unity and reform to God's church in head and members, legitimately assembled in the holy Spirit to the praise of almighty God, ordains, defines, decrees, discerns and declares as follows, in order that this union and reform of God's church may be obtained the more easily, securely, fruitfully and freely.

First it declares that, legitimately assembled in the holy Spirit, constituting a general council and representing the catholic church militant, it has power immediately from Christ; and that everyone of whatever state or dignity, even papal, is bound to obey it in those matters which pertain to the faith, the eradication of the said schism and the general reform of the said church of God in head and members.

Next, it declares that anyone of whatever condition, state or dignity, even papal, who contumaciously refuses to obey the past or future mandates, statutes, ordinances or precepts of this sacred council or of any other legitimately assembled general council, regarding the aforesaid things or matters pertaining to them, shall be subjected to well-deserved penance, unless he repents, and shall be duly punished, even by having recourse, if necessary, to other supports of the law.

Next, the said holy synod defines and ordains that the lord pope John XXIII may not move or transfer the Roman curia and its public offices, or its or their officials, from the city of Constance to another place, nor directly or indirectly compel the said officials to follow him, without the deliberation and consent of the same holy synod. If he has acted to the contrary in the past, or shall in the future, or if he has in the past, is now or shall in the future fulminate any processes or mandates or ecclesiastical censures or any other penalties, against the said officials or any other adherents of this sacred council, to the effect that they should follow him, then all is null and void and in no way are the said processes, censures and penalties to be obeyed, inasmuch as they are null and void. The said officials are rather to exercise their offices in the said city of Constance, and to carry them out freely as before, as long as this holy synod is being held in the said city.

Next, that all translations of prelates, or depositions of the same, or of any other beneficed persons, officials and administrators, revocations of commendams and gifts, admonitions, ecclesiastical censures, processes, sentences and whatever has been or will be done or accomplished by the aforesaid lord pope John or his officials or commissaries, since the beginning of this council, to the injury of the said council or its adherents, against the supporters or participants of this sacred council, or to the prejudice of them or of any one of them, in whatever way they may have been or shall be made or done, against the will of the persons concerned, are by this very fact, on the authority of this sacred council, null, quashed, invalid and void, and of no effect or moment, and the council by its authority quashes, invalidates and annuls them.

Next, it declares that the lord Pope John XXIII and all the prelates and other persons summoned to this sacred council, and other participants in the same synod, have enjoyed and do now enjoy full freedom, as has been apparent in the said sacred council, and the opposite has not been brought to the notice of the said summoned persons or of the said council. The said sacred council testifies to this before God and people.

5. The Council of Florence, Formula of Primacy[5]

We also define that the holy apostolic see and the Roman pontiff holds the primacy over the whole world and the Roman pontiff is the successor of blessed Peter prince of the apostles, and that he is the true vicar of Christ, the head of the whole church and the father and teacher of all Christians, and to him was committed in blessed Peter the full power of tending, ruling and governing the whole church, as is contained also in the acts of ecumenical councils and in the sacred canons.

Also, renewing the order of the other patriarchs which has been handed down in the canons, the patriarch of Constantinople should be second after the most holy Roman pontiff, third should be the patriarch of Alexandria, fourth the patriarch of Antioch, and fifth the patriarch of Jerusalem, without prejudice to all their privileges and rights.

6. The Four Gallican Articles, Declaration of the Church of France (March 19, 1682)[6]

1. St. Peter and the popes, his successors, and the Church itself have received dominion *[puissance]* from God only over things spiritual and such as concern salvation, and not over things temporal and civil. Hence kings and sovereigns are not by God's command subject to any ecclesiastical dominion in things temporal; they cannot be deposed, whether directly or indirectly, by the authority of the rulers of the Church; their subjects cannot be dispensed from that submission and obedience which they owe, or absolved from the oath of allegiance.

2. The plenitude of authority in things spiritual, which belongs to the Holy See and the successors of St. Peter, in no wise affects the permanence and immovable strength of the decrees of the Council of Constance contained in the fourth and fifth sessions of that council, ap-

proved by the Holy See, confirmed by the practice of the whole Church and the Roman pontiff, and observed in all ages by the Gallican Church. That Church does not countenance the opinion of those who cast a slur on those decrees, or who lessen their force by saying that their authority is not well established, that they are not approved, or that they apply only to the period of the schism.

3. The exercise of this Apostolic authority *[puissance]* must also be regulated in accordance with the canons made by the Spirit of God and consecrated by the respect of the whole world. The rules, customs, and constitutions received within the kingdom and the Gallican Church must have their force and their effect, and the usages of our fathers remain inviolable, since the dignity of the Apostolic See itself demands that the laws and customs established by consent of that august see and of the Churches be constantly maintained.

4. Although the pope have the chief part in questions of faith, and his decrees apply to all the Churches, and to each Church in particular, yet his judgment is not irreformable, at least pending the consent of the Church.

7. *Papal Primacy of Jurisdiction and Papal Infallibility According to Vatican I (1870)*[7]

Since the Roman pontiff, by the divine right of the apostolic primacy, governs the whole church, we likewise teach and declare that he is the supreme judge of the faithful, and that in all cases which fall under ecclesiastical jurisdiction recourse may be had to his judgment. The sentence of the apostolic see (than which there is no higher authority) is not subject to revision by anyone, nor may anyone lawfully pass judgment thereupon. And so they stray from the genuine path of truth who maintain that it is lawful to appeal from the judgments of the Roman pontiffs to an ecumenical council as if this were an authority superior to the Roman pontiff.

So, then, if anyone says that the Roman pontiff has merely an office of supervision and guidance, and not the full and supreme power of jurisdiction over the whole church, and this not only in matters of faith and morals, but also in those which concern the discipline and government of the church dispersed throughout the whole world; or that he has only the principal part, but not the absolute fullness, of this supreme power; or that this power of his is not ordinary and immediate both over all and each of the churches and over all and each of the pastors and faithful: let him be anathema. . . .

When the Roman pontiff speaks *ex cathedra*, that is, when, in the exercise of his office as shepherd and teacher of all Christians, in virtue of his supreme apostolic authority, he defines a doctrine concerning faith or morals to be held by the whole church, he possesses, by the divine assistance promised to him in blessed Peter, that infallibility which the divine Redeemer willed his church to enjoy in defining doctrine concerning faith or morals. Therefore, such definitions of the Roman pontiff are of themselves, and not by the consent of the Church, irreformable.

8. Episcopal Collegiality and Papal Infallibility According to Vatican II (Lumen gentium 22)[8]

Just as, by the Lord's decree, St Peter and the other apostles constitute one apostolic college, so in a similar way the Roman pontiff, Peter's successor, and the bishops, successors of the apostles, are joined together. The collegial character and nature of the episcopal order is shown in the very ancient practice by which bishops appointed throughout the world maintained communion with each other and with the bishop of Rome in the bonds of unity, charity and peace; this is also shown in the councils that were convened, by which all the most important matters were settled in common and a decision carefully arrived at through the counsel of many. This is clearly confirmed by the ecumenical councils that have been celebrated down the centuries. The same thing is already to be seen in that custom, going back to antiquity, of calling together several bishops to take part in raising a newly-elected person to the ministry of the high priesthood. A person is constituted a member of the episcopal body by virtue of sacramental consecration and by hierarchical communion with the head and members of the college.

However, the college or body of bishops does not have authority unless this is understood in terms of union with the Roman pontiff, Peter's successor, as its head, and the power of this primacy is maintained intact over all, whether they be shepherds or faithful. For the Roman pontiff has, by virtue of his office as vicar of Christ and shepherd of the whole church, full, supreme and universal power over the church, a power he is always able to exercise freely. However, the order of bishops, which succeeds the college of apostles in teaching authority and pastoral government, and indeed in which the apostolic body continues to exist without interruption, is also the subject of supreme and full power over the universal church, provided it remains united with its head, the Roman pontiff, and never without its head; and this power can be exercised only with the consent of the Roman pontiff. The Lord made Simon alone the rock and key-bearer of the church (see Mt 16, 18-19), and constituted him shepherd of his whole flock (see Jn

21, 15ff.). It is clear, however, that this office of binding and loosing which was given to Peter (see Mt 16, 19), was also granted to the college of apostles in union with its head (see Mt 18, 18; 28, 16-20). This college, in so far as it is composed of many, expresses the variety and the universality of the people of God, but in so far as it is gathered under one head it expresses the unity of the flock of Christ. In it the bishops, while faithfully maintaining the primacy and pre-eminence of its head, exercise their own proper power for the good of their faithful and indeed of the whole church, while the holy Spirit is constantly strengthening its organic structure and its harmony. The supreme power over the whole church which this college enjoys is solemnly exercised in an ecumenical council. There is never an ecumenical council which is not confirmed as such or at least accepted as such by the successor of Peter. It is the prerogative of the Roman pontiff to convoke these councils, to preside over them and to confirm them. The same collegial power can be exercised by the bishops throughout the world in conjunction with the pope, provided that the head of the college calls them to collegial action or at least approves of, or willingly accepts, the united action of the dispersed bishops in such a way that the result is a truly collegial act.

NOTES

[1]Alexander Roberts and James Donaldson, eds., *Translations of the Writings of the Fathers*, vol. 9 (Edinburgh: T & T Clark, 1880).
[2]Charles Joseph Hefele. *A History of the Councils of the Church from the Original Documents. vol. 2: A.D. 326 to A.D. 429*, tr. and ed. Henry Nutcombe Oxenhan (Edinburgh: T & T Clark, 1896).
[3]From E. Caspar, ed., *Das Register Gregors VII*, tr. Karl F. Morrison (Berlin, 1920–1923) Reg. II, 55a:202–08.
[4]Norman P. Tanner, S.J., ed., *Decrees of the Ecumenical Councils. vol. 1: Nicaea to Lateran V* (Washington: Georgetown University Press, 1990).
[5]Ibid.
[6]A. Degert, "Gallicanism," *The Catholic Encyclopedia*, vol. 6 (New York: Robert Appleton Co., 1909).
[7]Tanner, *Decrees of the Ecumenical Councils. vol. 2: Trent to Vatican II.*
[8]Ibid.

Index of Subjects

The following pages list the people, places, and events about which a pertinent statement is made in this book. By no means should this index be considered a complete listing of the scores of people, places, and events recorded in this book.

CPSIA information can be obtained
at www.ICGtesting.com
Printed in the USA
FFOW02n2121120416
23241FF

9 780814 65